Using Audition

Ron Dabbs

San Francisco, CA • New York, NY • Lawrence, KS

Published by CMP Books
an imprint of CMP Media LLC

Main office: 600 Harrison Street, San Francisco, CA 94107 USA
Tel: 415-947-6615; fax: 415-947-6015

Editorial office:
4601 West 6th Street, Suite B, Lawrence, KS 66049 USA
www.cmpbooks.com
email: books@cmp.com

Senior Editor:	Dorothy Cox
Managing Editor:	Gail Saari
Layout Design	James Hoyt
Cover Layout Design:	Damien Castaneda

Distributed in the U.S. by:
Publishers Group West
1700 Fourth Street
Berkeley, CA 94710
1-800-788-3123

Distributed in Canada by:
Jaguar Book Group
100 Armstrong Avenue
Georgetown, Ontario M6K 3E7 Canada
905-877-4483

For individual orders and for information on special discounts for quantity orders, please contact:
CMP Books Distribution Center, 6600 Silacci Way, Gilroy, CA 95020
Tel: 1-800-500-6875 or 408-848-3854; fax: 408-848-5784
email: cmp@rushorder.com; Web: www.cmpbooks.com

Printed in the United States of America
04 05 06 07   4 3 2 1

ISBN: 1-57820-240-X

CMP Books

Dedicated to my wife, Terry
and my children, Jennifer and Alexander,
without whom I would not have finished this work…
and to my parents, who taught me all I ever needed to know…
integrity, compassion, faith, and love.

During the writing of the book, our unborn child passed away.
I cannot help but add a special dedication to our Rachel.
Although we will surely miss the joys we would have shared on Earth,
we will laugh with you in heaven. Families are forever!

Table of Contents

Editor's Note

Audition…The word is intimidating and exciting at the same time. A successful audition suggests endless possibilities, whether for an actor, recording artist, student, or video editor looking for a better gig. We all have to reach the point of the audition.

Adobe's Audition is a wonderful tool, because regardless of the skill set of the user, it allows users to quickly become adept at the creation of great audio. Audition provides every tool conceivable (and some no one has ever thought of) that might be valuable in a recording session in any industry. It allows users to step to the stage, ready to take on any sort of project or product. Given dedication to all parameters of audio production, that user will finish with a great recorded product.

Adobe has long been associated with building great product suites, and the addition of Audition to the Adobe product line completes their dynamic media offerings. Like other Adobe products, this tool is terrific.

I'm honored to have had the opportunity to work with Ron Dabbs on this book project. Ron has meticulously assembled some great tips, tricks, and workflows for the Audition user, and he points out some of the various detours one might be tempted to take in the recording process. He gives a good overview of the good, the bad, and the ugly of digital recording. Ron's book truly sets the stage for a great recording project, and provides excellent direction for the finished cut.

I'm sure you'll enjoy reading and learning from this book as much as I did in working with Ron to bring it to you.

Happy editing,
SPOT
Douglas Spotted Eagle

Credits

One of the toughest tasks in writing this book came when I sat down to thank those involved in helping me with this project. The question that weighed on my mind was how to express the appreciation I felt. I realized I could not fit all those names on the front cover of the book.

As I leaned back and contemplated this thought, I looked around the remains of what was once an office and the impact of my wife's sacrifice was apparent. Terry ("the widow," as she may feel as of late) had kept all the affairs of home and family intact while I had immersed myself in seclusion. To her, I owe my thanks, my love…about six months worth of housework, and two dozen dates. I am also forever indebted to my parents, Thomas and Betty. Among so many other things, they patiently watched our dog and our son so that I could have some quiet time to work. I am so thankful to be blessed with this family.

A special thanks goes to Douglas Spotted Eagle who took time to not only provide technical editing, but was kind enough to take me under his wing offering suggestions on direction and style as well as technical comments. I am amazed that one person can have so much talent. Douglas, you are indeed a wealth of knowledge and a good friend.

Writing this book would have been much more difficult without the help of my friend and associate, Mike Newsome. Thanks for the constant encouragement and meticulous review of my writing.

Of course, the group at CMP Books, Paul Temme, Dorothy Cox, Gail Saari, Brandy Ernzen, Hastings Hart, James Hoyt, and Damien Castaneda not only made this project come into fruition, but also made it a very pleasant experience. You are truly pros. I appreciate your hard work in making this happen.

To the Adobe team, Jason Levine, Daniel Brown, Hart Shafer, Steve Fazio, Ron Day, Mat Chevez, and Michelle Love-Escobar, thanks for the quick responses to my frequent barrage of questions. Long live the future of audio production tools… Adobe Audition!

Clete Baker, my long time friend, associate, and mentor, for the lessons in audio production and mastering that you provided in my younger years and the use of your voice on some of the tutorials, you have my gratitude.

Chip Davis, Brain Ackley, Carol Davis, Rick Swanson, Steve Alex, Mat Domber, and Tim Mulaly composed and/or own the music used in the tutorials and offered their usage without any questions. I cherish not only the friendship we have, but also the trust you have shown.

There are also several people I would like to thank for their encouragement, advice, and support. Doug Franzen, Carl Evans, Mark Deal, Mary Anderson, Bruce Moore, Michael Watkins, Don Ulinski, Chad Jarae, and Rick Krainak. What a great group of people at Evatone! Bill Emener and Michael Newton, without your help, I would not have even started this project. A special thanks goes to two of my high school teachers: Paul Oertell for the recommendation that started my career in audio and Joe Burns for his insistence that a recording engineer still needed to study English.

The credits would not be complete without mentioning the host people that were so gracious in providing gear, software, and information. Diane Fleming, Kevin Walt, Vanessa Mering, Scott Kroeker, Antoni Ozynski, Axel Gutzer, Bob Reardon, Markus Jonsson, Daggan Stamenkovic, Flavio Antonioli, Andrew Green, George Jaroslaw, Jeff Bloom, Joe Kohler, Joerg Dieckow, John Calder, Joram Ludwig, Khaldhoun Ateyeh, Mark Ethier, Markus Jonsson, Massimiliano Tonelli, Matt Pelling, Michael Logue, Paul Titchner, Rob Martino, Robert Bielik, Robin Whitcore, Sascha Eversmeier, Cory Lorentz, Karen Abramian, Darrin Warner, Chris Donlon, David Bryant, C.H. Liljegren, Christina Burkhardt, Alfred Bantug, Amy Halm, and Daniel Graham. Jay Rose kindly gave permission for the use of Figure 1.2, reproduced from *Producing Great Sound for Digital Video*.

…and last, but certainly not least, a special little boy named Alex, who was extremely patient when Dad couldn't play with him.

Thank you all,

Preface

Let's face it: technology is fantastic, but it has traditionally gotten in the way of creativity. That's not to say technology does not foster ideas, but how many times have you sat down with a great concept or musical vision only to be trapped in figuring out how to make the software application do what you had in mind? You may have had an idea, but didn't even know if it was possible. Or you may have opened a program and sat wondering where to begin—perusing the menus and dialog boxes and wondering what a particular option or setting did. Did you ever wish someone could sit down with you for a couple of hours and just explain what different parts of the program are used for and how a professional would go about using the program?

In the summer of 2003, I was approached about writing a book on the newly released audio application from Adobe Systems, Inc., called Audition. I had been using the application in its former life as Cool Edit Pro and was already aware of the power bundled into this software. It was exciting to see the acquisition by Adobe and I took pleasure in speculating the possibilities of audio à la Photoshop. I realized I could not pass up the opportunity to proclaim the attributes of this incredible application and at the same time, do so in a manner that does not require a degree in physics.

You are now holding that attempt in your hands. *Using Audition* will introduce you to Audition and guide you through installation and optimization. It explains some basic analog and digital audio concepts essential to understanding how to get the most from the application, and it includes a description of audio file formats and typical format usage. An extensive use of screen shots will aid you in locating features of the application as the book details functions such as multitrack recording, editing, signal processing, looping, and mixing. *Using Audition* presents the specifics of each function, options, and some practical examples, as well as tips and tricks to help you really fine tune the production. Topics covered include MIDI, SMPTE synchronization, plug-ins, surround sound, scripting, and integrating workflow with other Adobe applications. From the first recording to the final mix or encode, *Using Audition* will be invaluable in helping you produce the best sounding tracks.

I hope you will enjoy using Audition as much as I do!

Chapter 1

Getting Into It!

THE MONOLOGUE

An Introduction to Audition

I remember the day we wheeled the brand-new 16-track recorder into the control room. We were amazed that you could get sixteen tracks onto a piece of 2-inch magnetic tape. We were also amazed at the price considering I had just purchased my first house for less than that box of tin and resistors on wheels. Eight-tracks had been the norm and now we had doubled that of any local competitor. We were lucky. Wow…things have changed.

Today, we are even luckier. Computer speeds are doubling every year while the prices are plummeting. The Internet has changed the whole dynamic of communication, and Adobe Systems has released an incredible new audio application called Audition.

If you have not already installed Audition, you will be in awe when you do. Audition is a feature-rich audio recording and production application that will allow you to explore almost every aspect of computer-based audio production. Many audio applications have made the claim of "studio-in-a-box," but Audition is the first program that really packs the entire recording studio into a PC. Audition offers an abundance of features including 32-bit processing, 128 stereo tracks, more than 45 digital signal-processing (DSP) tools, ReWire support, a complete range of sampling rates and file formats, built-in analysis tools, noise reduction, integration with other Adobe applications, and a host of other options. Another capability that helps set this application above the rest is the ability to create loop-based soundtracks. Best of

1

all, Audition ships with more than 4,500 royalty-free music loops of different genres that you can use to create your own compositions. Overall, Audition truly is a recording "Studio-in-a-box."

Whether you are a professional recording engineer, event videographer, musician, producer, scientist, or an amateur, Audition will become a powerful production tool for you. The video production company will learn how to use loops to create custom music tracks for their productions that are royalty-free. The employee in a corporate marketing department who has been tasked with assembling a training presentation will find out how easy it is to remove the obnoxious hum on a video. The musician with a limited vocal range can learn how to adjust the key to fit his range. The scientist can use the accurate and consistent analysis results for testing. The parent assembling an audio track for their first home video will discover how simple it is to add narration to the video. Whatever the need, both Audition and *Using Audition* will be a pleasing and satisfying experience.

THE AUDIO REPERTOIRE

Physics of Sound

In order to record, edit, and mix audio, one must have an understanding of the fundamentals of sound. These concepts are used throughout the audio production process.

Sound Pressure Level

Have you ever thrown a stone into a pond and noticed the waves that radiate from where the stone lands? As the waves travel farther from the center, they slowly fade away. Now instead of throwing a stone into a pond, imagine the stone as a drumstick hitting the head of a drum. Visualize waves of air traveling from where the stick hits the drum until they fade away. This is the essence of sound. In its simplest definition, sound is the compression and decompression of air molecules. The result of this compression and decompression is a change in air pressure called the sound pressure level or SPL. When the eardrum feels these changes in air pressure, it converts them to electronic impulses that your brain understands as sound.

Waveforms

Let's take a closer look at this concept. The stick hits the drum and forces the drumhead down, and the air under the drumhead is compressed. When the head returns to its original position, the air decompresses. The result is waves of air much like the waves in the water. The airwaves slowly fade away as the drum stops vibrating. If we look closer at the drumhead, we would see that the drumhead does not stop when it returns to its starting position. The drumhead continues moving upward the same distance it moved downward and repeats the cycle until it loses energy. Each time the air is compressed, decompressed, and the drumhead returns to the starting position is one cycle as shown in Figure 1.1. The number of cycles per second is referred to as the *frequency* and is measured in Hertz (Hz). The longer it takes to complete one cycle, the lower the frequency. The shorter the time required to complete a cycle, the higher the frequency. Frequencies of 1,000Hz and over are usually expressed in kilohertz (kHz).

Bass frequencies are found below 250Hz. The lowest string on a bass guitar moves slowly enough that you can see it vibrating. Hitting an orchestral triangle produces a high-pitched or high-frequency sound. It is vibrating so fast that its movement cannot be seen. Different instruments produce different ranges of frequencies, and almost all instruments fall within the range of human hearing, between 20Hz and 20kHz. Notice in Figure 1.2 that a new *octave* begins each time the frequency is doubled.

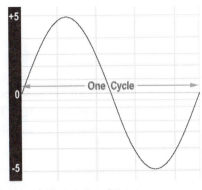

1.1   *One cycle of a wave*

Consider a painting with all the colors represented by different frequencies. Silence would correspond to black, and white would be the highest frequencies that stimulate the human ear. The lower frequencies begin with a very dark brown. The artist with a color palette of mostly browns or low frequencies is going to produce a painting that looks or sounds rather dark or muddy. The same result occurs when combining too many colors or sounds together. The piece becomes murky and tends to lose brilliance.

The easiest way to avoid this problem is to start with a good arrangement of instruments or soundtrack elements, but the architecture of a soundtrack can be complicated. It may

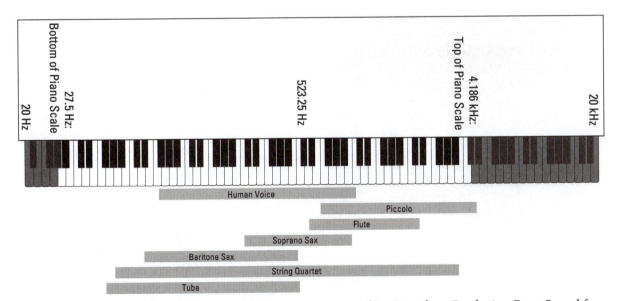

1.2   *Basic vibrations of common instruments. Image courtesy of Jay Rose from Producing Great Sound for Digital Video (CMP Books 2004).*

require a talented composer or sound designer to arrange the components so they don't mask the subtler tones. Fortunately, there is a way to add or subtract certain frequencies or bands of frequencies. The tool used to alter the frequencies is called an *equalizer*, and the process is called *equalization*. Equalizing particular bands of frequencies can help make a voice more intelligible, a guitar sound fatter, or a piano sound crisper. Equalization serves an important role in audio production and is used in many ways. Figure 1.3 depicts the type of sound that occurs in different ranges of frequencies.

1.3   *The common role of*
     frequency ranges

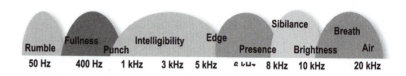

Sound is measured not only in frequency but also by loudness. Loudness is determined by measuring the amount the air is compressed. The more the air is compressed—remember the stone in the pond—the higher the wave will be. This is called the *amplitude* of the wave. Amplitude is measured from the peak of the cycle to the valley of the same cycle, as shown in Figure 1.4.

The human ear is incredibly sensitive. We can hear sounds over ten trillion times louder than the lowest audible sound. Because of this broad range and the way we perceive relative levels of loudness, a logarithmic scale was developed that expresses amplitude in decibel units, abbreviated as dB. The smallest change the mature human ear can typically discern is 1 dB.

Seldom is sound made up of one single wave. That's fortunate for us, because music would be very boring if it were all made up of a continuous tone, even if each track was a different tone. So what does happen when more than one stone is thrown into the pond at once? Image two stones thrown into the water at the same time. As the waves collide, they merge, creating

1.4   *Amplitude of a waveform*

1.5   *Typical decibel levels of*
     common sounds at a distance
     of three feet

Guns	140 dB
Jet Engine	120 dB
Lawn Mower	90 dB
Conversation	75 dB
Office	65 dB
Residence	50 dB
Whisper	20 dB
Total Silence	0 dB

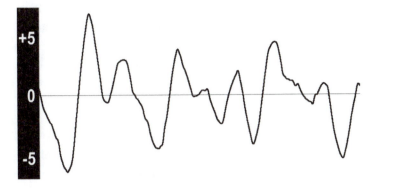

1.6   *A complex waveform*

a wave with varying peaks and valleys. This is a called a ***complex waveform,*** shown in Figure 1.6.

As some of these waves collide, even though they may be at the same frequency and amplitude, the timing may be such that one wave is peaking while the other is at its valley. When this occurs, they cancel each other and there is neither compression nor decompression. This is referred to as ***phase cancellation.*** The phase of a wave begins at 0° and continues through 360°. When a waveform is 180° ahead or behind another waveform, the waves are 180° out of phase. In Figure 1.7, the wave in the top panel begins at 0°. The wave in the next panel begins 90° out of phase, and the wave in the third panel is 180° out of phase. The peak of the wave begin-

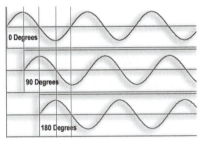

1.7   *Waves out of phase*

ning at 180° occurs at the same time as the valley of the wave beginning at 0°. The bottom wave is 270° out of phase.

No acoustic instrument produces a single continuous Sine wave. Even woodwind instruments that are relatively pure in pitch create a complex waveform by generating ***overtones.*** The overtones that are multiples of the fundamental frequency are called ***harmonics.*** Harmonics and instrument noise form the unique sound or color of an instrument that is referred to as ***timbre*** (pronounced TAM-ber).

Audio Signals

Until the mid-1980s, analog signals were the only way to work with audio in most professional recording studios. Digital audio was quickly accepted and for very good reasons. A minority of people will still argue that analog audio is more natural and sounds better, but most engineers prefer to work in the digital realm. Perhaps the best analogy to illustrate the difference between analog and digital signals is that of the children's game Telephone. One child is told what to bring to a birthday party and calls the next child. The instructions are passed in this way around the circle. The instructions given to the first child often have little resemblance to the instructions received by the last child. Analog audio tends to suffer from the same miscommunication, distortions, and even worse, noise. Digital audio might be analogous to giving the first child a list of numbers and having him write them down. The list can be passed through hundreds of generations, and as long as each child wrote the numbers down correctly, the list of numbers given to the last child will be identical to numbers given to the first child.

Analog Audio

Although we still work with analog signals, we will be working mostly with digital signals in Audition. You will probably record some tracks using a microphone. The microphone is an analog device that converts changes in sound pressure levels to electronic voltages. These voltages vary, closely mimicking the waveform. These voltage variations may be recorded to a magnetic tape or converted to a digital signal.

Digital Audio

Digital audio represents the value of the sound pressure level as a numeric value. The numeric value is determined by sampling the waveform amplitude at regular intervals. The result is a stream of numbers that describes the waveform as illustrated in Figure 1.8. The original analog waveform is represented by the bold line. During analog-to-digital conversion, voltage is measured at predetermined time intervals and stored in a binary format as a long string of ones and zeros. When the signal is reproduced from the numeric values, the voltages are played back at the same time intervals. Digital filtering is applied to smooth the waveform. Analog sources are converted to digital signals through an analog-to-digital converter (ADC). Reversing the signal from digital to analog requires a digital-to-analog converter (DAC).

TIP!! Digital converters vary in quality. It is important to select the best converter available, because the conversion step can significantly affect the quality of the sound.

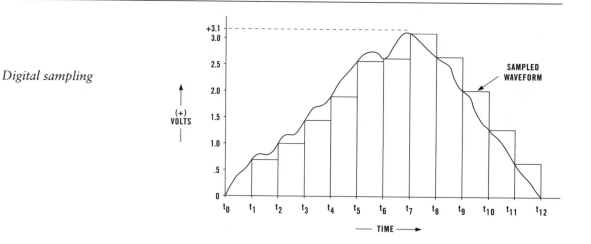

1.8   *Digital sampling*

Sampling Rate

Digital audio quality can vary significantly, depending upon the number of times per second that the level of the waveform is recorded. This is called the sampling rate. The higher the sampling rate or the greater the number of samples per second, the more accurate the reproduction of the original waveform. Low sampling rates can miss transients that occur quickly between samples. High sampling rates result in higher file sizes. A large file may not be a problem when creating a compact disc, but it can result in excessive download times for audio hosted on a web site. Compact disc audio requires a sampling rate of 44.1kHz. Table 1.1 lists sampling rates and common applications.

Nyquist Theorem

An engineer at Bell Labs named Harry Nyquist determined that the sampling rate must be at least twice that of the highest frequency. This concept, called the Nyquist Theorem, proved that a sample of both the positive and negative excursions of a wave is required to reproduce the wave.

Table 1.1   Sampling rates and common applications

Sampling Rate	Quality	Recommended Usage
6,000Hz	Telephone	Voice only for Internet or CD-ROM when file size is important.
11,025Hz	Telephone	Voice only for Internet or CD-ROM and multimedia presentation.
22,050Hz	AM radio	Voice mainly but can be used for music. CD-ROM and multimedia content. Internet usage when bandwidth is not an issue.
32kHz	FM radio	Voice or music. Consumer video, CD-ROM, and multimedia presentations.
44.1kHz	Compact disc	CD-quality. Standard sampling rate for CD.
48kHz	DVD-Video	Slightly better than CD quality. Standard for DVD-Video discs.
96kHz	DVD-Audio	Excellent quality. Standard for DVD-Audio discs.
192kHz	DVD-Audio	Best quality available for digital audio. Used only on DVD-Audio discs.

Resolution

Bit depth is another factor in the quality of the reproduction of the signal. This concept is very much like computer-monitor resolution. The higher the bit depth, the greater the number of colors the monitor can display. In digital audio, each sample is stored as a numeric value in a digital word and the length of the word is referred to as the resolution. The longer the word, the greater the number of reproducible levels or the greater the difference between the softest and loudest sounds. This difference is called the dynamic range. A bit depth of one bit would allow a resolution of two values, on or off. Not very useful unless used for Morse code. A bit

> ### *Binary System*
>
> A computer can ultimately only recognize two states: off and on. These two states are used to represent numeric values through a binary numbering system. Each binary digit, 0 or 1, is called a bit. Combining eight bits can result in 256 different values. Combining 16 bits can produce 65,536 unique values. It is through this binary system that computers are able to calculate and process values.

depth of eight bits provides 256 levels. Compact discs have a bit depth of 16 bits or 65,536 discrete levels, and 24-bit audio allows more than 24 million distinct values.

FILE FORMATS

All computer instructions or data are stored as bit streams in a container referred to as a file. Audio is no different. The audio file consists of a contiguous stream of ones and zeros representing the amplitude value of each sample. There are too many audio file formats to discuss here, and many are obsolete, so we will discuss the supported formats. File formats can be divided into two categories: those with header information and those without header information. A header is the data placed in the file that describes the content and format. The header information is used by the application to set up specific parameters when opening the file.

A file with a header has what is called a self-describing format. It generally includes the number of channels, sampling rate, and bit depth; however, some formats can include much more data, such as artist name, engineer, copyright holder, tempo, and a wide range of file-related data.

The headerless format is referred to as a raw file. Raw files generally do not contain information about the waveform's characteristics. Although the sampling rate may be changed on these files, the other parameters are usually fixed.

Most audio file formats can be converted to another format. Audition supports the most commonly used audio formats and can frequently open unsupported file formats by attempting to open the file as an ACM or RAW file type. Most compressed audio formats are decompressed when the file is opened in Audition.

Compression can have two meanings in audio production. Prior to computer-based audio production, compression meant reducing the dynamic range of the analog signal. Today, compression also means reducing the file size. The majority of file compression techniques take the form of removing information that the human brain does not perceive. For example, a bass drum and a bass guitar hit a note at the same time. The attack of the bass drum masks the sound of the bass guitar for a split-second and the bass guitar is not heard during that instance. There are also other times that the brain expects to hear a sound and creates it even though the sound is not present. This phenomenon is called psychoacoustics, and the encoding technique is referred to as perceptual coding. MP3 is a common example of this type of compression. This type of compression is known as lossy since the original data cannot be reclaimed.

Many file formats offer another method of compression by using bits as necessary instead of using them at a constant rate. This method of varying the bit rate is called variable bit rate (VBR). The standard method is referred to as constant bit rate (CBR) and requires that bits be allocated at a constant rate regardless of the content. The term kbps or kilobits per second is used to represent the bit rate.

Once the coding is complete, the file is compressed using traditional file-compression techniques.

> **Algorithms**
>
> Any file that is compressed by a computer using a formula or algorithm. The application that plays back the file needs a similar algorithm to decompress or decode the file. The set of computer instructions that uses the algorithm to encode or decode the file is called a *codec*.

Commonly Used Formats

The most commonly used audio file format is the WAV format. It is the standard Microsoft Windows format for working with high-quality audio files. Apple Macintosh users should be familiar with the AIF or AIFF file formats, which are the most common formats on that platform. mp3 files have gained an incredible popularity based on reasonable quality for a small file size, but the quality does not meet professional standards.

It is beyond the scope of this book to discuss all formats and format options. I have selected the most common formats and provided a brief overview of the format, settings, and usage. Following that section is a summary of other supported formats. The Audition manual provides additional information on specific formats, and there is a list of sources for additional reading at the end of this chapter on page 14.

Apple AIFF (.aif, .snd)

The format name is an acronym for Apple Interchange File Format. The data is not compressed, and the format supports mono or stereo with sampling rates up to 192kHz in 8-bit and 16-bit resolutions. Although AIFF files can be used to provide cross-platform compatibility, any metadata (non-audio information) will be lost when opened in Audition.

Application: Most common usage is for compact disc audio. Format is frequently used in multimedia.

Typical settings: 16-bit, 44.1kHz, stereo for compact disc and 8-bit, 8kHz, mono for multimedia.

Audition Loop (.cel)

The Audition Loop file format stores loop files. The file is stored as an mp3 or mp3Pro file except that Audition includes the loop information, and Audition does a little housekeeping

File Association in Windows and Macintosh

Microsoft Windows uses the three-character extension following the period in the file name to associate a file to an application. The extension will not be seen if the **Folder Options/View** is set to **Hide Extensions for known file types**.

Apple Macintosh computers use a file format that is comprised of the data file and a hidden file called a resource fork. The resource fork contains a unique creator code and file type code that associate the file with an application. Microsoft Windows does not recognize the resource fork. Although this does not prevent the file from opening or saving on a PC and it will probably open on the Macintosh, you should confirm that the resource fork is not required by the Macintosh application that will play the file back. Simply opening the file and saving it again on the Macintosh will create a new resource fork.

necessary to ensure smooth loops. The .cel extension is added to the filename. The loop settings are found in the **Loop Info** tab of the Waveform Properties window, and the mp3PRO options are available from the **Options** button in the **Save Waveform As** window.

Application: loop files for use in the **Multitrack View** of Audition.

Typical settings: 320kbps, 44.1kHz, stereo.

mp3PRO (.mp3)

The mp3/mp3PRO file format was developed for use with MPEG (Motion Picture Experts Group) video. The format takes it name from the MPEG-1/Level III specification. Because of the small file size and reasonable quality, the format caught on as a method to transfer music across the Internet and for use in portable music devices. The data is highly compressed using perceptual encoding techniques, and the format supports mono or stereo with a wide range of bit rates including CBR and VBR.

Audition also supports an advanced mp3 encoding format called mp3PRO, which offers better sounding compression with lower bit rates. However, if the file is played back on a player that does not support mp3PRO, the enhanced quality will not be heard.

There are a number of mp3/mp3PRO options. Several of these options reduce file size by sacrificing quality. Descriptions of the functions will appear in the mp3/mp3PRO **Encoder Options** window when the option is selected. Once the settings are satisfactory, the settings can be saved as a user preset by clicking the **Add** button.

Application: Most common usage is for portable audio devices and Internet download.

Typical settings: 128 kbps, 44.1kHz, stereo for MP3 or 96kbps, 44.1kHz, stereo for mp3PRO.

PCM Raw Data (.pcm, .raw)

The PCM file format is usually a headerless format. The format name is an acronym for Pulse Code Modulation. The data is not compressed, and the format supports mono or stereo with sampling rates up to 192kHz and resolutions up to 32-bit. Because the format is headerless, it does not support metadata, but it does support writing header information to a DAT file, making it easier to open the file later. There are several options available for saving PCM files. Audition does not require the .pcm extension to open a file.

Application: Professional Digital Audio Workstation (DAW) format.

Typical settings: 16-bit, 44.1 or 48kHz, stereo.

Windows PCM (.wav)

The Windows PCM file format is a Microsoft Windows file format and carries the .wav extension. It is by far the most common file format used in audio production. The format name is an acronym for Windows Audio Video format. It conforms to the Resource Information File Format (RIFF) specifications. The data is not compressed, and the format supports mono or stereo with sampling rates up to 192kHz in up to 32-bit resolutions. Metadata is fully supported in Audition; however, caution should be used if the WAV files are intended for burning compact discs. If metadata is saved with the file, it can cause audible clicks or pops on the CD. There are several options available for saving WAV files.

> **PCM Format:** Opening a file as PCM will open almost any audio file format. Because the PCM format is headerless, it may take several attempts to guess the file parameters. Once the file is open, check for any clicks caused by header information and remove any noises.

Application: Most common usage is for compact disc audio. Format is frequently used in multimedia.

Typical settings: 16-bit, 44.1kHz, stereo for compact disc and 8-bit, 8kHz, mono for multimedia.

Windows Media Audio (.wma)

The Windows Media Audio file format is a Microsoft Windows file format designed as an alternative to the mp3 format. The data is highly compressed using perceptual encoding techniques, and the format supports mono or stereo with a wide range of bit rates including CBR and VBR. WMA also supports a lossless option that produces a smaller file size than the standard WAV file with comparable quality.

Application: Most common usage is for portable audio devices and Internet download and streaming. However, many software applications are supporting the WMA format as an editing format.

Typical settings: 128kbps, stereo for portable devices. Internet settings vary according to content and available bandwidth.

Other Supported Formats

ACM Waveform (.wav): The ACM Waveform provides a range of options. Almost any file that is supported by the Microsoft Compression Manager (ACM) can be used in Audition. There are a multitude of format setting and options. However many of these options are not available unless the waveform meets the format requirements.

TIP!! The ACM Waveform codec may open files that are not officially supported by Audition.

ACSII Text Data (.txt): The ASCII Text format is a standard text file. Audio data can be written or read to the file. The format allows saving the file with a header, and the audio can be normalized before saving.

Amiga IFF-8SVX (.iff, .svx): The Amiga IFF format is an 8-bit signed format created for the Commodore Amiga computer.

A/mu-Law Wave (.wav): The A-Law and µLaw (pronounced "mu-law") file formats are 8-bit formats typically used for telephony applications. The µLaw format is the international standard (CCITT standard G.711) for telecommunications, and A-Law is a European version.

Creative Soundblaster (.voc): The Soundblaster format was developed for use with Creative Labs Soundblaster and Soundblaster Pro PC audio cards. The format provides options for older 8-bit VOC files and newer 16-bit sound files.

Dialogic ADPCM (.vox): The Dialogic ADPCM format is primarily used for telephony applications.

DiamondWare Digitized (.dwd): DiamondWare Digitized is a format for use with the DiamondWare Sound Toolkit. The toolkit is used by programmers to add sound to games and multimedia applications.

DVI/IMA ADPCM (.wav): The DVI/IMA ADPCM file format was developed for the International Media Association. The acronym is derived from Adaptive Differential Pulse Code Modulation. Because the compression method used makes some predictions rather than simply compressing the audio, it can reproduce the audio with fewer bits; however the risk of inaccurate results is also present. It is similar to Microsoft's ADPCM, only faster.

Microsoft ADPCM (.wav): Microsoft ADPCM is a format suited for compression of voice. The quality is similar to DVI/IMA ADPCM, however the option of making two passes to encode the audio give it an edge.

Next/Sun (.au, .snd): The AU file format is frequently used for Java and Internet applications. The format supports 8-bit and 16-bit files. The format offers several options for saving including Linear PCM, A-Law, and µLaw.

SampleVision (.smp): The SampleVision file format is a native format of the application of the same name published by Turtle Beach. This is a 16-bit mono format that supports loops.

8-bit Signed (.sam): The 8-bit Signed file format is frequently used for MOD files. MOD files take their name from the word module and can contain sets of samples (the instruments) and sequencing information. The original MOD format rose from the Commodore Amiga computer and has a developed a cult following.

64-bit doubles (.dbl): The 64-bit doubles file format stores 8 bytes or 16 bytes per mono or stereo sample respectively. The file is stored as a headerless PCM file. This format uses the .DBL extension.

Adobe Audition also supports several video formats including .AVI, MPEG, DV, and .WMV/.ASF. See the Audition manual for more specific information on the specifications and available options.

 Audition can also support other file formats through the use of third-party filters such as the MPEG-4 AAC filter from Imagine Technologies. Check out the Third-Party Filters demos on the CD-ROM included with this book.

 An undocumented feature of Adobe Audition is the ability to import audio from .vob (Video Object) files on a DVD. Choose Import while in **Multitrack View** mode making certain the Files of type: field in the Import dialog box is set to All Files (*.*). Navigate to the desired .vob file on the DVD and click the **Open** button.

Metadata

Audition provides access to metadata, an extensive set of information that may be included with the file. The additional information can identify compositions, sampler settings, automate playback and tracking in broadcast applications, and other file-specific data. The user can modify most fields; however some information is written routinely as the file is created or saved. None of the information is mandatory. In fact, do not save the file with metadata if the destination is a compact disc. Figure 1.9 shows the **Text Fields** tab of the Wave Properties window.

Text Fields : The **Text Fields** tab contains fields used to identify the filename, title, origination, comments, and other file-specific information. Selecting the dropdown list labeled **Text Field Names** allows you to choose between **Standard RIFF** fields, **Radio Industry** fields, and MP3 (ID3 Tag) information for mp3 files. The **Radio Industry** fields hold much of the same identifying data, start time, stop times, automation cues, and a description of the last few seconds of the track referred to as the outcut. This information facilitates broadcast automation and daily programming. The **Fill *** fields automatically checkbox fills the **Software Package** and **Creation Date** fields with "Audition," year, and the current date, respectively.

1.9 The Wave Properties window

Loop Info: The **Loop Info** tab contains the settings that control the file actions in Audition. The **Loop** and **One Shot** options determine whether the file will loop or simply play once. You can select tempo and key selection here, and the method of scaling or stretching the length of the file. Audition can also help you find the key. See Chapter 7, "On-Cues, Loops, and Sounds" on page 141, for more information on loops.

Sampler Info: The **Sampler** tab provides access to fields that contain sampler-specific information. It is possible to map a sample to a key, change the sample rate, and sample length. This tab allows modifying the sample start and end times, loop functions, and it provides the ability to find the note of the sample.

Misc: The **Misc** tab associates a bitmap (BMP) or Device-Independent Bitmap (DIB) file with the Audition file. You can obtain the best results by using an image 32×32 pixels.

EBU Extensions: The **EBU Extension** tab permits access to fields used for compatibility with the EBU (European Broadcast Union) standards.

Cart: The **Cart** tab is for use with broadcast automation systems. The data requirements are specific to each system. Consult the automation system for specifics.

File Info: The **File Info** tab provides the filename, folder name, file type, size, format, and length. You cannot change any fields in this tab.

FOR MORE INFORMATION

Modern Recording Techniques 5th Edition, David Mile Huber and Robert E. Runstein, Focal Press, 2001

Principles of Digital Audio, 4th Edition, Ken C. Pohlmann, McGraw-Hill Professional, 2000

Chapter 2

Setting the Stage

FIRST AUDITION

First-time Adobe Audition users will find that the installation is simple and painless. Audition is packaged as a two-disc CD set. Disc 1 contains the installers for Audition, Adobe Acrobat Reader, Microsoft DirectX, and a User Guide in PDF format. Disc 2 contains thousands of royalty-free music loops. Audition cannot run from the CD and must be installed on a computer to operate, but the loops can be used directly from the CD. If hard drive space is available, copying the loops to a directory on the hard drive makes opening them faster and eliminates the need to have Disc 2 in the CD-ROM drive when working with loops.

Once installation is complete, check the Adobe and Microsoft web sites for updates or newer versions of the software. These updates may contain added features or fix minor problems discovered after the software was published.

Installing Audition

Audio production requires some serious number crunching, and Audition will definitely give your computer a workout. Every time an edit is made or an effect applied, the processor must calculate the result, display the waveform on the monitor, and possibly play the sound at the same time. It may not sound like it, but this is a lot to accomplish and will push most computer systems to the limit. A computer equipped with the minimum requirements listed will run Audition, but you may find yourself in the break room frequently while some of the processes finish.

Minimum system requirements are:

- 400MHz processor
- 64MB RAM (Random Access Memory)
- 55MB of hard drive space
- Video card (capable of a pixel display of 800×600)
- Stereo sound card
- CD-ROM drive
- Speakers
- Microsoft Windows 2000, XP Home, or XP Professional

> **Note** Microsoft Windows XP is required for WMA Multi-channel Import. DirectX 9.0 or later is required for importing video files.

There are many advantages to using a system that exceeds minimum requirements, but the primary advantage is speed. Although Audition will run on a slower processor, the application shines on a faster CPU. Applying effects over a long track can take several minutes, even on a fast processor. Another factor to consider is the workspace in Audition. Although Audition uses the screen space very efficiently, the screen can still become cramped when working with multiple tracks, effects, and control windows. Higher-resolution monitors provide the extra screen space for those windows, but dual monitors are ideal when working on complex projects. Working with a stereo sound card is all that many projects call for; however, surround-sound mixing requires a multichannel sound card. The following are recommended system components.

Recommended system requirements:

- 2GHz or faster processor
- 1GB RAM
- 4 GB hard drive space
- Video card (capable of pixel display of 1,024×768)
- Multichannel sound card

Sound Cards: When purchasing components or upgrading a system, the importance of the sound card or audio interface should not be ignored. The sound card handles one of the most critical tasks of converting analog to digital and vice versa. There is a distinctly audible difference between low-end and high-end sound cards. Although I have my favorites, there are a number of excellent sound cards and audio interfaces on the market. The most well-known may not necessarily be the best. Do your homework. It will be well worth the time.

- CD/DVD-Recorder
- 5.1 Surround-Sound Speakers
- Microphones
- Windows XP or above
- DirectX 9.0 or later

 Adobe Audition can take advantage of multiple processors.

 If possible, install your sound card and all hardware before installing Audition. Also, check the hardware manufacturer's web site and install any updated drivers before beginning Audition installation.

 To determine the currently installed version of DirectX, select **Run from the** Windows **Start** menu and type *dxdiag* to open the Microsoft DirectX Diagnostic Tool. The installed version is listed on the **System** tab.

Installation Procedure

Audition provides the standard Adobe-type installation method. A few moments after inserting the installation disc into the CD-ROM drive, the splash screen shown in Figure 2.1 will appear. If not, explore the Adobe Audition CD-ROM and double-click *AutoPlay.exe*. The splash screen presents options to install Audition, Acrobat Reader, or to explore the CD-ROM. Clicking the **Explore** button reveals other options including detailed installation instructions.

2.1   *Splash screen for the Adobe Audition Installation CD*

To begin the installation, make certain that all other applications are closed. Click the **Adobe Audition 1.5** button and the InstallShield Wizard will begin the installation. Continue through the installation prompts and enter the requested information as shown in Figure 2.2. The serial number is located on the back of the CD case.

The next screen shows the default location that Audition will be installed on the hard drive. Clicking the **Change** button and selecting another location can change this location, but changing the destination can make future updates more complicated. Leaving the default location is recommended.

The screen shown in Figure 2.3 determines whether Audition will be the default application called to open files with particular extensions. For example, Audition does not open .WMA files by default. Another application such as Windows Media Player may be associated

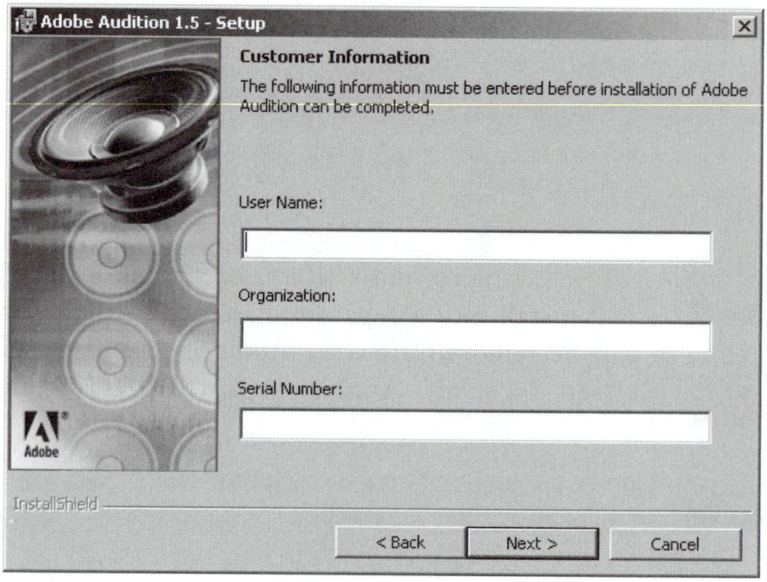

2.2 User information screen

with .WMA files. Selecting the **Associate** button next to **Windows Media Audio (.wma)** will cause any .WMA file to open in Audition instead of Windows Media Player.

TIP!! File associations can always be modified later via the **File Views** tab in the **Folder Options** control panel in Windows.

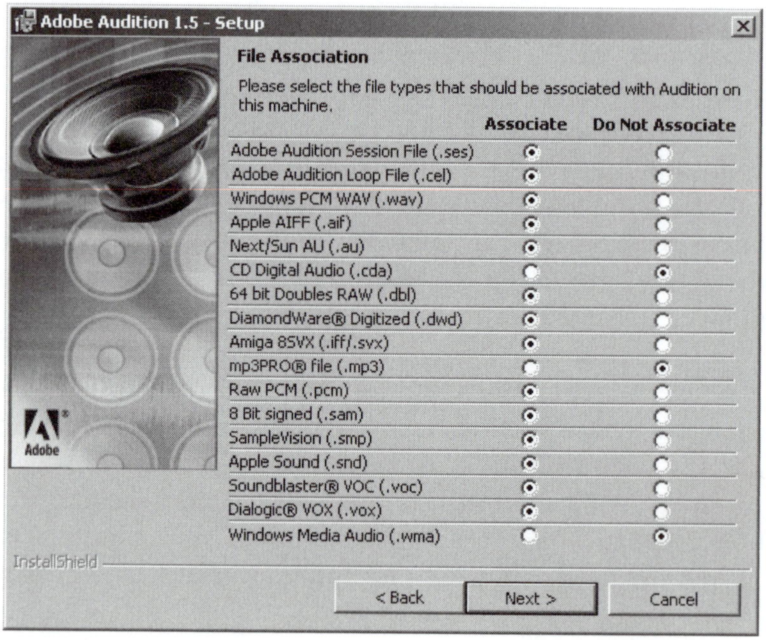

2.3 File association screen

Once file associations are chosen, click the **Next** button, finish the installation, and remove the installation CD. Rebooting may not be necessary, but it is a good habit to practice after installing any software.

Upgrading Audition

Users of Cool Edit Pro need to leave the Cool Edit Pro application on their computer until after Audition is installed. Audition will install into a separate directory so that Cool Edit Pro can be removed after the Audition installation is complete. Users of Adobe Audition 1.0 will be prompted through the upgrade steps.

The Ins and Outs

Getting signal in and out of Audition depends upon the hardware installed or connected to the computer. Let's take a look a the various ways to hook up with Audition.

Audio Connections

There are two forms of audio signal that sound cards can accept; analog and digital; however, there are many different types of connectors in use. The longer you have been working with audio, the more types of connectors and cables you will have lying around the studio. I have mine in a tackle box.

The standard connector for analog audio is a 1/8-inch stereo mini-plug. This type of connector is common on consumer sound cards such as the SoundBlaster and personal computer systems from companies such as Dell, Gateway, and Hewlett-Packard. The same plug is used for Aux (Auxiliary) and Line In inputs. Microphone inputs typically use a mono version of this plug. You may also find sound cards using RCA connectors for audio. The higher-end sound cards generally use 1/4-inch phone jacks or even XLR or Cannon type connectors. These connectors are usually balanced to reduce potential noise problems.

cv2, flt, and xfm

There are three types of files that may be added to the Adobe Audition application directory by third-party developers. Files with the extension of .cv2 are used by external controllers such as the Tascam US-428 or US-224. Filters that provide the ability to import foreign audio formats use the .flt extension, and effects or transforms use the .xfm extension.

In addition, a separate VST Plug-Ins directory is provided for third-party VST effects should a VST plug-in directory, which is not installed as part of another Host application, not be found on the system.

Noise and Audio Cables

Audio cables are very susceptible to noise in a manner similar to an antenna. To reduce the noise, a third conductor wire is integrated into the cable. The hot signal is split into two signals and sent down two separate wires with one of the signals flipped 180° out of phase. The ground travels down the third wire. When the signals reach the other end of the cable, the phase is reversed again and added back together. The noise picked up along the cable is out of phase and therefore cancels itself out when added together.

Digital audio connectors also come in several flavors. The most common connector found on sound cards is an RCA connector. Other connectors such as BNC, and 1/4-inch Phone, and the optical TosLink (Toshiba Link), connectors can also carry the SPDIF (Sony/Philips Digital Interface) digital signal. XLR connectors are most often used for a balanced digital signal called AES/EBU.

Once the necessary cables have been rounded up, start by connecting the inputs and outputs. The task of connecting the equipment can range from extremely easy to very complex depending upon the outboard gear available. There are a few simple rules. Connect digital signals to digital connections and analog signals to analog connections. Microphones require a preamp. If the sound card has a "Microphone in," then the sound card has a preamp on it. If not, you will need to run the microphone through another piece of equipment to get it up to line level. Do not plug line-level equipment into microphone inputs. It will distort.

MIDI

MIDI interfaces come in a flock of shapes and sizes from build-your-own to controllers with keyboard and audio interface. The connections have remained simple. Five-pin mini-DIN is the standard for connecting MIDI devices, and USB is the latest standard computer connection, but many sound cards have the older joystick/MIDI port connection. Either connection offers full support of the MIDI protocol.

Audio Monitors

The difficulty in hooking up an audio monitoring system is not so much in the connections as in getting the wiring out of the way. It is not hard when using a set of stereo speakers

2.4 *Different types of audio connectors. © 2004 by Monster Cable Products, Inc., used with permission.*

Preamplifier

The voltage output of a microphone is only a few millivolts; however most audio circuits look for about 750mV. A preamplifier (preamp) is used to boost the microphone level to what is referred to as line level.

2.5 *M-Audio Delta IIO soundcard. © 2004 by M-Audio, used with permission.*

2.6 *USB and mini-DIN connectors*

MIDI

The acronym MIDI is derived from Musical Instrument Digital Interface. MIDI is a protocol that allows computers, lighting devices, and other type of electronics to communicate and work in a synchronized manner. It's used mostly in synthesizers.

because the speaker cables can be hidden behind the computer, but putting in a surround-sound system increases the challenge. Most sound cards use a 1/8-in. stereo mini-jack connector for speaker output, and higher-end sound cards provide balanced outputs.

Many of the "home theater" speaker systems are self-powered, meaning that you do not need an additional source of amplification, but an amplifier or receiver may be required to offer a suitable listening volume.

THE BEST PERFORMANCE

There is an old cliché that is appropriate here: "Time is money." Preparing Audition and your computer system for optimum performance cannot only save time but also the cost of more than a few cups of coffee. Speed is important whether it is your own time or someone else's, so take the time to set your system up for maximum performance.

Audition, like a new sports car, will run on most systems without any modifications, provided that the system meets the minimum requirements. However, the professional driver knows how to pop the hood and tweak the engine.

You can achieve a performance boost by optimizing in two ways. The first way is by setting up the application preferences. Many of these preferences are set-it-and-forget-it options. The second way is by optimizing your system hardware. Keeping your hardware at peak performance also requires some regular maintenance steps. One word to the wise: if you don't know what it does, don't touch it until you do, and don't be afraid to call in a computer "mechanic."

Settings

The **Audition Settings,** or application preferences, are located under the **Options** menu. The **Settings** dialog box contains different tabs that divide the application settings into groups of

Audio Monitoring System Out of Phase?

Your audio monitoring system can also be out of phase. If you don't make certain your speakers are hooked up in phase, some of your sound will be canceled out as one speaker is pushing while the other is pulling back. Check and see if the speakers are wired in phase by confirming that the positive terminals of your amplifier are both connected to the positive terminals of your speakers. To make certain that your speakers are in phase, momentarily connect the positive and negative terminal of a 9-volt battery to the matching terminals of each speaker and verify that the speakers move in the same direction. You can also tell if your speakers are out of phase by listening to the vocals on most recordings. If you cannot seem to pinpoint where the voice is located in the stereo image, then your speakers are probably out of phase. Loss of low-end sound is another hint that your monitoring system may have phase issues.

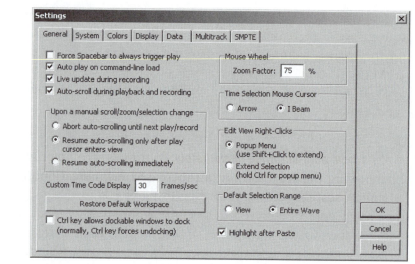

2.7   General tab of the Settings dialog box

similar functions. Changes to the look, response, and performance are made through these tabs. The following sections describe the functions of each tab.

General Tab

The **General** tab provides access to options controlling playback display, cursor and mouse behavior, and a few common application parameters (see Figure 2.7).

Force Spacbar to always trigger play: causes Audition to toggle between playing the waveform and stopping playback regardless of the currently active window or function.

Auto play on command-line load: allows Audition to launch and play back a file from the **Run** command above the **Start** menu. Most users find it easier to double-click the file; however, using this feature can open the file faster if the file type is associated to an application other than Audition.

Live update during recording: renders the waveform as the audio is being recorded. This is a great feature and provides the ability to see not only the amplitude of the waveform, but also the frequency content when the waveform is viewed via the **Spectral View**.

Auto-scroll during playback and recording: automatically keeps the segment of waveform displayed in sync with the segment being recorded or played back when zooming in. The **Live update during recording** checkbox must also be selected for this feature to function during recording. This feature is more useful during recording, but it has its applications during playback. For example, while recording guitar track, the producer asks if the player was in the groove at the beginning. Without stopping and possibly wasting the take, the beginning of the tracks can be visually reviewed for sync with other previously recorded tracks.

Upon a manual scroll/zoom/selection change: controls whether and when **Auto-scroll during playback and recording** resumes.

- ***Abort auto-scrolling until next play/record:*** deactivates the auto-scrolling until another recording or playback is initiated.

- ***Resume auto-scrolling only after play cursor enters view:*** causes the waveform to scroll when the cursor comes back into view. This setting offers the most benefit by allowing the view of waveform segments and returning to a scrolling view afterwards.

- ***Resume auto-scrolling immediately:*** continues scrolling right after zooming. This is great for viewing the waveform at an increased magnification; however, it prevents viewing specific locations during recording or playback.

 Live updating and auto-scrolling are handy features, but they come at a significant cost. Turn these features off if recording or playback skips.

Custom Timecode Display: sets the number of frames per second in the **Custom Time Format**.

Restore Default Workspace: returns all Audition windows in the current workspace to the default size and positions.

Ctrl key allows dockable windows to dock: allows you to press the **Control** key to dock windows. Otherwise, the **Control** key will permit undocking windows.

Mouse Wheel: adjusts the zoom factor when turning the wheel on Intellipoint-compatible mice. The default of 33 percent works fine, but higher numbers zoom in faster for extremely accurate editing or track mark placement.

 There are a number of different pointing devices on the market from quad-button mice to drawing tablets that provide a substantial gain in ease and speed. Check your local computer store.

Time Selection Mouse Cursor: selects whether to display the cursor as an I-beam or an arrow when the cursor is on the waveform.

Edit View *Right-Clicks*: determines what happens when you right-click on the waveform. One option will present a pop-up menu, and the other option will extend the selected segment.

Default Selection Range: determines the part of the waveform that is selected if no manual selection is made. This is an important setting. When **View** is chosen and no part of the waveform is selected, an effect or level adjustment is applied only to the segment that can be seen in the window. When **Entire Wave** is chosen and no part of the waveform is selected, the effect or level adjustment is applied to the entire waveform whether it is currently viewable or not.

Highlight after Paste: highlights any segment that is pasted or copied into the waveform. It can be difficult to tell where or whether a segment has been added if this option is turned off.

 Double-click the waveform to select the segment in the window. Triple-click the waveform to select the entire waveform.

System Tab

The **System** tab allows modification of settings that directly relate to the computer system resources, mainly memory and storage space. Audition will run on most systems without changing these parameters, but there are systems that will benefit by altering these options. Caution should be used when making changes to these parameters because some modifications could hurt performance.

Edit View *Play/Record Buffer:* adjusts the amount of RAM used for recording and playback. The buffers store audio data as it transfers to and from devices. The default of 2 seconds using 10 buffers works on most systems, but these values may need to be increased if skipping or dropouts occur. Increasing the buffer size reduces the amount of memory available for other processes or applications and can cause recording errors. Faster systems can benefit from lowering buffer values.

EV Preview Buffer: sets the minimum memory used to preview effects in **Edit View**. Setting the minimum buffer size too low will result in skipping or dropouts, and setting the minimum too high will cause sluggish response. 1,000 milliseconds is the suggested minimum, but 250 milliseconds is often acceptable.

2.8 *System tab of the Settings dialog box*

Wave Cache	Installed RAM
8192	64 MB
16384	128 MB
32768	256 MB
32768	512 MB

2.9   Wave cache recommendations

Wave Cache: stores blocks of the waveform as it is processed. The value depends upon the amount of installed RAM. Figure 2.9 shows the appropriate values. Values above 32,768 have diminishing returns and fail to provide appreciable results.

Use System's Cache: permits Audition to use the system cache instead of the *Wave Cache*. Audition handles memory more efficiently, so using the system cache is not recommended.

Use Sound Card Positioning Info: This option is used for sound cards that cannot record or playback at 44.1kHz. Use this option only if the cursor does not sync with the audio.

CD Device Options: Audition provides two options for communication with CD and DVD drives. ASPI (Advanced SCSI Programming Interface) and SPTI (SCSI Pass Through Interface). SPTI is Microsoft's development and is operational on Windows 2000 and Windows XP. ASPI as written by Adaptec and requires installation of the ASPI drivers.

Temporary Folders: designates paths to the directories used by Audition to store temporary files when modifying audio. Although only one *Temp* folder is required and it can reside on the system drive, performance can be improved by placing the directory on a secondary drive. You can achieve even greater improvements by placing the *Secondary* folder on a third hard drive.

 You should not set a *Secondary Temp* folder if your computer has only one hard drive.

Reserve: maintains the value entered for hard drive overhead. Audition will leave this much space free on your hard drive. Every hard drive needs some space to store directory listing and file-location information. File corruption or drive failure could result if the drive becomes full and is unable to perform this housekeeping.

Some drive manufacturers have recommended not allowing the free space to fall below 100MB, but 25–50MB should be sufficient reserve for most drives.

Enable Undo: enables reversing the last change or edit. This feature should be enabled.

Levels (minimum): sets the minimum number of previous changes or edits that can be reversed. Each edit or change is considered as a level. Because every level of undo requires disc space and time to save those levels to disc, it does affect performance, but the cost is well worth it…that is, unless you don't make mistakes. Five is a good setting, and much consideration should be given before lowering this number.

Purge Undo: deletes all temporary undo files. This is a useful feature when working on complex projects and with limited system resources, but think twice before using it. Pressing this button will immediately remove all undos.

Delete clipboard files on exit: Dumps all data copied to the clipboard memory. This should remain off unless the data needs to be accessed specifically from the clipboard by another application.

 When copying statistical data from Audition to another application, open the other application and copy the data before closing Audition.

Force complete flush before saving: Disables Audition's quick save feature. Check this option if you're unable to save changes back to the same file name. Enabling this feature will result in extended save times and should be used only if necessary.

Colors Tab

We live in an age of individuality, and Audition offers the ability to give the application a unique appearance. The **Colors** tab permits customization of the color scheme. Bright colors should be avoided if the application is to be used for extended periods of time to avoid eye fatigue.

Waveform Tab: permits changing colors of the waveform components presented in the **Waveform List** window (see Figure 2.10).

- *Selection:* Colors can be inverted with the **Invert** checkbox, and the component opacity can be adjusted with the **Transparency** slider. Transparency can also be entered as a numeric value.

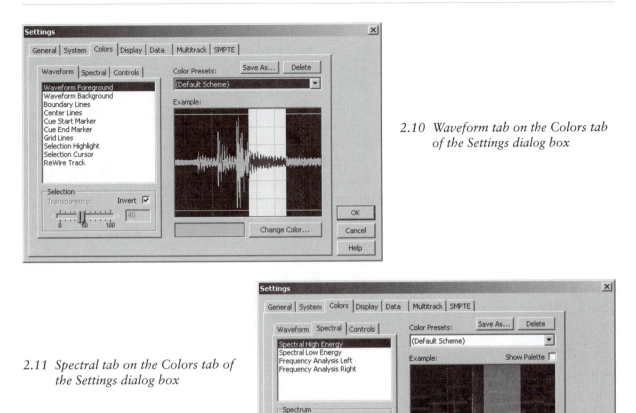

2.10 *Waveform tab on the Colors tab of the Settings dialog box*

2.11 *Spectral tab on the Colors tab of the Settings dialog box*

Spectral Tab: permits changing colors of the **Frequency Analysis** and **Spectral Energy** components displayed in the **Edit View/Spectral View** window (see Figure 2.11).

- **Spectrum:** The **Reverse Direction** checkbox inverts the colors displayed in the color spectrum much like a photo negative, and the **Gamma** adjusts the range of the color spectrum. A value of 1.8 should be satisfactory for most monitors.

- **Selection:** Colors can be inverted with the **Invert** checkbox, and the component opacity can be adjusted with the **Transparency** slider. Transparency can also be entered as a numeric value.

- **Show Palette:** displays the color palette used by the spectrum display.

2.12 Controls tab of the Colors tab on the Settings dialog box.

Controls Tab: permits changing colors of the Audition's interface controls.

- **Segmented Progress Bar:** determines whether the progress bar will be one continuous tone or a segmented bar.

- **White Progress Background:** sets the progress bar background to white.

- **Dockable Windows:** has three options that vary the color of the **Dockable Windows**, depending upon the Microsoft Windows theme currently in use or the color specified in the color palette.

Color Presets: allows selection of a preset color scheme. There are a number of stock presets, and Audition allows the option of modifying, saving, and deleting color schemes with the pop-up list and **Save As** and **Delete** buttons.

Change Color: allows you to select custom colors for each component. The standard Microsoft Windows color palette appears.

Display Tab

The **Display** tab options control the methods used to display both the **Spectral View** and **Waveform View**. Adjustments to peak files are also made in this tab (see Figure 2.13).

Spectral Display: Determines display properties of the view when **Spectrum View** is selected in the **Edit View** workspace. The **Spectrum View** exhibits frequencies over time as a spectrograph as shown in Figure 2.14.

- **Windowing Function:** selects the algorithm used for the **Spectral Display**. Each curve is weighted differently. The Blackmann-Harris weighting curve is the broadest curve, and although it is not quite as accurate as other curves, it is the easiest to use for most users.

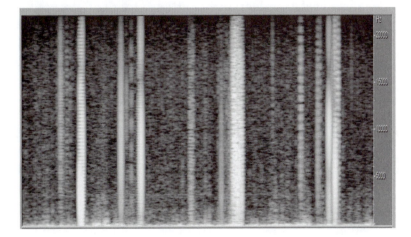

2.13 *Display tab of the Settings dialog box*

2.14 *Spectrograph viewed in Spectral View mode*

- **Resolution:** determines the number of bands in which the frequencies are grouped for display. The larger the number of bands, the more precise the frequencies displayed. However, this places more demand on the CPU. A value of 256 works well and provides a good overview of the file. High values can be used to acquire information that is more specific.

- **Window Width:** sets the percentage of the frame used for analysis. Smaller values yield higher-frequency resolution and lower time resolution, and lower values reduce frequency resolution and increase the precision of the time scaling. A value of 60 is suggested.

Plot Style: sets parameters for plot display of the spectrograph.

- *Logarithmic Energy Plot:* specifies the plotting in a decibel-based logarithmic scale. The range value determines the scale. This scale works well for extreme details in low-level material.

- *Linear Energy Plot:* specifies the plotting in a percentage of maximum amplitude. The **Scaling** value determines the sensitivity. This scale works well as an overview.

Waveform Display: turns on ond off the waveform display guides such as **Cue Markers, Grid Lines,** and **Center Lines.** The guides are a valuable aid in the production process and should remain checked, but they can be shut off.

- *Show Cue and Range Lines:* turns on the vertical dotted lines that define **Cue Marker** and **Range Lines.**

- *Show Grid Lines:* turns on the grid that delineates the time and amplitude scales.

- *Show Center Lines:* turns on the center line that marks zero amplitude.

- *Show Boundary Lines:* turns on lines that can be used as level guides. In addition to the level meters, these guides are used to provide a visual cue when levels cross a preset amplitude. For example, by setting the display lines at –3dB, you can easily see any levels that are within 3dB of clipping or distorting during recording.

  Display Lines at: sets the decibel value on the vertical scale that the **Boundary Line** defines.

Peak Files: determines how quickly files are displayed. Peak files contain the data necessary to render the waveform representation on the monitor. They carry the .pk extension and are not required to open audio files, but they will make files open significantly faster.

- *Peaks Cache:* sets the number of samples per block used to store a graphic representation of the waveform. The default setting is a numeric value of 256 and is recommended for song length audio files. Increase the value to 1,024 or 2,048 when working with longer files.

- *Save Peak Cache Files:* enables the saving of .pk files. The default is enabled. Disabling this feature will result in markedly longer file load time.

- *Rebuild Wave Display Now:* scans the current waveform and renders a new peak cache file.

Data Tab

The **Data** tab grants access to the options that control how Audition processes audio files (see Figure 2.15).

2.15 *Data tab of the Settings dialog box*

Embed Project Link data for Edit Original functionality: enables Audition to link project data to other Adobe applications such as Adobe Premiere Pro and After Effects 6.0 and above. Checking this box is recommended when working on video or DVD projects.

Auto-convert all data to 32-bit upon opening: enables automatic conversion of all files to 32-bit files when the files are opened in Audition. Setting this option depends on the typical content and workflow. Leave this option off unless specifically needed. Enable this option to take advantage of the extended dynamic range provided in 32-bit mode when applying effects or mixing tracks.

Interpret 32-bit PCM .wav files as 16.8 float: allows compatibility with files saved in version of Cool Edit 1.2 and older. Uncheck this option unless required.

Dither Transform Results (increases dynamic range): enables dithering on the processed signal. Leaving this on is recommended. Because all processing such as adding an effect require mathematical calculations, Audition uses more than 16 bits to do the computations and then uses dither as the waveform is rendered back to 16 bits. The outcome with **Dither Transform Results** enabled is less distortion, but a minor amount of white noise is added to the signal.

Use Symmetric Dithering: causes dithering to produce an equal amount of positive and negative samples. The results are generally inaudible, but it is suggested that this option remain enabled.

Smooth Delete and Cut Boundaries: enables a smoothing of edit transitions by matching levels and thus eliminates potential clicks caused by sudden changes in level. This should be checked. A value of 2 milliseconds is the default.

Smooth all edit boundaries by crossfading: causes a small cross-fade during each edit or effect transition. Crossfading smoothes the transition and eliminates potential clicks caused by sudden changes in level. This option should be checked, and a numeric value should be entered in the millisecond field following the option. The default is 5 milliseconds.

Auto-convert settings for Paste: enables automatic sample conversion to the format of the waveform into which the data is pasted.

- ***Downsampling quality level:*** reduces the sampling rate. Values between 30 and 1,000 are accepted, but 200 is a good starting point. Higher values will preserve more high-end sound but may cause a ringing of high frequencies. Lower values can result in loss of high frequencies.

- ***Pre-filter:*** turns on signal filtering before downsampling and reduces the potential for aliasing and artifacts. Leaving this on is recommended.

- ***Upsampling quality level:*** increases the sampling rate. Values between 30 and 1,000 are accepted, but 120 is a good starting point. Higher values will preserve more high-end sound but may cause a ringing of high frequencies. Lower values can result in loss of high frequencies.

- ***Post-filter:*** turns on signal filtering after upsampling and reduces the potential for aliasing and artifacts. Leaving this on is recommended.

Dither amount for saving 32-bit data to 16-bit files: enables or disables dithering when pasting 32-bit audio to 16-bit. The default value of **1** enables dithering, and **0** disables dithering.

Allow for partially processed data after cancelling effect: determines whether a partially rendered effect is saved when canceled. The ability to render part of an effect for review can be an advantage when the preview is too short.

Multitrack Tab

The **Multitrack** tab permits setting multitrack recording and playback options and some mixdown settings.

Play/Record: contains the options that affect sound card or device playback and record performance.

Crossfades

Crossfades, sometimes referred to as *segues*, are common in audio production. A crossfade occurs at the transition between two segments of audio. The crossfade can be any length and begins as the first segment begins fading and the second segment gradually increases in amplitude until the desired level is achieved. This effect is heard routinely on the radio as one song transitions to another.

2.16 Multitrack tab of the Settings dialog box

- *Playback Buffer Size:* determines the number of seconds allocated for playback buffering. Increasing the buffer size stores more data in the buffer, requiring less processing time to move data, but doing so uses more of the available memory. The default is one second.

- *Playback Buffers:* sets the number of buffers used for multitrack playback. The size and number of buffers work together. Try decreasing the number of buffers if skipping or dropouts occur during playback. Default is 10.

- *Recording Buffer Size:* determines the number of seconds allocated for record buffering. Try increasing the buffer size if problems result during recording. Default is two seconds.

- *Recording Buffers:* sets the number of buffers used for multitrack recording. Default is 10.

- *Background Mixing Priority:* sets the priority level of background mixing in relation to other processes. Background mixing takes advantage of any available CPU clock cycles to render effects or changes made to tracks. Setting a lower numeric value forces a higher priority. This value can also be set by right-clicking on the **Background Mixing Gauge.**

Sound cards may require different buffer settings to achieve the best performance, but the default settings work for most. Before adjusting the buffers, make sure the problems still occur when background mixing is complete. The **Background Mixing Gauge** provides a progress bar to indicate progress, and right-clicking on the **Background Mixing Gauge** allows you to choose **Background Mixing of Entire Session**. If skipping or dropouts occur on playback., try lowering the number of playback buffers or increasing playback buffer size. If problems occur during recording, try increasing the number of recording buffers or recording buffer size. Finding the correct combination of buffer size versus number of buffers may take some experimentation.

- *Open Order:* determines the sequence of open commands issued to the sound card driver. As with any input/output device or file, an open command is issued to ready the device for operation. Because recording and playback are separate but simultaneous functions, both functions must be opened. Most sound cards do not require a specific order; however there are a few that do.

- *Start Order:* determines the sequence of start commands issued to the sound card driver. Because recording and playback are separate but simultaneous functions, both functions must be started. Most sound cards do not require a specific order; however there are a few that do.

> Digital Audio Labs CardD and Soundblaster cards require an Open Order of Rec, Play. CardD also requires a Start Order of Play, Rec, and Soundblaster cards require a Start Order of Rec, Play. Check your sound card's manual.

- *Correct for Drift in Recordings:* causes Audition to compare sync between the master sound card or device (first output device is usually on **Track 1**) and the recording sound card or device. If significant drift occurred, the recorded track will be resampled to correct the drift once the recording is stopped. Disable this check box on sound cards or devices that use the same clock source or support sample accurate devices.
- *Correct for Start Sync in Recordings:* causes Audition to calculate the difference between the master playback device start time and the recorded track start time. The recorded track is adjusted by the difference so that the tracks are played back in sync. Disable this checkbox if sound cards or devices use the same clock source.

Merging: merges the selected take into the waveform when using **Punch-In** record mode.

- *Delete old takes after merging:* deletes all outtakes (takes that were not selected as the final take).
- *Crossfade Time:* accepts a numeric value that determines the number of millisecond crossfade at the beginning and end of a **Punch-In** take. The default of 30 milliseconds works well.

Mixdowns: determines whether the mixdown will be 16-bit or 32-bit. The default of 16-bit is more than adequate for radio and most video productions. For high-end music projects, use 32-bit until outputting as Red Book (compact disc audio) audio. Remaining in 32-bit mode retains the highest fidelity and provides the most flexibility for repurposing the audio, but there is also a performance cost due to increased file sizes. (Dithering options are discussed in depth in Chapter 10 on page 244.)

Defaults: sets the track defaults when engaging the record mode in the **Multitrack View**.

- *Track Record:* selects whether the track will be recorded in 16-bit or 32-bit mode and whether the track will be recorded as a stereo or mono track.

- **Pre-Mixing:** determines whether pre-mixing will occur in 16-bit mode or 32-bit mode. Because the processor requirements of mixing multiple tracks can bring even the faster systems to their knees, Audition processes or mixes as many of the tracks in advance of playback. Pre-mixing in 32-bit is recommended for systems with a single sound card. Systems with multiple sound cards can see a performance boost by switching to 16-bit pre-mixing mode.

- **Panning Mode:** selects the result of panning the signal between channels.

  L/R Cut (log) enables a method that logarithmically decreases the signal of the right channel when panning left or decreases the signal to the left channel when panning right. The panning will not result in an increased signal gain.

  Equal-power Sine enables a method that maintains constant power and results in a signal gain when panning. Because of this potential gain increase, clipping may occur in 16-bit mode.

Auto Zero-Cross Edits: smoothes or matches the levels nearest zero level on edits or transition points. This prevents clicks or pops.

Smooth auto-scrolling during playback: enables a smoother scrolling of the tracks during playback by continuously updating the screen. The effect is similar to watching movie credits scroll on the screen instead of appearing page at a time. There is a performance cost for smoother scrolling.

Save locked track files after closing sessions (for faster session loads): saves tracks that have been locked during the session. This feature enables faster reloading of session files, and the locked tracks will remain locked.

SMPTE Tab

The SMPTE Tab contains parameters to adjust system response when synchronizing to other machines using SMPTE (Society of Motion Picture and Television Engineers) or MTC (MIDI Timecode). See "Synchronization" on page 286 in Chapter 12 for a detailed discussion of SMPTE and synchronization.

Lead Time (to prepare wave driver): sets the amount of time in milliseconds that Audition has to sync with timecode. Lower values cause quicker transport response, but could result in inhibiting successful synchronization. The default value is 200 milliseconds, but 500 is recommended.

Stopping Time (freewheel-audio stops after no input detected for this time): determines the amount of time Audition will continue playing after timecode ends. The default is 1,000 milliseconds. A frame or two of timecode could be corrupt or missing, so with a value of 1,000, playback will

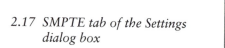

2.17 SMPTE tab of the Settings dialog box

continue. Missing one second or more of timecode generally signals the end of the program or a serious issue with the timecode signal.

Lag Time (constant time difference between sound card driver's reported position and actual): permits correction of the delay between the timecode and audio caused by the sound card buffers. The lag time varies with different sound cards. This value is entered in samples.

Slack (time error allowable before repositioning play cursor): sets the maximum number of frames that Audition can be out of sync before repositioning the cursor or executing a full resynchronization. The default and recommended value is one frame. Values greater than two can be entered, but that will probably result in audible synchronization issues between tracks.

Clock Drift Correction Time (crossfade length to use when adjusting playback position): establishes the number of samples to crossfade when adjusting playback position. The default is 200 samples.

Reposition playback cursor when shuttling: resets the cursor position when shuttling. Repositioning occurs when sync is greater than the amount set in the **Slack** option.

Full re-sync when shuttling: executes a full resync when sync is greater than the amount set in the **Slack** option.

Device Properties

The **Device Properties** dialog box provides access to sound card or device settings. Digital audio, MIDI, and external controller parameters are set in one of five tabs.

2.18 Wave Out tab of the Device Properties dialog box

Note ASIO, a protocol that specifies a standardized method of communication between software applications and hardware devices, is not supported by Adobe Audition.

Wave Out Tab

The **Wave Out** tab is used to set digital audio playback options. A pop-up list allows selection of the device or sound card output. Preferences for each output are separate and operate independently (see Figure 2.18).

Order: sets the preferred order of the sound card or device that is used for playback. Pressing the **Change** button opens the **Device Order** dialog box. Zero indicates that the device will not be used for recording. See the "Device Order" on page 42 for a discussion of available options.

Use this device in Edit View: determines the sound card or device used for waveform playback when in the **Edit View** workspace. Only one device is used for playback in **Edit View,** so in multidevice systems, checking this box will deselect any other previously selected device.

Limit Playback to: limits sound card playback to 8-bit or 16-bit. The playback can also be limited to mono. Some devices may not support 32-bit playback. Check the **Supported Formats** table on the right of the dialog box to see if the formats are supported by the device. The **Limit Playback to** options allow playback of unsupported formats. For example, when the Supported Formats table does not list any 32-bit formats, select the 16-bit checkbox to play back a 32-bit waveform. The audible quality will not sound as good, but at least it makes playback possible.

Send 32-Bit Audio as: allows selection of the supported output formats of 32-bit audio.

Try as WDM: enables WDM (Win32 Driver Model) driver extensible wave format. Enable this checkbox if supported by the hardware unless experiencing problems with the sound card or device.

2.19 Wave In tab of the Device Properties dialog box

Enable Dithering: turns on dithering. Dithering helps resolve an anomaly that occurs as a result of the digitization of the audio signal. Dithering adds a low-level noise to the signal that masks the anomaly. Dithering should be used when reducing the bit depth of the waveform, for example, when outputting a 16-bit track for use on compact disc from a 32-bit waveform. Dithering and dithering options are discussed in depth in Chapter 10 on page 244.

Supported Formats: displays the digital audio formats supported by the selected device.

Wave In Tab

The Wave In tab is used to set digital audio recording options. A pop-up list allows selection of the device or sound card input. Preferences for each input are separate and operate independently.

Order: sets the preferred order of the sound card or device used for recording. Pressing the **Change** button opens the **Device Order** dialog box. Zero indicates that the device will not be used for recording. See the "Device Order" on page 42 for a discussion of available options as well as Figure 2.19.

Use this device in Edit View: determines the sound card or device used for waveform recording when in the **Edit View** workspace. Only one device is used for recording in **Edit View,** so in multidevice systems, checking this box will deselect any other previously selected device.

Get 32-bit audio using: allows selection of the supported formats of 32-bit audio.

Try as WDM: enables WDM (Win32 Driver Model) driver extensible wave format. Enable this checkbox if supported by the hardware unless experiencing problems with the sound card or device.

Multitrack Latency: allows entering a value in milliseconds to compensate for timing delays between multiple sound cards.

Adjust to zero-DC when recording: enables automatic elimination of DC (Direct Current) bias during recording.

Supported Formats: displays the digital audio formats supported by the selected device.

MIDI Out Tab

The **MIDI Out** tab controls the default device used to output MIDI and SMPTE.

MIDI Output: selects the MIDI output device.

SMPTE Output: selects the SMPTE timecode output device.

Order: sets the preferred order of the sound card or device that is used for MIDI. Pressing the **Change** button opens the **Device Order** dialog box. Zero indicates that the device will not be used for MIDI. See "Device Order" on page 42 for a discussion of available options.

MIDI In Tab

The **MIDI In** tab controls the default device used to input MIDI.

The Problem with DC Offset

A complex audio waveform is typically made up of alternating positive and negative voltages at varying frequencies. Sound cards, particularly the less expensive cards, allow some direct current (DC) voltage to leak into the audio signal. This leakage is added to the signal and causes the waveform to be offset from the center line or zero voltage. Figure 2.20 shows an audio signal with a severe DC offset followed by a signal with the offset reduced to near zero. DC offset can cause clicks and pops and can affect the level metering. Audition provides the ability to remove the DC offset during the recording and allows adjustment of the offset on existing files.

2.20 *Signal with DC offset followed by audio signal with DC offset removed*

2.21 *MIDI Out tab of the Device Properties dialog box*

2.22 *MIDI In tab of the Device Properties dialog box*

SMPTE Slave Device: determines the MIDI slave device. The SMPTE slave device is the device that will chase or slave to the master device during synchronization.

Use Internal Timestamps: enabling this checkbox can help correct sync problems when using Sample Accurate devices. Appendix A on page 293 provides a brief overview of a few of the available external surface controllers.

Ext. Controller Tab

The **External Controller** tab selects the external controller device supported by Adobe Audition. External controllers can be used to control most of the functions in Audition (see Figure 2.23).

External Control Device: selects the controller device from the dropdown list.

Volume Increment (dB): specifies the **Volume Increment** in decibels that will be used by the external controller.

Configure: presents the external controller configuration dialog box when an external controller is connected.

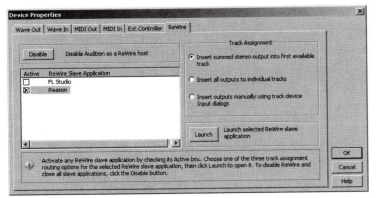

2.23 *Ext. Controller tab of the Device Properties dialog box*

ReWire Tab

The **ReWire** tab is used to configure Adobe Audition as a ReWire host. Applications that support ReWire are selected and launched from this tab. Note that ReWire can be used only in **Multitrack View.** The **ReWire** tab will not be displayed in the **Device Properties** window when Audition is in the **Edit View** mode.

Enable: toggles the status of Audition as a ReWire host. Any available ReWire slave applications can be selected from the **Active ReWire Slave Application** list below the button.

Track Assignment: determines the track assignments of the ReWire slave application. The stereo output or individual outputs can be automatically patched to the next available tracks in **Multitrack View,** or the slave applications outputs can be assigned to each track manually in the **Input Device** window in **Multitrack View.**

Launch: starts the selected ReWire slave application.

ReWire

ReWire is a relatively new technology developed by Propellerhead Software that allows ReWire-compliant applications to communicate in real time. The ReWire technology is a virtual wiring harness between the applications that permits two-way communication of audio, MIDI, and transport functions.

ReWire has become a standard for cross-application operation and is supported by a growing list of software applications. No installation is required, because the code is incorporated into programs that support it.

2.24 *ReWire tab of the Device Properties dialog box*

2.25 Device Order dialog box

Device Order

The **Device Order** dialog is used to set the sound card or devices that are used for recording, playback, and MIDI. There are four tabs: **Playback Devices, Recording Devices, MIDI Output Devices,** and **MIDI Input Devices.** Each tab controls which devices are used in **Edit View** and **Multitrack View** workspaces and the preferred order of the devices (see Figure 2.25).

The **Use** and **Remove** buttons move the device between the **Unused Playback Devices** list and the **Multitrack Device Preference Order** list. **Move Up** and **Move Down** permit arrangement of the preferred order when used in the **Multitrack** workspace. The **Use in EV** button sets the device as the default device used in the **Edit View** workspace and places an **EV** in brackets next to the device name. The **Properties** button opens the **Device Properties** dialog box.

System Resources

Processors

Upgrading to the fastest processor available is the best way to increase performance, but over-clocking is not recommended. Processors with large L2 caching are recommended. L2 caching stores frequently used system commands in memory on the CPU and speeds processing by reducing the number of trips the CPU has to take to the hard drive to retrieve recently used commands.

Memory

Increasing RAM has a point of diminishing returns around 512 MB, but installing more cannot hurt. Letting the operating system manage virtual memory or swap files is recommended for systems, but you can change these settings manually. Suggested virtual memory settings are 1.5–2 times the amount of RAM installed.

DMA

Direct memory access (DMA) relieves the CPU of hard drive data transfer tasks that can take a toll on the processor. Enabling DMA on hard drives can make a significant improvement in performance.

> **TIP!!** DMA settings are set by the **Device Manager** in Microsoft Windows. To access the **Device Manager**, click Start and select **Control Panel**. Double-click the **System** icon, choose the **Hardware** tab, and click the **Device Manager** button. Expand the IDE ATA/ATAPI controllers, right-click the desired controller channel, and pick **Properties**. The **DMA Transfer Mode** option, if available, is under the **Advanced Settings** tab.

Hard Drives

Hard drives have a great impact on Audition's performance. There are several things to consider about how Audition uses drive storage. The first way Audition uses hard drives is for file storage. Because CD-quality stereo audio requires about 10MB per minute, drive space can be depleted quickly. Storage requirements for a full audio CD are about 650MB. Fortunately, hard drive space is relatively inexpensive. One might think it would be prudent to install the largest hard drive they could afford. Instead, consider purchasing two smaller drives or adding another drive instead of replacing the system drive. By running two drives, each drive could be set up on a separate drive controller thereby reducing the data bottleneck and speeding up the data transfer. Optimum performance is achieved when Audition and the operation system are located on one drive and the *Temp* folder is on the second drive. Temporary storage preferences are found in the **System** tab of the **Settings** dialog box. If three physical drives are available on the system, keep the edited or audio data file on the second drive and put the *Temp* folder on the third drive.

When purchasing a new drive, select a drive with a minimum spin speed of 7,200RPM (revolutions per minute) and look for an access time of no more than 10 milliseconds. A 2MB buffer is acceptable, but many of the newer drives have at least an 8MB buffer. The buffer acts like a data bucket. The drive fills the bucket with data, and the drive controller gets data from the bucket. Even if the drive slows or goes about another task, the bucket will still have data in it to feed to the controller. This process also works in reverse. It is important when recording or playing a file back that the data stream is not interrupted. An interrupted data stream will cause a click, pop, or worse, the loss of the recording.

Most professionals prefer to use a SCSI (Small Computer System Interface) drive, but most PCs ship with an IDE (Integrated Drive Electronics) drive. SCSI drives have always offered faster transfer speeds; however, newer IDE drives such as the SATA (Serial AT Attachment) drives are offering transfer speed rivaling all but the fastest SCSI drives. SCSI also offers the ability to write and read simultaneously. This coupled with the capability of adding up to 15 drives to a controller make SCSI the better choice for professional usage.

Drive Formats

Windows 2000 Professional and later support the NTFS (New Technology File System) drive format. NTFS offers a more robust file system than FAT16 or FAT32. NTFS provides some fault tolerance. It automatically corrects certain types of drive errors. and although it can become fragmented like FAT16 and FAT32, NTFS is able to locate and access the fragments faster.

Drive Maintenance

One of the best ways to keep your system running at its peak is to defragment hard drives frequently. All drives eventually become fragmented. Fragmentation occurs as files are written to the drive and then deleted. Fragmentation would not happen if all files were the same size, but like empty seats in a half-filled theatre, there are not always enough seats to accommodate everyone in a group, and the group has to split up and fill the available seats. Defragmentation rewrites the data with all the data for each file grouped together so that the drive head does not have to zip back and forth across the drive looking for fragments of the file. The drive can be reformatted as an alternative to defragmenting the drive, but be careful, because formatting a drive will erase all data on the disc.

 Disk Defragmenter is a utility supplied with Microsoft Windows and is found at **Start > All Programs > Accessories > System Tools**. The path will vary slightly depending upon the version of operating system. There are also third-party utilities (such as PerfectDisk from Raxco Software) that may handle these tasks more efficiently.

Monitor Settings

Refreshing the waveform on the monitor can require enough time to be noticeable. If so, reduce the screen bit depth to 16-bit. The visual difference should only be perceptible when viewing color photos or high-resolution images, but the screen will redraw faster. Reducing the **Hardware Acceleration** to **None** on the graphics card can also improve performance and elimination possible sound card conflicts and possible system errors.

 The **Graphics Card Accelerator** setting is accessed by selecting the **Display** icon in the **Control Panels**. Click the **Advanced** button and then the **Troubleshoot** tab.

Networks

Networks will not usually have a noticeable affect on performance; however, depending upon the amount and type of network traffic, performance could suffer. If application performance is not acceptable, test the system with and without network connections by simply disconnecting the network cable. You may need to reboot with the network cable plugged in to reestablish a network connection on some operating systems.

System Options

Animated cursors, windows, and tool tips certainly give the desktop more personality, but at what cost? These options steal clock cycles from the processor. Put simply, a 400MHz processor can execute 400 million instructions per second. Enabling a number of these visual toys could make a 400MHz run like a 350MHz processor.

Disable the Windows sounds. Windows sounds are the sounds that play when the system boots up, shuts down, or sounds alerts on an error condition. Failing to disable the Windows sounds results in wasted clock cycles, and can interfere with professional sound card drivers. It may cause ear damage when one of the system alert sounds accidentally plays.

Auto-Insert Notification is a feature that automatically plays a CD when inserted into the CD-ROM drive. Unfortunately, this process requires the computer's attention at frequent intervals. Shutting this feature off is recommended, but be aware that CDs will not begin automatically once this feature is disabled. Turning **Auto-Insert Notification** off in Windows 9.x is easy, but Windows 2000 and later require registry modification. Modifying the registry can have disastrous results if done incorrectly. More information on this feature is available at http://www.microsoft.com, but be certain to consult with an expert before making any changes to the registry.

Background Processes

Background processes can rob the system of necessary resources and slow or even stall Audition. Remove any processes such as screen savers, fax software, schedulers, instant messengers, and any other processes that are not required for system operation or running Audition. It is beyond the scope of this book to list the processes that can be safely removed or how to disable them, but most can be researched by simply typing the name of the process in the search field at www.google.com. Caution should be taken when removing or disabling any service to make sure it is not required for system operation.

> **TIP!!** Windows XP has a valuable feature that reverses any changes to the operating system by restoring the system to a point in time. For example, suppose a new device driver was installed today and the scanner no longer works. Using the **System Restore** feature reverts the system back to yesterday's state, and the scanner now functions properly. More information is available by performing a search on "System Restore" in Microsoft Windows Help and Support.

There are many more ways to optimize your system, but these tips provide a solid starting point. Keep the system optimized by checking for software and the operating system updates and upgrade hardware when possible. A search on www.google.com will result in much more information on optimizing your system for audio.

Housekeeping

Maintaining an organized file system is key to achieving peak performance from Audition, and it will help with your own sanity as well. Develop a naming scheme for your folders and files and stick with it. The hard drive is more efficient with shorter files names, but make them long enough to indicate the contents and try not to nest the folders more than a few levels deep.

Take the time to set up project folders before each session and do the housekeeping afterwards. Save and backup files frequently. Saving outtakes is a good idea, but try to separate them and store them on a CD-R or DVD-R and purge unusable material.

 Computers are good at repetitive chores. Take advantage of the scheduled tasks offered in Microsoft Windows to perform routine tasks. Windows has a backup utility that can be configured to backup file and folders at a scheduled time allowing backups to happen automatically while you're not using the computer. Defragmenting drives can also occur automatically using the **Scheduled Tasks** utility and Visual Basic Scripting such as the *drag_all2.vbs* available free at www.dougknox.com.

Housekeeping is important to optimizing performance; however there are times when even the cleanest systems require alternatives. Audition provides some options for those situations.

Flush Virtual File

Audition opens audio files into RAM and can prevent other applications from using the same audio file. The **Flush Virtual File** option located under the **File** menu forces Audition to make a copy of the file in the *Temp* directory and releases control of the original file.

Audition uses the temp directory to store copies of waveforms while editing. These temp files carry the prefix *Audx* followed by a unique four-character code. This temporary copy used by the **Undo** command to restore the audio to a previous state. These temp files are normally deleted when Audition closes; however they may not be deleted if the system crashes. Manually purging these files can free up more hard drive space.

Manage Temporary Folder Reserve Space

It may become necessary to clear some of the temp files Audition uses for undoing changes. The **Manage Temporary Folder Reserve Space** provides the means to clear **Undo** items or close waveform files. The command is accessed from the **File** menu and opens a dialog box

2.26 *The Manage Temporary Folder Reserve Space dialog box*

that shows the path and space of each temporary directory and the total drive space available (see Figure 2.26).

Files can be closed by highlighting the file name in the list and pressing the **Close File** button. **Undo** levels are shown in the **Undo History** list and allow deletion of **Undo** items.

<u>Chapter 3</u>

Moving around the Stage

THE STAGE

Moving around in Adobe Audition can seem complicated at first, but navigation is easy once you are familiar with the work flow. There are two main workspaces in Audition: **Multitrack View** and **Edit View**. A third workspace called **CD Project View** is available for preparing a project for output to compact disc. The screen layout, menus, and available options depend on the current workspace; but controls, time display, and metering will remain the same in both **Edit View** and **Multitrack View**. The **CD Project View** displays only the controls used in creating a compact disc.

Multitrack View is the primary workspace in Adobe Audition and is used to composite and mix multiple tracks. **Edit View** functions on only one track at a time; however, it provides many more editing and effect options. Perhaps a good analogy would be directing a Broadway play. **Edit View** allows you to work with individual actors, editing their dialog, directing their performance and fine-tuning their inflections. **Multitrack View** places all the actors on stage, enabling you to balance the overall performance, lighting, timing, and stage positions. There is one big difference between Audition and a play: in Audition, you can go back and make precise changes with a guaranteed repeat of the previous performance. Try that with a group of actors.

Begin by opening Adobe Audition. Double-click the Adobe Audition application on the desktop. If there is not a program icon, select the Adobe Audition application from the **Programs** menu on the **Start** menu. Audition should open in the **Multitrack View** workspace. If

49

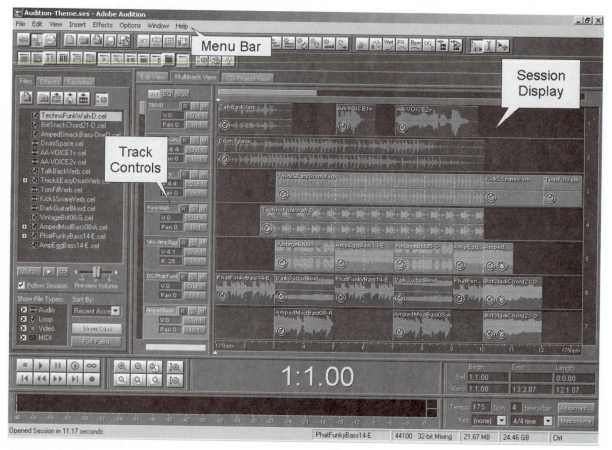

3.1   Multitrack View workspace with multiple tracks open

not, press **F12** on the keyboard, or select **Multitrack View** from the **View** menu. Locate and try the functions as we proceed through this chapter.

Multitrack View

The **Multitrack View** is the default workspace in which Audition opens. There are three elements of this workspace that are unique to **Multitrack View**: the menu bar, the track controls, and the session display. These three elements are labeled in Figure 3.1. The track controls affect only the waveform or file contained in the horizontal panel to the right of the track controls, and both track controls and panels are numbered accordingly.

Edit View

Press **F12** or select **Edit View** from the **View** menu to change the workspace to the **Edit View** mode. There are two elements that are distinct to the **Edit View** workspace. The menu bar will change to reflect available menu choices in the **Edit View** mode, and the waveform display

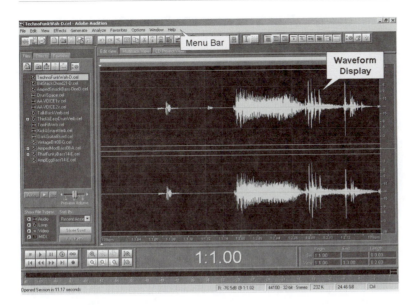

3.2   *Edit View workspace with a single stereo track open.*

area displays only the waveform of a single track, although the single track can be mono or stereo. These two elements are labeled in Figure 3.2.

CD Project View

Press 0 (zero) or select the **CD Project View** tab to change the workspace to the **CD Project View** mode (see Figure 3.3). The track list display area shows specific information about each track, and the column to the right contains controls to manipulate track properties and sequence. The menu bar will change to reflect available menu choices in the **CD Project View** mode.

3.3   *CD Project window*

The interface elements of the **Multitrack View, Edit View,** and **CD Project View** modes will be discussed in much more detail, but first let's review some of the basic navigation and control techniques.

GIVING DIRECTION

Like the actors in a play, Adobe Audition needs a director. That director is you, and you can communicate your vision to Audition through a number of ways. The method of giving direction to a computer that most of us are familiar with is the mouse, but Audition can accept commands from external devices such as synthesizers, dedicated MIDI controllers, and drawing tablets. Audition also provides many keyboard shortcuts and toolbars that can be customized to individual preference.

Mousing Around

A two-button mouse with a scrollable wheel is recommended, but any Windows-compatible mouse will work adequately. A four-button mouse may be programmed to execute common tasks in Audition, and HUI devices such as the Contour Shuttle Pro V2 allow for even greater control.

Clicks

Clicking the left mouse button in a window activates the window, control, or field. Holding down a key modifier such as the **Shift** key while clicking can change the result of the action.

Double-clicking the left mouse button enables many different features in Audition depending upon where the double-click occurs. Double-clicking on the window title bar minimizes or maximizes the window, on the level meters enables monitoring, and on the waveform selects the entire waveform. Another useful action is changing the time format by double-clicking the horizontal ruler. There are many more double-clicking actions that will be covered in later chapters, but don't hesitate to experiment with double-clicking. You can always change it back or use the **Undo** command by pressing **Ctrl+Z**.

Right-clicking just about anywhere in Audition reveals a pop-up menu or other available options. Right-clicking can also be used to move an entire track or set of tracks horizontally in time or vertically to another track or set of tracks.

3.4   *Right-clicking on a window often displays pop-up menus.*

Right-click and drag on the horizontal or vertical position bars when the cursor turns into a magnifying glass to zoom in on a segment as shown in Figure 3.5. Practice these techniques while working through the examples.

Key Modifiers

Many mouse functions assume another role when combined with a keystroke or key modifier. Hold down the **Control** key and click in **Multitrack View** to select multiple segments or combine the **Control** key with a right-click and drag to copy a segment. Extending a segment selection by pressing the **Shift** key while dragging the end of the segment is another example of a key modifier. Other key modifiers will be discussed in the appropriate chapters.

3.5 *Right-click on the horizontal or vertical position bars and drag to zoom in on a segment of the waveform.*

Scroll Wheel

IntelliPoint-compatible devices with a scroll wheel are well worth the cost. Rolling the scroll wheel while the cursor is over the waveform display quickly zooms in or out of the waveform. Clicking the scroll wheel in **Edit View** mode turns the cursor into a double arrow as shown in Figure 3.6 and permits quick forward or backward navigation of the waveform.

3.6 *Cursor produced with a scroll wheel*

Keyboarding

Audition does not require a pointing device to execute commands. Although using a mouse may be quicker for some commands, the keyboard can initiate almost any routine required. For example, as long as the waveform or session has focus, pressing the spacebar starts or stops playback. The **Home** button moves the cursor to the beginning, and the **End** button moves the cursor to the end of the track. A set of default keyboard shortcuts is included as part of the application (see Figure 3.7).

Audition allows you to modify these shortcuts. **Alt+K** opens the **Shortcuts** dialog box. See "Shortcuts and MIDI Triggers" on page 271 in Chapter 12 for an in-depth discussion of shortcuts.

> Wave Properties... Ctrl+P

3.7 *Standard keyboard shortcuts to menu selections appear next to the menu item.*

> ### Mnemonics
>
> Mnemonics. Don'cha love that word, even though it is not an easy word to pronounce (nĭ-mŏn´-ĭks). It is the key to becoming quick with Audition. Mnemonics are keyboard shortcuts for commands that tend to aid in remembering the correct shortcut key for the command. Using a keyboard command instead of selecting menu items can be much faster. For example, **Ctrl+N** is much quicker than mousing up to the **File** menu and selecting **New**. Perhaps the easiest to shortcut to remember is **Ctrl+Q**, which quits the application.

MIDI Controllers

Musicians will appreciate the ability to control menu selections, transport controls, and other functions with a keyboard. In fact, any MIDI controller can be used, even another computer. Implementing MIDI controllers is discussed in detail in Chapter 12 beginning on page 267.

Note Tascam, Mackie, and Event Electronics manufacture mixers called *surface controllers* that provide an even greater level of control than a MIDI keyboard. See Appendix A on page 293 for a brief description of these surface controllers.

Toolbars

The toolbars can display up to three rows of buttons providing quick access to specific functions, eliminating the need to find the desired task from the menu bar. The toolbar appears across the top of the screen directly below the menu bar as shown in Figure 3.8, and changes according to the selected workspace. Placing the mouse over the button for a few seconds displays a tool tip describing each button's function.

3.8   *Toolbars provide quick access to the most commonly used functions.*

View Buttons

The **View** buttons quickly change modes between **Edit View**, **Multitrack View**, and **CD Project View** workspaces. Views can also be changed quickly from the keyboard by pressing the number keys **8**, **9**, and **0**. The **F12** key toggles between **Edit View** and **Multitrack View** modes.

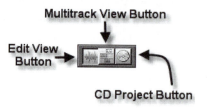

3.9   *View buttons switch between workspaces*

CHANGING THE SCENE

Audition has many options to customize the workspaces to the user's workflow. Windows can be opened, closed, resized, and moved as in most other Microsoft Windows programs. Toolbars, the status bar, and controls are also highly adaptable.

The **Edit View, Multitrack View,** and **CD Project View** workspaces are separate views, and changes to the layout in one do not affect the other. This enables you to create an extremely customized view for each mode.

Customizing the View

Audition uses the standard windows resizing routines and **Minimize/Maximize, Restore,** and **Close** button functions. Audition also adds some windows-docking functionality, providing a flexible workspace.

Resizing Windows

The main window of Audition can easily be resized. Place the cursor on the window border, and the cursor will change to the shape shown in the first row of Table 3.1. Once the cursor changes shape, left-click and hold the mouse button while dragging the window in or out. Moving a side will resize the window horizontally or vertically, and dragging on a corner resizes both width and height at the same time.

> The default window positions can be restored by selecting the **Settings** dialog box (function key **F4**) and pressing the **Restore Default Windows Layouts** button on the **General** tab.

Audition allows resizing windows within the main window. For example, drag the cursor to the left edge of the session display area until the cursor changes to the shape shown in the second row of Table 3.1. Hold the left mouse button down and drag. The selected window will enlarge as the adjacent window or windows shrink.

Table 3.1   Changing cursor

Right-click and drag on the border to resize the window.	
Resize windows by dragging the edge.	
Docked windows such as the Time Display window can be undocked.	

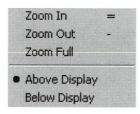

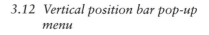

3.10 *Docked windows such as the Time Display window can be undocked.*

3.11 *Horizontal position bar can be located above or below the waveform or session display areas. (center)*

3.12 *Vertical position bar pop-up menu*

Docking Windows

Audition offers the ability to move windows or dock them. Docking a window causes it to occupy space in the main window instead of simply covering it. Move the cursor over the **Time** window shown in Figure 3.10 until the cursor changes to the shape in the third row of Table 3.1.

Horizontal Position Bars

The horizontal position bar controls the amount and position of the waveform in the display area. It is located in its default location at the top of the waveform and session display windows. The bar can be moved to the bottom of the display area by right-clicking on the horizontal position bar and selecting the desired location as shown in Figure 3.11.

Vertical Position Bars

The vertical position bar is available only in **Multitrack View** and controls the tracks viewed in the session display area. The bar can be located to the **Left Of Track** controls, **Left Of Display**, or **Right Of Display** by right-clicking on the bar as shown in Figure 3.12.

Horizontal Ruler

The horizontal ruler is present in both **Multitrack View** and **Edit View** (see Figure 3.13). It displays a time scale in one of a number of formats including **Decimal** (minutes, seconds, and thousandths of a second), **Compact Disc**, various formats of SMPTE Timecode, digital audio samples, and musical **Bars and Beats**. Formats are easily changed by selecting **Time Display Format** from the **View** menu or right-clicking and choosing from the pop-up menu. The grid also changes to reflect the current time format.

3.13 *Horizontal ruler displayed in Compact Disc 75fps Time Display Format.*

TIP!! Compact discs are written in frames, with each second containing 75 frames. Starting a track in the middle of a frame can cause an audible click or pop. Set the **Time Display Format** to **Compact Disc 75 fps** when placing cue marks for compact disc. This prevents tracks from starting in the middle of a frame, helping to prevent pops and clicks.

Vertical Ruler

In **Edit View,** the vertical ruler displays the amplitude of the waveform in one of four formats: **Sample Values, Normalized Values, Percentage,** and **Decibels.** The scale is expressed as Hertz in **Spectral View.** Formats are easily changed by selecting the **Vertical Format** from the **View** menu or right-clicking and choosing from the pop-up menu. The grid also changes to reflect the selected **Vertical Scale Format** (see Figure 3.14).

Multitrack View shows the numbers of the currently viewed tracks in the vertical ruler.

TIP!! The cursor will change to a hand when the mouse is over a bar or ruler of the waveform that is in a magnified or zoomed mode. Drag the hand to scroll the waveform or session display without changing the current zoom level.

3.14 Vertical ruler displayed in Decibel format.

Status Bar

The status bar provides a wealth of information at any given instant. Display options include the file size and time, free disk space in both size and time, sample format information such as sample rate, bit depth, and track configuration. Keyboard modifiers and SMPTE slave stability can be shown, but one of the most useful features is the **Data Under Cursor** status. Moving the cursor over a track will display the file name in **Multitrack View.** Moving the cursor over a waveform in **Edit View** shows the channel, amplitude, and absolute location. Any or all of the options or the status bar can be hid by right-clicking the status bar and selecting the desired options or selecting **View>Status Bar.** The status bar can appear only at the bottom of the screen.

| Completed in 0.09 seconds | | L: -25.8dB @ 21013 | 44100 · 32-bit · Stereo | 472 K | 0:01.371 | 44.56 GB free | 8:52:43.161 free | 00.0% SMPTE |

3.15 Status bar displaying file loading time, channel, amplitude, location under cursor, file size, file length, free disk space, free disk space measured in time, and SMPTE slave stability

Customizing the Toolbar

The toolbars are grouped by function. Available toolbar groups are dependent upon the work-space mode. Display of toolbar groups are turned on and off by the **View Menu>Toolbars** menu option as shown in Figure 3.16. Currently displayed toolbar groups are indicated by a checkmark.

The toolbar can be restricted to display one, two, or three rows. The number of rows the toolbar occupies on the screen can be limited by selecting the desired rows from the menu. Right-clicking on the toolbar also presents the customization options.

Customizing the Organizer Window

The **Organizer** window is a multipurpose tool. Think of it as an area to list assets or files for use in the current project or session. It can be used to import, open, and close files. It can also be used to insert files into a track or into the **Edit View** waveform area for editing, and it provides options for filtering and sorting the asset list. Pressing the **Control** key while clicking on files allows you to insert multiple noncontiguous files into separate **Multitrack View** tracks at the same time. **Effects** and **Favorites** functions can be quickly accessed from this window.

The **Organizer** window, like the other Audition windows, can be moved, resized, docked, and undocked. The **Organizer** is divided into three tabs: **Files**, **Effects**, and **Favorites**.

Files Tab

The **Files** tab displays a list currently open files or assets. There are six buttons under the tabs. The first two buttons open and close audio files respectively. The next button inserts the selected files into the highlighted tracks or next available tracks. The fourth button inserts the selected files into the **CD Project View**, and the fifth button readies the file for editing by switching the mode to **Edit View** and displaying the selected file in the waveform display area. The last button toggles display of the **Advanced Options** pane in the **Organizer** window.

When the **Advanced Options** pane is displayed, it appears at the bottom of the window and controls the type of assets that are displayed and the order the files are listed. Only file types with a checkbox in front of them will be shown in the list. The types are **Audio, Loop, Video,** and **MIDI**. A plus sign appears before the file name of any files that contain cues. Individual cues can be displayed in the **Organizer** window by clicking on the plus sign. The **Sort By** pop-up list orders the listed files by the selected option: **Recent Access, File Name,** file type listed in order of the most recently opened file, and file type sorted alphabetically by file name. The **Full Paths** button shows the complete file path to the file, and can be used to quickly locate a file. However, because the path displays left to right, displaying the full path tends hide the file name. For example, the default size of the **Organizer** window will not display the file name of the following path: *C:\Projects\Scoring\mFx Video\mFx Final Mix.wav*.

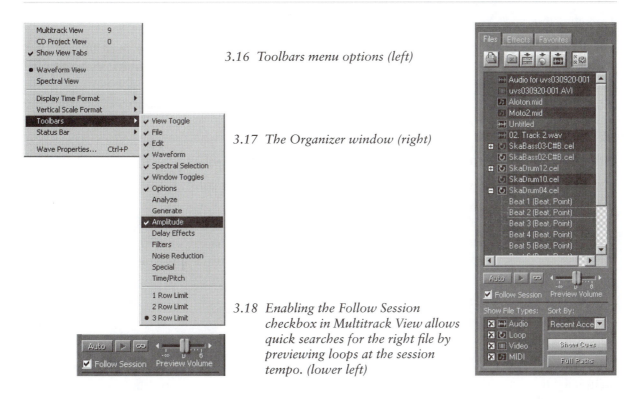

3.16 *Toolbars menu options (left)*

3.17 *The Organizer window (right)*

3.18 *Enabling the Follow Session
checkbox in Multitrack View allows
quick searches for the right file by
previewing loops at the session
tempo. (lower left)*

The **Advanced Options** pane also allows playback of Audition files directly from the **Organizer** window. The **Auto** button activates automatic playback when a file is selected in the **Organizer** window. The **Play** button enables manual playback when the **Auto** button is not activated, and enabling the **Loop** button repeats playback of loop files until stopped. The **Preview Volume** control adjusts the playback volume independent of the **Multitrack View** levels. This volume control combined with enabling the **Follow Session** checkbox allows auditioning of loops at the session tempo before importing them.

Effects Tab

The **Effects** tab lists all effects currently available for use in Audition. The list of effects will differ when switching between **Multitrack View** and **Edit View** modes. Effects that are not ready for use are dimmed. Some effects will be become enabled and change appearance when a segment of a waveform is selected. For example, **Apply Silence** is dimmed in **Edit View** until an area of the waveform is highlighted. **Apply Silence** brightens when the segment is selected.

The **Group By Category** button organizes the effects into collections by function in the same manner as the effects are grouped in the **Effects** menu. Pressing **Group Real-Time Effects** sorts the effects into two groups: processes that can work in real time, without having to wait for the effect to render, and processes that require offline rendering before playback.

Favorites Tab

The **Favorites** tab provides another method of quickly accessing frequently used or favorites effects, scripts, or external applications. Clicking the **Edit Favorites** button at the bottom of the **Organizer** window opens the **Edit Favorites** dialog box. The same options are presented in the **Favorites** menu. Chapter 12 on page 278 contains a detailed discussion describing the usage and customization of the **Favorites** items.

Other View Elements

The default Audition view layouts include several other elements: time window, transport controls, zoom controls, the selection/view controls, level meters, session properties, and track controls. All of these elements support resizing and docking and undocking, although track controls will remain accessible in the original position as well as the new location. Expanding the track controls window also reveals more of the individual track controls and options.

Each of the elements will be discussed in more detail later in this chapter as well as in the chapters that use their functions.

THE STAGE CREW

Most theatrical performances would not be received well by the audience if there were not technical support on the stage to open the curtain, operate the sound and lighting, and make changes to the set and props. Audition has a large stage crew to manage the technical aspects of running the program. This crew is made up of the options available under the **View** menu and the **Windows** menu. Access to almost every area of the Audition stage is available through these options.

Let's begin by discussing the **View** menu options followed by the **Windows** menu options.

THE VIEW MENU

The **View** menu hosts a number of options. The options are interactive and change to display only those options that are pertinent to the active workspace.

Multitrack View: Selection of this option switches the workspace to the **Multitrack View**. This is also accomplished without accessing the **View** menu by pressing the number **9** key or the **F12** function key. Note that **F12** toggles between **Edit View** and **Multitrack View** modes. Views can also be switched using the **View** tabs if the **View>Show View Tabs** option is enabled.

CD Project View: Highlighting the **CD Project View** places Audition in the **CD Project** mode for creating and burning compact discs. The **CD Project View** can also be accessed from the keyboard by pressing the **0** key. Chapter 11 on page 252 contains a tutorial demonstrating how to use the **CD Project View** and burn a CD.

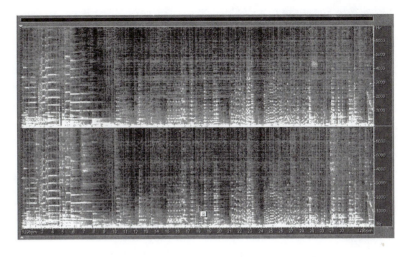

3.19 *Spectral View shows distribution of frequency content with higher amplitudes depicted as brighter areas.*

Show View Tabs: There are a handful of ways to switch between the three main views. Leaving the **Views** tabs on can take up some valuable screen space. The **Show View Tabs** menu option toggles showing and hiding the **View** tabs.

Edit Waveform View: This menu selection changes the workspace to the **Edit View** mode. Pressing the number **8** key or the **F12** function key also switches the mode to **Edit View**. F12 toggles between **Edit View** and **Multitrack View** modes. Views can also be switched using the **View** tabs if the **View>Show View Tabs** option is enabled.

Waveform View: The **Edit View** workspace offers two graphical representations of the waveform: **Waveform View** and **Spectral View**. The default is **Waveform View**, and the file is presented as a graph of time versus amplitude. The Y-axis scale displays amplitude, and the X-axis represents time. Both units and methods of representing each scale can be altered with the **View>Display Time Format** or **View>Vertical Scale Format** options. Switch between the **Waveform View** or **Spectral View** while in the **Edit View** workspace by pressing F9.

Spectral View: **Spectral View** presents an alternative view of the waveform. In this mode, the waveform is depicted as frequency versus time as shown in Figure 3.19. The amplitude is still displayed. However, rather than showing it on an axis, it is symbolized by colors, with brighter colors representing higher levels. Frequencies are shown on the Y-axis scale in Hertz with low frequencies starting at the bottom. The X-axis represents the time scale. The units representing the time scale can be altered with the **View>Display Time Format** options. Toggle between the **Waveform View** or **Spectral View** by pressing F9 while in the **Edit View** workspace.

Show Pan Envelopes: Displays a visual representation of panning applied to a track. Panning determines the amount of signal present in the left and right channels at a given time. Panning is not limited to stereo and applies to multichannel mixing. **Enable Envelope Editing** must be enabled to change the envelopes.

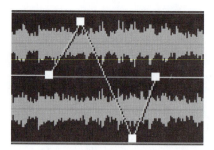

Show Volume Envelopes: Displays a visual representation of volume applied to a track. **Enable Envelope Editing** must be enabled to change the envelopes.

3.20 *Panning Envelope illustrates stereo track panning beginning in the center and panning to full left and then to full right before retuning to center.*

Show Wet/Dry Mix Envelopes: Displays a visual representation of effects applied to a track. The higher the point on the track, the more effects are applied, or the more "wet" the track. An end point at the bottom of the track indicates no effect; the track is "dry." **Enable Envelope** Editing must be selected to change the envelopes.

Show FX Parameter Envelopes: Displays a visual representation of certain effect parameters applied to a track. **Enable Envelope Editing** must be selected to change the envelopes.

Show Tempo Envelopes: Displays a visual representation of the tempo applied to a MIDI track. **Enable Envelope Editing** must be enabled to change the envelopes. Individual envelope nodes cannot be edited on a MIDI track.

Enable Envelope Editing: A check next to this option indicates that all envelope modes can be manually edited. Edit points or nodes appear on the envelope lines when this option is enabled and the values are displayed as the points are changed. Envelopes and editing envelopes are discussed in more detail in Chapter 10 on page 241.

Enable Clip Edge Dragging: This option toggles the **Clip Edge Dragging** option on and off. Grabbing the edge of a clip and dragging while this option is operating enables you to shorten or lengthen the clip. The clip cannot exceed the length of the original using this method.

Enable Clip Time Stretching: This option toggles the **Clip Time Stretching** option on and off. Grabbing the edge of a clip and dragging while this option is enabled allows you to shorten or lengthen a clip without altering the pitch of the clip. See Chapter 6 on page 132 for more details on using **Clip Time Stretching**.

Display Time Format: The **Display Time Format** menu selection presents a submenu with numerous time format options. A dot next to the format indicates the currently selected format. This option affects how the time is displayed in the time display window, horizontal ruler, **Selection/View** control window and status bar, and any other location that displays time. The time format will be consistent throughout the application. The following formats are available.

- *Decimal:* displays the time in hours, minutes, seconds, and 100ths of a second.
- *Compact Disc 75 fps:* displays time in hours, minutes, seconds, and 75 frames per second. Select this option when mastering for compact disc.
- *SMPTE 30 fps:* displays time in SMPTE standard hours, minutes, seconds, and 30 frames per second.
- *SMPTE 29.97 fps:* displays time in SMPTE standard hours, minutes, seconds, and 30 frames per second with without dropping frames.
- *SMPTE Drop (29.97 fps):* displays time in SMPTE standard hours, minutes, seconds, and 30 frames per second with one frame dropped at certain intervals.
- *SMPTE 25 fps (EBU):* displays time in SMPTE standard hours, minutes, seconds, and 25 frames per second using the European Broadcast Union specification.
- *SMPTE 24 fps (film):* displays time in SMPTE standard hours, minutes, seconds, and 24 frames per second to match the film frame rate.
- *Samples:* displays the time in samples per second based on the file sample rate.
- *Bars and Beats:* displays time in musical bars, beats, and ticks.
- *Custom (nn frames/sec):* recalls the frame rate of the last selected time format.
- *Edit Tempo:* provides an option for setting the tempo and automatically determining the tempo of a selected segment. The Edit Tempo option is detailed in Chapter 7 on page 153.
- *Define Custom Frames:* opens the **General** tab of the **Settings** dialog box, where the custom frame rate field can be changed. Choosing the proper format is important and is discussed in later chapters.

Vertical Scale Format: The **Vertical Scale** options allow selection of the amplitude scale in **Edit View** mode. Only track numbers are displayed in **Multitrack View**. Four format options are available: **Samples, Normalized Values, Percentage,** and **Decibels**.

Toolbars: The **Toolbars** menu option displays the desired toolbar groups on the toolbar as discussed in the first section of this chapter on page 54. The total numbers of toolbar rows is selected here. A checkbox next to the option indicates that the option is on.

Status Bar: This menu option toggles the display of the status bar on and off. A checkbox indicates the options that are currently displayed on the status bar.

Free space based on 74 min CD: Select **Free space based on 74 min CD** when using 650MB/74-minute CD recordable media to display the remaining time and space on the disc. This option only appears when the **CD Project View** is active. The **Free Space** and/or **Free Space (time)** must also be enabled on the status bar.

Free space based on 80 min CD: Select **Free space based on 80 min CD** when using 700MB/80-minute CD recordable media to display the remaining time and space on the disc. This option only appears when the **CD Project View** is active. The **Free Space** and/or **Free Space (time)** must also be enabled on the status bar.

It is not recommended to exceed 79:40 when creating a Pre-MasterCompact Disc (PMCD) for use as a master for CD replication.

Chapter 11 starting on page 251 discusses the mastering process and specifics of outputting to a compact disc.

Track Properties: **Track Properties** appears only in the **CD Project View** mode. Selecting this option while a track is highlighted opens a dialog box to change the CD parameters for the selected track.

Wave Properties: The **Wave Properties** menu option opens the **Wave Properties** window. **Wave Properties** contains non-audio information called metadata and is discussed in Chapter 1 on page 13.

Advanced Session Properties: The **Advanced Session Properties** menu option opens the dialog box of the same name. Five option tabs are presented in the dialog.

- ***General Tab:*** allows you to set options for **SMPTE Start Time Offset**. The offset is the absolute time location where Audition will playback when synchronizing as a slave to other devices. The format of the offset can be changed by clicking the **Format** button (see Figure 3.21). The **Key** pop-up menu sets the session's musical key. Any loops with a specified key will be transposed to the session key.

3.21 General tab of the Advanced Session Properties window

- ***Mixing Tab:*** determines whether pre-mixing will occur in mode or 32-bit mode. Pre-mixing is extremely processor-intensive. Setting pre-mixing to 16-bit in systems with multiple cards is recommended if performance becomes an issue. Pre-mixing in 16-bit mode does not cause any quality or data loss, and the final mix can still be done in 32-bit mode (see Figure 3.22).

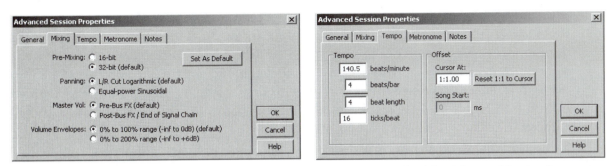

3.22 *Mixing tab of the Advanced Session Properties window*

3.23 *Tempo tab of the Advanced Session Properties window*

Panning selects the result of panning the signal between channels. **L/R Cut logarithmic** (default) decreases the signal of the right channel when panning left or decreases the signal to the left channel when panning right. The panning will not result in an increased signal gain. **Equal-Power Sine** maintains constant power and results in a signal gain when panning. Because of this potential gain increase, clipping may occur in 16-bit mode.

Master Volume positions the **Master Volume Fader** before the effects bus or after the effects bus. This preference affects the level sent to effects and is discussed in Chapter 10 on page 236. **Volume Envelopes** can be set for a range of 0–100 percent or 0–200 percent.

All preferences in this tab can be set as defaults for future sessions by pressing the **Set As Defaults** buttons after the desired settings have been selected.

- *Tempo Tab:* adjusts beats per minute, beats per bar, beat length, and ticks per beat. Beats per bar and beat length comprise the time signature used in music notation (see Figure 3.23). The offset features in the **Tempo** tab allow lining the tempo up with a previously recorded song and are discussed in Chapter 7.

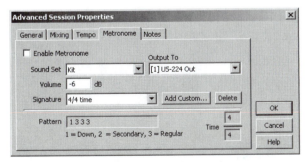

3.24 *Metronome tab of the Advanced Session Properties window*

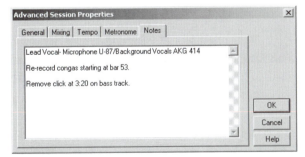

3.25 *Notes tab of the Advanced Session Properties window*

- *Metronome Tab:* controls the metronome parameters. Checking the **Metronome** checkbox turns the metronome on and assigns the output to the device selected in the **Output To** pop-up menu. The **Sound Set** pop-up menu sets the sound of the metronome, and the **Volume control** field is directly below. Time signatures are selected from the pop-up menu, and custom time signatures and patterns are created by pressing the **Add Custom** button (see Figure 3.24). Creating and using custom time signatures are described in Chapter 7.

- *Notes Tab:* provides an area to record any comments or notes about the session (see Figure 3.25).

TIP!! The **Notes** tab of the **Advanced Session Properties** window provides a great place to store information such as microphone used, special setup information, things left to do before mixing, or any other items that we tend to keep on small pieces of scrap paper or the back of the track sheet or score.

Multichannel Encoder: Audition provides a multichannel encoder capable of automated panning and full surround-sound mixing and WMA encoding. In addition, this encoder can output files in the most popular formats for final encoding in Dolby Digital and DTS. Selecting this menu option opens the **Multichannel Encoder**. A detailed discussion of this feature and usage is discussed in Chapter 10.

Note A third-party encoder is necessary for encoding in Dolby Digital and DTS formats.

THE WINDOW MENU

The **Window** menu is a standard implementation of the **Window** menu found in most PC applications. It is used to manage the currently displayed and active windows. It provides an alternate way to activate a window and bring that window to the front. In the same manner as the **View** menu, the available options are interactive and change to display only those options that are pertinent to the active workspace. A tear-off tab appears when the **Switch To** submenu is selected, allowing display of more than the limit of 10 under the submenu.

Session Properties: The Session Properties option enables display of the **Session Info** window. **Alt+3** also brings up this window. Tempo, beats per bar, time signature, and key are displayed and modified in through this dialog box. Pressing the **Metronome** button toggles the metronome on and off. The **Advanced** button calls the **Advanced Session Properties**

3.26 Session Info window

dialog box that is discussed earlier in this chapter on page 64. **Session Properties** and **Advanced Session Properties** are discussed in more detail later in this book.

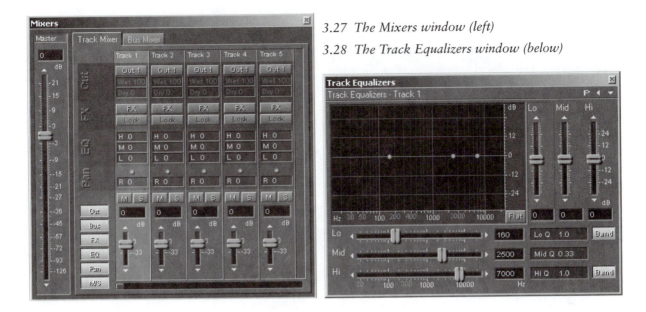

3.27 *The Mixers window (left)*

3.28 *The Track Equalizers window (below)*

Mixer: The **Mixers** window works with the **Track EQ** and **Track Properties** windows. It offers quick and easy access to most mixing parameters such as volume, panning, equalization, effects, output device, mute and solo buttons, and a master volume control. The window provides the ability to hide controls not currently in use and a tab to display the **Bus Mixer.** Pressing **Alt+2** also opens the **Mixers** window (see Figure 3.27).

Track Equalizers: The **Track Equalizers** window controls frequency response for the selected track. Three bands of variable band and Q equalization are provided (see Figure 3.28). EQ control is available through the **Mixers** window; however, **Track Equalizers** offers greater manipulation of the equalization. The **Track Equalizers** window can also be called by double-clicking the **EQ** button in the **Mixers** window or pressing **Alt+5**.

Track Properties: The **Track Properties** window allows track naming, input and output device selection, and volume and panning control (see Figure 3.29). **Record, Solo,** and **Mute** are also available in this window. Effects selection and effects properties are also controlled in this window. **Alt+4** opens the **Track Properties.**

More details on the usage of the **Mixers** window, **Track Equalizers** window, and **Track Properties** window are included in the chapters that follow.

Organizer: Selecting the **Organizer** option toggles display of the **Organizer** window. This window can be called from the menu or pressing **Alt+9**. A checkbox to the left of this menu item indicates that the **Organizer** window is open. See the "Customizing the Organizer Window" on page 58 for a detailed discussion of the **Organizer** window features.

3.29 Track Properties window (left)

3.30 Cue List window (below)

Cue List: The **Cue List** menu option toggles display of the **Cue List** window, although pressing **Alt+8** may be a quicker method of activating the window. A check to the left of this menu item indicates that the **Cue List** window is open (see Figure 3.30).

Cues are marks that tag a point in the waveform. For example, one type of cue point called a track mark indicates the beginning of a compact disc track. Two cue points can be used to create a section between the points called a range.

The **Cue List** window presents the cues and ranges in a list view and offers various options for manipulating and modifying the cues. Figure 3.30 shows the **Cue List** window. Chapter 7 describes cues, ranges, and the **Cue List** window in detail.

Play List: The **Play List** menu selection opens the **Play List** window (see Figure 3.31). The **Play List** window allows the organization of cues for playback. Playback of cues in the list will be seamless. In other words, no gaps will be heard between cues. The playback sequence can be rearranged, and a cue can be looped a number of times before the next cue begins playback. The loop count for each cue is noted in parenthesis at the left of the cue name. The total length of the playback list is displayed at the bottom of the window. A check to the left of this menu item indicates that the **Play List** window is open.

- ***Show Cue List:*** displays the **Cue List** window. Once the **Cue List** window is displayed, the button name changes to **Insert Cue(s)**.

- ***Insert Cue(s):*** highlighting a cue or multiple cues in the **Cue List** window and clicking the Insert Cue(s) button adds the selected cues to the **Playback List**.

- ***Remove:*** deletes a cue from the **Playback List**. This does not delete the cue from the **Cue List**.

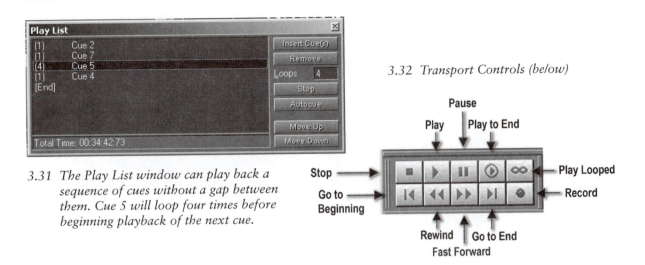

3.31 *The Play List window can play back a sequence of cues without a gap between them. Cue 5 will loop four times before beginning playback of the next cue.*

3.32 *Transport Controls (below)*

- **Loops:** repeats concurrent playback of the selected cue by the number of times entered in the **Loops** field.
- **Play:** begins playback from the highlighted cue or the first cue in the list if no cues are selected. Button label will change to "Stop" when in play mode.
- **Stop:** ceases playback immediately. Button label will change to **Play** when in stop mode.
- **Autocue:** stops playback after the currently selected cue and highlights the next cue in the list.
- **Move Up:** moves the highlighted cue up in the list.
- **Move Down:** moves the highlighted cue down in the list.

Transport Controls: The **Transport Controls** handle the motion of the playback and recording much like a VCR control. Stop, play, record, rewind, and six similar functions are controlled by these buttons. A check next to the menu option indicates that the controls are in display mode.

- **Stop:** halts playback or recording. **Alt+S** stops the playback or recording as well.
- **Play:** begins playback from the location of the cursor. **Alt+P** will also begin play. Right-clicking displays a pop-up menu with playback options.
- **Pause:** stops playback temporarily. Clicking the **Pause** button a second time continues from the same cursor location where the **Pause** button was initially pressed.
- **Play to End:** enables the play function the same way the **Play** button does, but a different stopping point can be set by right-clicking the button and selecting the desired option from the pop-up menu.

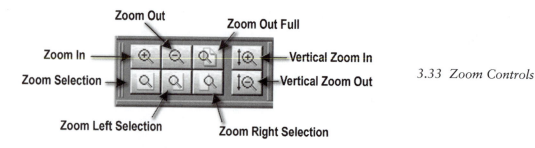

3.33 Zoom Controls

- ***Play Looped:*** repeats play of the selected segment. Right-clicking opens a pop-up menu that displays options for looping the section of the waveform currently in view or looping the entire waveform. Either option is overridden when a selection is highlighted and only the selection will repeat.

- ***Go to Beginning:*** moves the cursor to the beginning of the current cue. This button can be used to quickly navigate back to the beginning of an earlier cue point. This function is also enabled by pressing the **Control** key and **Left Arrow** key simultaneously.

- ***Rewind:*** moves the cursor location backwards. The rate at which the cursor rewinds in controlled with options in a pop-up menu accessed by right-clicking on the **Rewind** button.

 The J key and L key can be used to control rewind and fast-forward functions, respectively.

- ***Fast Forward:*** moves the cursor location forward. Right-clicking displays a pop-up menu with options controlling the fast forward speed.

- ***Go to End:*** moves the cursor to the end of the current cue. Continuing to click this button will advance through the remaining cue until the end of the track or session is reached. Holding the **Control** key and pressing the **Right Arrow** key also performs the same function.

- ***Record:*** places the enabled track or tracks into the record mode and begins recording. There are three recording options accessible in a pop-up menu. Those options are discussed in the next chapter.

Zoom Controls: The **Zoom** controls direct the horizontal and vertical magnification of the waveform and session display much in the same way that a set of binoculars work. These buttons or shortcuts are one of the most frequently used controls in Audition. Zooming in or magnifying a waveform enables accurate editing to the sample level.

- ***Zoom In:*** magnifies the waveform or track view using the cursor location as the center.

- ***Zoom Out:*** reduces the magnification level of the waveform or track view.

- ***Zoom Out Full:*** returns both horizontal and vertical views to the default position with the entire waveform or track shown in the display area.

- **Zoom Selection:** magnifies the selected area or the waveform or track, filling the entire display area with the selected area.
- **Zoom Left Selection:** magnifies the left end of the selected waveform or track.
- **Zoom Right Selection:** magnifies the right end of the selected waveform or track.
- **Vertical Zoom In:** magnifies the waveform vertically.
- **Vertical Zoom Out:** reduces the vertical magnification level of the waveform or track.

> Use the equal (=) key to zoom in and the minus (−) key to zoom out horizontally. Holding the **Alt** key while pressing these keys zooms in and out vertically.

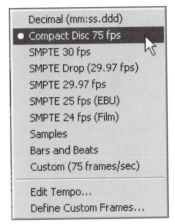

3.34 *The Time window*

3.35 *Time Display Format options*

Time : The **Time** window displays the current location during recording or playback or the left edge of a selected segment. The **Time** window is dockable like most other Audition windows and toggles on and off by selecting this menu option. A checkbox next to this selection indicates that the **Time** window is open.

Time can be displayed in many formats by right-clicking on the **Time** window or selecting **View>Display Time Format** from the menu bar (see Figure 3.35). The dot to the right of the format indicates the current display format.

Selection/View Controls: The **Selection/View Controls** window shows significant waveform or session points (see Figure 3.36). The top row, named **Sel,** lists the beginning point of the current selection, the end point of the current selection, and the total length of the current selection.

The bottom row, named **View,** shows the beginning point of the current view, the end point of the current view, and the total length of the current view. The locations of the points can be modified by changing the current view or selection or entering a location in the fields.

3.36 *Selection/View Controls*

Level Meters: The **Level Meters** option toggles the **Level Meters** window on and off. The level meters display the instantaneous peak amplitude during recording or playback. The meters window carries the usual Audition windows attributes and can be docked and resized. The meters can also be displayed horizontally or vertically as shown in Figure 3.37. The top segment of the left channel of the meter shows that the signal hit 0dB Full Scale and may result in a clipped signal. The peak indicators shown as horizontal lines between −6dB and −12dB denote recent peak levels. The solid bar ending between –12dB and –24dB shows the current levels. The horizontal lines in the current level bars are the valley indicators or lowest levels that occurred. The level meters have a number of display options.

- **Monitor Record Level:** enables metering of the input signal and aids in setting levels during rehearsals. This option can be enabled by double-clicking on the meters, from the **Options** menu, or the **F10** function key.

- **Show on Play and Record:** enables metering on both record and playback.

- **Clear Clip Indicators:** clears the **Clip Indicators** segments located at the top of the meters above the **0 dB** mark. Clicking on the **Clip Indicator** segments or on the edge of the meters also clears the clears **Clip Indicators**. The **Peak Indicators** and **Valley Indicators** are also reset whenever the **Clip Indicators** are cleared.

- **Adjust for DC:** compensates for any DC offset and provides for accurate metering if DC is present in the signal.

- **Show Valleys:** marks the minimum amplitudes with a pink horizontal line. Clicking on the clip indicator segments, the edge of the meters, or **Clear Clip Indicators** will reset the valley indicators.

3.37 *Level Meters window in a vertical display position (left)*

3.38 *Right-clicking on the Level Meter window opens the metering options on a pop-up menu. (left)*

- **Range:** provides six decibel-range scales. The **120dB** range provides the widest dynamic range and should be used for extremely dynamic material. The **24dB** range is useful for highly compressed material such as the current heavy metal music rage. The ranges provide for more accurate level monitoring.

- **Dynamic Peaks:** mark the hottest peak levels with a yellow horizontal line. The dynamic peak indicators automatically reset every 1.5 seconds.

Metering All Devices

Level Meters options in **Multitrack View** allow metering of all input and output devices. This is a great feature for multitrack recording; however, be aware that metering multiple devices is demanding on the processor and may result in poor performance or even worse dropouts in the recordings. Users with slower systems may want to disable this feature to ensure clean and accurate recordings.

- *Static Peaks:* marks the hottest peak levels with a yellow horizontal line. Static peaks will remain until manually reset by clicking on the clip indicator segments, the edge of the meters, or **Clear Clip Indicators**.

> Choosing **Static Peaks** during rehearsals can help in setting up record levels. For example, if the static peaks are at −10dB at the end of the rehearsal take, you can probably safely increase the level by 5–7dB.

Load Meter: The load meter appears in the default position under the time display window. It functions like a progress bar or level meter and indicates the current load on the CPU.

Video: Audition provides the ability to work with video tracks in the AVI, DV, MPEG, and WMV/ASF formats. Selecting this option opens the video into a dockable window. Right-clicking on the **Video** window opens a pop-up revealing several playback options including display sizes and playback quality.

Frequency Analysis: Selecting this option or pressing **Alt+Z** opens the **Frequency Analysis** window. An alternative is to open this window by selecting **Analyze>Show Frequency Analysis**.

3.39 *Video track displayed in a docked window*

Phase Analysis: Selecting this option opens the **Phase Analysis** window. The same window is opened by selecting **Analyze>Show Phase Analysis**.

Placekeeper: There are times when a gap between windows needs to be filled to keep the desired screen layout. These are similar to rack panel covers on an equipment rack. Up to four placekeepers can be open in a view. Right-clicking on the placekeeper opens a pop-up menu that offers the options for panel textures: **Nothing, Cool Texture,** and **Squares**. The textures are shown in Figure 3.40.

3.40 *Three placekeeper panels. No texture is on the first, Cool Texture is on the second panel, and Squares is on the third panel.*

Chapter 4

The Opening Act

THE CASTING CALL

The stage is set, the crew is ready, but a cast is still needed. In Audition, the cast members are the assets, and the assets come in several forms: audio files, MIDI files, video files, loop files, and session files. Calling these cast members is commonly done by opening these assets using the **Open** command on the **File** Menu, but there are other ways these performers can appear on the stage.

Let's take a moment to discuss ways to open, close, and save files. Consider the file system on the computer as a large file cabinet capable of storing tens of thousands of files. Each hard drive is a file cabinet drawer and is called the root directory or folder. Files and folders can be placed into other folders or nested like the files and folders in a file cabinet.

Most computer applications have few options for handling files. Typically, it is as simple as open, close, and save. Audition offers these methods and several other ways of manipulating files with **Append, Import, Insert,** and **Extract.** The available options change with the work-space mode. For example, the **Insert** choice is available only in **Multitrack View,** and the **Extract** command is available only in **Edit View.**

We'll begin with a review of the commands available in **Edit View** followed by a look at the choices in **Multitrack View.** The commands available from the **CD Project View** are the same commands available in **Edit View** and **Multitrack View,** so they will not be covered separately. It is not necessary to follow along with the examples in the section; however, should you desire to work with some files, some example are included on the CD that accompanies this book. The examples are in the directory named *Chapter 04-Audio*.

THE EDIT VIEW CAST

Edit View is used primarily to work with a single file or asset at a time; however, it is possible to open more than one file into the waveform display using the **Open Append** command. **Edit View** also provides the ability to extract audio from compact disc or video, and all open files can be closed from the **File** menu. All file-handling commands are found under the File menu in **Edit View**.

Press **F12** to switch to the **Edit View** workspace if you're in **Multitrack View**.

New

The **New** command does what the command name implies. It initiates the process of creating a new waveform. Selecting the **File>New** or pressing **Ctrl+N** presents the **New Waveform** dialog box as shown in Figure 4.1. The desired sample rate can be entered directly into the **Sample Rate** field or selected from the list below the field. Mono or stereo channel configuration and bit depth or resolution are chosen by radio buttons. Click **OK** once the parameters are set, and an empty waveform appears in the waveform display.

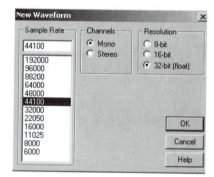

4.1   *The New Waveform dialog box*

To Create a New Waveform

1. Press **Ctrl+N** or select **File>New**.

2. Select the sample rate from the list or enter the rate in the **Sample Rate** field.

3. Select **Mono** or **Stereo**.

4. Choose the resolution.

5. Click the **OK** button.

 Shortcuts such as **Ctrl+N** will not function if the wrong window has the attention or focus of the application. You can determine which window has focus by pressing **Alt+ /** (forward slash) and watching which window handle flashes momentarily.

4.2   The Open dialog box

Open

The **Open** command functions like that of most Windows-based applications. Select **File> Open** or **Ctrl+O**, and the **Open** dialog box appears. A list of recently accessed folders is displayed in the pop-up menu at the top of the window. This is a time saver if files are deeply nested in other folders or drives. The **Look in** pop-up list allows navigation of hard drive directories and the **Files of type** pop-up menu can be used to filter out undesired file types. For example, selecting **Windows PCM (*.wav)** will list only files with the .wav extension regardless of how many files are in the directory, whereas selecting **ALL files (*.*)** will display all files in a directory. Checking the **Don't ask for further details** checkbox prevents Audition from querying for any other format information. Instead, Audition will use the last setting used if necessary. The **Show File Information** checkbox shows pertinent file information such as type, sample rate, resolution, and length. The **Auto Play** checkbox enables automatic playback of the highlighted file. The **Play** button toggles between **Play** and **Stop** states. Checking the **Loop** checkbox will continuously repeat the highlighted selection until stopped.

To open an existing waveform:

1. Press **Ctrl+O** or select **File>Open**.

2. Use the Look in pop-up list to navigate to the desired file or asset. In this example, locate the *CH04-Example 01.wav* in the *Chapter 04-Audio* directory on the CD-ROM that accompanies this book.

3. Highlight the *CH04-Example 01.wav* file.

4. Double-click or press the **Open** button, and the waveform will appear in the waveform display.

Double-clicking on the **Organizer** window is another way to open or import files.

Audition creates another file with the same name as the audio file and an extension of .pk. The .pk file does not contain audio but instead describes the waveform graphically, enabling Audition to quickly render the waveform on the screen. If the .pk file is lost or corrupted, Audition will automatically create a new one when the file is opened.

Open As

The **Open As** command looks and works the same as the **Open** command with one exception. Once the file is selected, a dialog box is presented, prompting for sample rate, channel configuration, and resolution.

The preferred method is to open the file in its original format and choose **Edit > Convert Sample Type**, which uses filtering rather than changing the format. This will result in a higher quality conversion.

Open Append

The **Open Append** command looks and acts the same as the **Open** and **Open As** command except that rather than opening each file separately, each file is appended to the next in the waveform display.

Multiple files can be opened at once using the **Open** and **Open As** commands; however, only the first file in the list will appear in the waveform display. Hold down the **Shift** key and drag to select sequential files and the **Control** key to select files that are not sequential.

Open Audio from Video

The **Open Audio from Video** command separates the audio from a video file and places it in the waveform display just as if an audio file were opened. The dialog box is virtually identical to the **Open** dialog box. Audition supports AVI, DV, MPEG, and WMV/ASF formats.

Extract Audio from CD

Audition can open track on a compact disc through the **Open** and **Open As** commands by opening the desired track with a .cda (CD Audio) extension, but Audition provides a cleaner method with the **File>Extract Audio from CD** command. The command opens the **Extract Audio from CD** dialog box as shown in Figure 4.3.

4.3   *The Extract Audio from CD dialog box shows the configuration for ripping three tracks to a single waveform.*

The **Device** pop-up menu allows selection of the source ROM drive. All CD-ROM or DVD-ROM drives in the computer will appear in this list.

There are several selections in the **Interface Options** area of the dialog box. Select **ASPI/SPTI** as the first choice. ASPI (Advanced SCSI Programming Interface) and SPTI (SCSI Pass Through Interface) are the most common and work with most drives. Switch to **Generic Win32** only if you have problems with audio extraction. The **Read Method** commands work only with the ASPI/SPTI interfaces. **MMC - Read CD** should work with most newer drives, but some experimentation with other methods may be required if the drive is an older drive or has problems ripping. Maximum speed allows the drive to rip as fast as possible; however, slower speeds can be selected if errors become a problem. The **Buffer Size** enables faster rips since the data is stored to RAM, but larger buffers can also introduce errors. **Swap Byte Order** should remain unchecked for Microsoft Windows. **Swap Channels** reverses the left and right channels during the rip. Leave the **Spin Up Before Extraction** disabled unless you experience problems at the beginning of the rip.

The **Source Selection** area determines the locations and length of data that will be extracted. Extract tracks by choosing the **Track** radio button and highlight the desired tracks. Each track will be opened as a separate waveform unless the **Extract to Single Waveform** checkbox is enabled. Choosing the **Time** radio button allows ripping a particular range of time from the CD. The **Start** and **Length** fields must be filled with the start and length calculated in frames. Remember that there are 75 frames per second, so multiply the number of minutes by 60, add the seconds, and multiply the sum by 75. For example, to rip the first 3:21 of a CD, use the formula $((3 \times 60) + 21) \times 75$, or you could just plug in a rough guess and check the time display above the **Start** and **Length** fields.

In the **Error Correction** area, CDDA Accurate is sufficient for most drives; however, **Jitter Correction** may be necessary for some older drives that have difficulty reading the disc.

The **Preview** button allows you to listen to the audio before extraction, and the **OK** button begins extraction. The first track will open in the waveform display, and the remaining tracks will be available in the **Organizer** window.

 Ripping compact discs with the **Extract to Single Waveform** checkbox enabled will automatically place cue marks at the beginning of each track. This can be very handy for revising or compiling CDs. Note that the cue placement is not exact, so double-check each cue mark before burning another disc.

Close

The **Close** command closes the file currently open in the waveform display. To close a waveform, press **Ctrl+W**, or select **File>Close** to close the example file.

Close Only Non-Session Media

The **Close Only Non-Session Media** command closes all files not currently inserted into a track in the **Multitrack View** workspace. This command functions as more of a housekeeping task to close or remove files not in use in the current session. Not a bad habit to practice.

Close All

The **Close All** command closes all open files. Use this command before beginning a new session.

Save

The **Save** command can be executed by pressing **Ctrl+S** or selecting **File>Save**. The **Save** command saves any changes to the existing waveform. This habit cannot be practiced too frequently.

 A selected waveform can be saved as a new file by right-clicking on the waveform and selecting **Save Selection** from the pop-up menu.

Save As

The **Save As** command is used to save the waveform in a different format. The **Save As** command is accessed from the **File** menu or with the key combination of **Ctrl+Shift+S**. Upon selection, the **Save Waveform As** dialog box is opened. The dialog box is not unlike the other file-handling dialog boxes. **Recent Folders** can be quickly chosen from the pop-up menu at the top of the window, and you can navigate to the desired directory or folder through the **Save In**

4.4 *The Save Waveform As dialog box*

pop-up menu. **Save as type** determines the format, and the **Options** button presents the appropriate parameters for the chosen format. The free space on each drive is listed in a column to the right of the window. Checking **Save extra non-audio information** stores metadata with the file. This option should be disabled if the audio is to be output on compact disc.

Save Copy As: The **Save Copy As** command looks and works like the **Save As** command except that the file format and location of the last **Save Copy As** command becomes the default settings for the new file. This command is accessed by **File>Save Copy As** or **Crl+Alt+S**.

Save Selection: The **Save Selection** saves the active selection to a file. The **Save Waveform Selection** dialog box presents the same options as the **Save As** command. This command is also available by right-clicking on the waveform.

Save All: The **Save All** command saves all open files that have been modified since the last save. This includes waveforms and sessions.

Revert to Saved: The **Revert to Saved** is a valuable command. **Choosing File>Revert to Saved** discards all changes to the waveform since the last time the file was saved.

Insert Into Multitrack: The final command to be discussed in the **Edit View** section is the **Insert into Multitrack** command. This command can be accessed in a number of ways, but perhaps the easiest is to press **Ctrl+M**. Right-clicking also displays a pop-up menu with an option to **Insert into Multitrack**. This command places the waveform to a track in the **Multitrack View**.

Adjust Sample Rate: This function located at the bottom of the **Edit** menu. The **Adjust Sample Rate** function allows you to change the sample rate playback of the sound card. It does not alter the rate of the sound file and is only for playback purposes. Select the desired playback rate and click **OK**. The result is instant.

Convert Sample Type: The abundance of audio formats and standards causes a frequent need to convert audio sampling rates. The **Convert Sample Type** function provides a method to

4.5 Convert Sample Type dialog box

change the sampling rate of the waveform while retaining the highest quality; however, higher quality settings will require more time to convert. Using the **Pre/Post** filter is recommended when upsampling (increasing the sample rate) or downsampling (reducing the sample rate) for the cleanest conversion.

In addition to the sampling rate, resolution rate and channel configuration can be changed. A qausi-mixer determines the amount of each channel used for a mono conversion. Values are expressed as a percentage of signal used. Negative values reverse the phase of the signal used in the conversion.

Dithering parameters are discussed in detail in Chapter 10 beginning on page 229.

THE CAST OF THE MULTITRACK VIEW

Multitrack View is truly the stage where all the cast and crew work together to present the final performance. Audio, video, and MIDI files can perform together in the **Multitrack View** in a forum Audition calls a session. Although individual files and assets can be inserted into tracks in the **Multitrack View**, most of the file-handling functions deal with sessions. All session, importing, and exporting commands are located in the **File** menu, and the asset commands are in the Insert menu.

Press **F12** to switch to the **Multitrack View** workspace if you're in **Edit View**.

New Session

The **New Session** command prompts you to save the current session before clearing any previously opened tracks and opens a **New Session** dialog box as shown in Figure 4.6. To start a new session, press the shortcut **Ctrl+N** or select **File>New Session**.

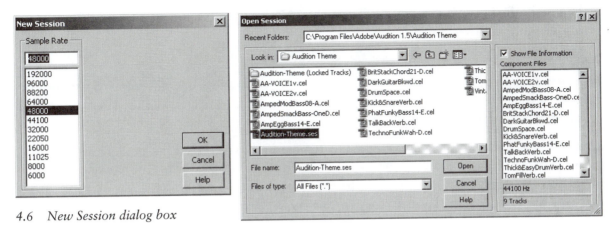

4.6   *New Session dialog box*

4.7   *Open Session dialog box*

To Create a New Session:

1. Press **Ctrl+N** or select **File>New Session**

2. Select the sample rate from the list or enter the rate in the **Sample Rate** field.

3. Click the **OK** button.

> **TIP!!**
>
> Creating a new session clears any existing tracks but does not close the previously opened files. Use the **Close Only Non-Session Media** command if you want to clean house and close all the previous session files.

Open Session

Ctrl+O or **File>Open** Session opens the **Open Session** dialog box. Recent folders can be found quickly in the **Recent Folders** pop-up menu. The **Look in** pop-up menu is used to navigate to the desired folder, and the **File of type** pop-up menu defaults to filter out display of all files except Multitrack Session (*.ses) files. The **Show File Information** checkbox displays a listing of the session components or assets, sample rate, and number of tracks currently used in the session.

To Open a Previous Session:

1. Select **File>Open** Session.

2. Locate the Audition Theme folder from the Look in pop-up menu.
   This path is *C:\Program Files\Adobe\Audition 1.5\Audition Theme* if the default installation was selected. The session file is also located in the Audition Theme Folder in the *Chapter 04-Audio* folder on the CD that accompanies this book.

3. Highlight the file named *Audition-Theme.ses*. Notice the **Component Files** on the right side of the window.

4. Double-click the filename or press the **OK** button.

Append to Session: The **Append to Session** command looks and works like **Open Session**; however, the selected session is appended at the beginning of the timeline, and the assets are placed on consecutive tracks starting with the first open track.

Close Session: The **Close Session** command removes all assets from the tracks but leaves the files open. The **Close Session** command shortcut is **Ctrl+W**, or it can be selected from **File>Close Session**. Use this command to begin work on a new composition using the same assets as the session being closed.

Close Session and Its Media: The **Close Session and Its Media** closes the session and any associated components. Any other waveforms remain open and available for use.

Close Only Non-Session Media: The **Close Only Non-Session Media** is the inverse command to **Close Session and Its Media**. Using this command closes all assets that are not components of the current session.

Close All: The **Close All** command closes all session files whether the files are components of the session or not.

Save Session: **Ctrl+S** issues the **Save Session** command saves the open session. Any changes to the session will be saved.

Save Session As: The **Save Session As** command is a carbon copy of the **Save As** command in **Edit View** except that the **Save Session As** saves all assets or files called components that are used in the session. The dialog box also offers the option of saving copies of all the session files. This feature is enabled by checking the **Save copies of all associated files** checkbox. If saving copies is chosen, the **Option** button can be called to modify the properties of the copies as shown in Figure 4.8.

4.8   The Session 'Save Copies of all files' Options dialog box

Copies of session files are saved in their native format unless the **Save all copies in this format** checkbox is enabled, which allows selection of alterative file formats and format options. The sample rate of the copies can be modified by checking the **Convert Sample Rate** checkbox. Dithering and other parameters are set through the **Conversion Properties** button, and the current settings can be saved by enabling the **Remember these settings for next time** checkbox.

Save All: The **Save All** command saves the session file and all components of the session.

Import: The **Import** command is almost the same as the **Open** command in **Edit View** with the exception that **Import** supports several video formats. The **Import** command can be called from the **File** menu or by the pressing **Ctrl+I**. Right-clicking in the **Organizer** window also opens the **Import** dialog box.

Export: The two submenu choices of the **Export** command are literal. The **Export>Audio** command is used to mix the session audio to the desired format. The **Export>Video** is only available when the session includes a video track and exports both video track and the session mix to a supported video file format.

- *Audio:* Selecting **Export>Audio** is essentially a mix-down command. The command opens a dialog box identical to the **Save As** window except that the **Option** button allows you to set parameters for the chosen file format. The session mix is stored to the location and filename entered in this window.

Audition defaults to 16-bit mix-downs. This setting can be changed on the **Multitrack** tab of the **Settings** window. Pressing the **F4** key opens the **Settings** window.

- *Video:* The **Export>Video** command functions the same as the **Export>Audio** command, but the audio is exported with the video track. The **Options** button presents a list of audio codecs installed on the computer.

Default Session

Set **Default Session** functions as a template command allowing the session configuration to be saved and recalled for future sessions. The **Default Session** submenu choices either sets the current session settings as the default for future sessions or clears the current default settings.

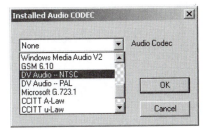

4.9   *DV Audio-NTSC is a common codec used for MiniDV video files.*

Insert Menu in Multitrack View

The **Insert Menu** provides an easy way to place assets into position on a track in **Multitrack View.**

Empty Wave: Inserts an empty wave into the selection area of the currently selected track or in all tracks armed and ready to record.

Audio: Inserts the selected audio file into the highlighted track at the current cursor location.

MIDI: Inserts the selected MIDI file into the highlighted track or the next available track at the current cursor location.

Video: Inserts the selected video file into the highlighted track at the current cursor location with audio inserted into the next consecutive track. Placement of the audio track will remain in sync with the video.

Audio from Video : Inserts only the audio from the selected video file into the highlighted track at the current cursor location.

File/Cue List: Inserts the file selected from a pop-up menu of open assets into the highlighted track at the current cursor location.

 Although many of the **File** menu and **Insert** menu commands lack a default shortcut, you can easily create your own through **Options > Keyboard Shortcuts and MIDI Triggers**. See Chapter 12 on page 271 for more information on customizing shortcuts.

Chapter 5

Laying Tracks

THE FIRST ACT

Recording audio is usually the first act in creating a soundtrack. Recording a track can be the easiest or the most difficult task depending upon the location and talent. Although Audition makes the technical aspect of recording fairly simple, an understanding of basic recording techniques is recommended and can significantly affect the outcome of your efforts. We will discuss some basic recording and miking techniques in this chapter; however, it is beyond the scope of this book to provide an in-depth discussion of the topics. Additional sources of information are provided in Appendix B on page 297 and on the CD that accompanies this book contains some additional reading material.but here are some considerations to keep in mind.

First, microphones are wonderful pieces of equipment. Each type of microphone has unique characteristics that cause it to hear the sound differently. Building an array of microphones to give you the option of selecting the one that provides the desired quality can make the difference between a mediocre recording and a superb one.

Second, when you begin to lay down tracks, realize that unless you are the composer you may not have a full idea of what the finished project is intended to sound like. So avoid using extremes in compression, equalization (more commonly called *EQ*), or any type of signal processing. Attempt to capture the sound as naturally as it occurs with enough substance to alter later during the mix, if necessary.

5.1   *Each microphone has a unique personality and hears sound differently. ©2004 by Shure Incorporated, used with permission.*

Third, pay attention to gain-staging. Set recording levels and the levels of any devices between the microphone and other sound sources to make sure that the gain at each stage is at its optimum level. Each device or stage adds noise to the signal, and improper gain-staging will result in increased noise as each stage is added or amplified by the next stage.

Last, listen for the "magic." Unless you're recording narration, where the words and pronunciation leave little room for error, when you have a take with a magical performance, keep it! Good sound can help make a hit song, but bad sound never stopped one.

RECORDING MODES

Audition offers the ability to record a single track in the **Edit View** workspace or simultaneous recording of multiple tracks in the **Multitrack View** workspace.

Unlike traditional multitrack tape recorders that could record only in mono, each track can be configured to record in either mono or stereo. Although Audition can record up to 128 tracks, recording in stereo provides 256 channels of audio. Various sampling rates up to 192kHz and resolutions to 32-bit are available depending upon the soundcard or audio interface capabilities. Audition can support rates up to 10MHz, but you'll have a tough time finding one of those cards today.

Recording and working in 32-bit resolution and reducing the bit depth during the final output will retain the best quality; however, the higher resolution will place much greater demand on the CPU. The added overhead will probably not be worth it if the result is a mix used on a radio spot, television commercial, or corporate video.

Recording at the highest supported sampling rate will yield the best results when recording tracks. 96kHz is considered satisfactory for even the most discriminating ear. 48kHz is recommended for commercial or corporate video projects to provide the best compromise between quality and performance.

Table 5.1   Typical sampling rates for compact disc, digital video, and DVD

Media	Sampling Rate
Compact disc	44.1kHz
Digital video	48kHz
DVD-Video	48kHz
DVD-Audio	96kHz

Table 5.2   Approximate file size of one minute of stereo audio at different sampling rates. Tracks recorded in mono require half the space.

Sampling Rate	16-bit	24-bit	32-bit
44.1kHz	10.6MB	16.9MB	21.2MB
48kHz	11.5MB	17.3MB	23.0MB
96kHz	23.0MB	34.6MB	46.0MB

Selecting **View > Status Bar > Free Space** or **Free Space (time)** will show the available drive space for recording.

Recording in Edit View

Once Audition has been installed and the computer system has been configured for optimum performance, you are ready to begin recording. So fire up the application, and let's get started.

Poor equipment connections, wrong connections, or finding the end of the cable lying on the floor next to the device are the most common reasons Audition does not work properly. You'll save yourself many headaches by making sure the connections are correct and in working order as one of your first steps in troubleshooting.

Selecting Sound Devices

Audition permits you to select a preferred device for recording and playback when multiple soundcards or devices are available. The preferred recording device does not have to be the same device as the preferred playback device.

Selecting the **Device Order Preference** need be set only once. Audition will retain the settings unless a device is removed or disabled.

1. Press **F12** or select **View>Edit Waveform View** if not already in the **Edit View** mode.
2. Select **Options>Device Order**.
3. Click the **Playback Devices** tab and highlight the device or soundcard desired for audio playback when in **Edit View** mode.
4. Press the **Use in EV** button. The letters **EV** will appear next to the device name indicating that it is the device that will be used for playback when in **Edit View** mode.

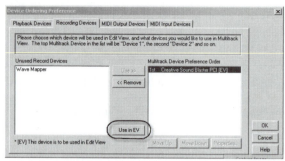

5.2   *Selecting the preferred device for use in Edit View mode*

5.3   *Enabling "Adjust to zero-DC when recording"*

5. Click the **Recording Devices** tab and highlight the device or soundcard desired for recording audio when in **Edit View** mode as shown in Figure 5.2.

6. Press the **Use in EV** button. The letters **EV** will appear next to the device name indicating that it is the device that will be used for recording when in **Edit View** mode.

7. Click **OK**.

8. Select **Options>Device Properties**.

9. Click on the **Wave In** tab.

10. Enable the **Adjust to zero-DC when recording** checkbox (see Figure 5.3). (**DC Offset** is discussed on page 39, and although enabling is not mandatory, it is recommended.)

11. Click **OK**.

Device Properties and **Device Order Preferences** settings are discussed in more detail on page 36 in Chapter 2.

Adjusting Monitor Volume

Microsoft Windows has a standard interface for controlling monitor volume. The **Volume Control** function can be accessed by clicking the speaker icon on the task bar in the lower right corner of the screen (see Figure 5.4). If the icon is not visible, select **Start Menu>Control Panel>Sounds and Audio Devices** and click the checkbox that places the volume icon on the task bar. (The name of the control panel and checkbox description varies slightly depending on the version of Microsoft Windows you have.)

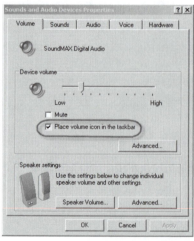

5.4   *Sound and Audio Devices Properties Control Panel in Microsoft Windows XP. Checking the Place volume icon in the taskbar checkbox makes the speaker icon appear in the task bar for easy access.*

Click on the speaker icon in the task bar to open the volume control. The monitor volume can be easily adjusted or muted, and the balance of signal between left and right channels can be varied. Right-click on the speaker icon and select **Open**

Volume Controls to adjust channel balance and output levels of individual devices such as CD players, software synthesizers, or other input devices.

 While in the **Sound and Audio Devices control** panel, select the **Sounds** tab and choose **No Sounds** from the **Sound Scheme** pop-up menu. This will help avoid severe ear damage when the monitors are cranked up and a Windows system beep sounds. Besides, the infamous Microsoft Windows startup sound is copyrighted, so you don't want it in your recordings.

5.5 *Volume Control allows convenient adjustment of overall monitor volume.*

Configuration of which individual volume controls appear in the volume control window is done in the **Volume Control Properties** window. The window is accessed by selecting **Options>Properties** from the **Volume Control** window. Select the mixer device from the pop-up menu and choose **Playback** under **Adjust volume for.** Enable checkboxes to show the desired devices in the **Volume Control** window.

Setting Recording Levels

Audition does not provide direct input level control. Input levels are controlled much like the monitor volumes through the **Windows Recording Mixer.** Select **Options>Windows Recording Mixer** to open the **Recording Control** window. Enable the checkbox of the desired recording source and adjust the volume fader until the desired levels are seen on the level meters.

5.6 *Open Volume Control adjusts overall volume and individual output levels.*

 If you experience poor mic levels, your sound card may offer the ability to boost the mic level through the **Advanced** button in the Windows Recording Mixer. Note that built-in or inexpensive sound cards may produce unacceptable noise when boosted because of inferior electronics.

Griffin PowerMate

The PowerMate from Griffin Technology is an inexpensive substitution for the **Volume** control panel, and you might find a few other uses. It's a USB device and programmable.

5.7 *The PowerMate from Griffin Technology is just plain cool. ©2004 by Griffin Technology.*

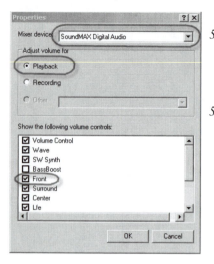

5.8   *The Properties window permits selection of devices that will be shown in the volume control. (left)*

5.9   *Microphone input is selected in the Recording Control dialog box of the Windows Recording Mixer. (right)*

TIP!! Many high-end sound cards offer their own software mixers that provide advanced features and a higher degree of control. Consult the sound card documentation for specific configuration and control options.

Working with the Level Meters

The level meters are a visual gauge of the input recording levels. Attention to metering is imperative for achieving the best recordings. Like most ideas, there are two camps on where

5.10 *Selecting Option>Properties while in the Recording Control window allows configuration of the desired recording devices that appear in when the Windows Recording Mixer is selected. (above left)*

5.11 *Wave mixer for Digigram VX222 sound card (above right)*

to set the levels for the purest digital signal. Regardless, the fact remains, levels that are too low will be noisy, and levels that are too hot, even if only for a split second, will result in a type of distortion. I subscribe to the theory of recording the levels as high as possible while leaving enough headroom or margin for error should the performance peak a little hotter than the rehearsal. Setting input levels so that peaks are around 6dB below the maximum level of 0dBFS is a good starting point. Leave more headroom for instruments or performances that are dynamic. Practical experience will enhance your level-setting skills, but these are important guidelines to follow as you get started.

Levels that are too hot and exceed the limit of recordable level produce a distortion called clipping. Clip indicators at the top of the meters will light up when the signal clips and will remain on until manually cleared by clicking on the clip indicator or selecting **Clear Clip Indicators** on the pop-up menu. Clearing the indicators will also clear peak and valley indicators.

Right-click on the level meters to display a pop-up menu with a number of metering options (see Figure 5.12). Enabling the **Monitor Record Level** allows the input signal to loop through the meters without having to go into the record mode. This option can be enabled from the pop-up menu or by selecting **Options>Monitor Record Level**, but double-clicking

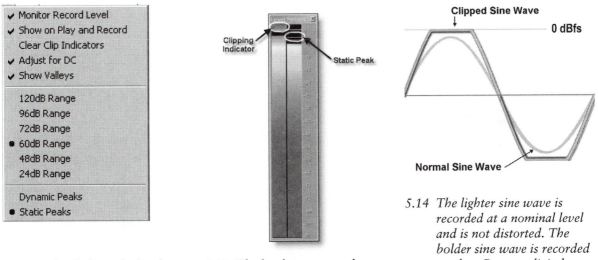

5.12 Right-click on the level meters to change the range, clear clip indicators, and change the peak and valley display modes, among other options.

5.13 The level meters can be moved, resized, and placed vertically or horizontally. Many engineers find that placing the level meters vertically makes them easier to read.

5.14 The lighter sine wave is recorded at a nominal level and is not distorted. The bolder sine wave is recorded too hot. Because digital audio cannot exceed 0dBFS, the signal is simply chopped off or clipped at 0dBFS. The level meters can be moved, resized, and placed vertically or horizontally. Many engineers find that placing the level meters vertically makes them easier to read.

Digital versus Analog Recording:

Digital recording is not forgiving as analog recording is when it comes to levels that are recorded too hot. In the analog world, as recording levels reached the maximum signal the tape could handle, the tape would begin to saturate and produce varying degrees of noticeable distortion. In fact, saturating the analog tape was sometimes a desirable effect that caused a soft form of compression. Not so with digital signals. When a digital signal hits 0dBFS (Zero decibel Full Scale) for more than a few consecutive samples, it clips the signal and produces a noise that is not only audible but also even obnoxious. The distortion occurs since the digital signal cannot exceed 0dBFS. It is impossible. An analogy might be to imagine a drinking glass with the top of the glass being 0dBFS. You can fill the glass without a problem until it reaches the top. Once the liquid reaches the top, the glass cannot physically contain any more. Attempting to add any more to it simply causes it to spill over the edges, and the liquid that spilled is lost.

---

the meters or pressing **F10** are quicker ways to enable the meters. Chapter 3 on page 71 contains more detailed information on level meters and metering options.

 Static Peaks and **Show Valleys** metering options hold the hottest and lowest levels until the meters are cleared. Using these options during rehearsal will provide a good idea of how much the levels can be adjusted for the optimum recording level.

 Enabling **Live update during recording** is a cool feature that draws the waveform on the screen as it is recorded. However, it does decrease performance and should not be enabled if skipping or dropouts occur. This option can be enabled or disabled by pressing **F4**, selecting the **General** tab, and checking or unchecking **Live update during recording**.

 If you're both the talent and the engineer, use good quality headphones for monitoring, and make sure they are turned down to avoid feedback or bleed.

Recording a New Track

Before beginning the section, make sure that you have plugged in a microphone or another input device and that your monitoring system volume is at a comfortable listening level. If not already in **Edit View** mode, press **F12** to switch workspaces.

1. Select **F10** or double-click on the level meters to monitor the source input levels. This will allow you to set maximum recording levels without actually starting the recording.

2. Make sure the **Option>Show Levels on Play and Record** is enabled. Checking this option allows the level meters to display levels during recording and playback.

3. Select **Options>Windows Recording Mixer** or your sound card or device's mixer.

4. Enable the **Select** checkbox of the desired input. This can include the internal CD-ROM drive, but digital extraction or ripping generally provides better quality.

5. Adjust the **Volume** fader on the selected device until the level meters are within an acceptable range.

6. Press **F10** to disable the **Monitor Record Level** and click on the clip indicators to clear the level meters.

7. Press the **Record** button or **Ctrl+spacebar**.

8. Choose the sample rate, channels, and resolution from the **New Waveform** dialog box.

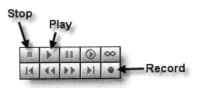

9. Click **OK**, and recording will begin.

10. Once the performance is complete, press the spacebar or use the **Stop** button to end the recording.

5.15 Clicking the Record button begins recording at the current cursor location. The Stop button or spacebar is used to end the recording.

11. Click the **Play** button to audition the recording.

12. Select **File>Save As** to save the recording to the hard drive or hit the **Home** Key to return the cursor to the start Reset the level meters beginning, clear the waveform selection, and click the **Record** button to record the track again. Note that recording again will erase the previous recording.

> **TIP!!** Press **F8** during recording to note any locations where there are anomalies such as microphone pops, noises, or the beginnings of program segments. A visual cue mark will be placed in the file, allowing quick location during playback.

> **TIP!!** You may have noticed that Audition saved another file beside the .wav file with an .pk extension. That file is a peak file, which contains data used to draw the waveform in Audition. The peak file is not required, and Audition will create a new one when the file has been deleted or is missing, but the peak file helps Audition open the file and draw the waveform on the screen more quickly.

Timed Record

Audition provides a very handy feature for unattended recording called Timed Record mode. It's a great alternative to baby-sitting a DAT (Digital Audio Tape) file while it loads into Audition or recording a radio or Internet broadcast without having to be there to start and/or stop the recording.

This option is enabled by selecting **Options>Timed Record Mode** or by right-clicking the **Record** button and selecting the option from the pop-up menu. Once the feature is enabled, clicking the **Record** button presents a dialog box for configuring the start and stop times. After the times are entered, click **OK** and press the **Record** button. If the recording is not set to start right away, the **Record** button will flash until the desired time and the recording will start and stop according to the times entered in the **Recording Timed Record Mode** window.

5.16 Timed recording allows scheduling unattended recording.

 Audition has a 4GB file limit when recording in **Edit View**. This typically won't be an issue because that equates to more than six hours of stereo recording or over 12 hours of mono recording.

 It's a good idea to register your software to prevent the registration reminder from popping up in the middle of your recording and causing clicks, pops, and other problems. The same holds true for any other services that happen automatically such as desktop photo subscriptions or any other automatic updates.

Life will be much easier if you keep notes on recordings such as microphone used, compression, EQ, and other pertinent information that may help jog your mind six months later when the client's legal department needs to change a few sentences. Press **Ctrl+P** to open the **Wave Properties** dialog box after the recording and add any information, comments, or other metadata to the **Text Fields** tab. The information will stay with the original file as long as the **Save extra non-audio information** checkbox is enabled.

Recording in Multitrack View

Edit View permits recording only a single track at a time. **Multitrack View** can record multiple tracks simultaneously. In fact, the number of tracks that Audition can record simultaneously is limited far more by the computer power and hardware devices than the 128-track limit of Audition.

Recording in **Multitrack View** offers the ability to record one or more tracks and play those tracks while recording more tracks. Each of those tracks can be recorded in mono or stereo.

Les Paul's Invention

Multitrack recording was pioneered in the 1940s by Lester Polsfus, or Les Paul as most of us know him. Yes, the same Les Paul of Les Paul Guitars fame. Les Paul first referred to this process as sound-on-sound because it allowed recording another sound on the same tape while playing back a previously recorded track.

Imagine connecting a number of cassette decks together in such a way that you could start, stop, rewind, and fast forward them all at the same time. Add the ability to record on any of the cassette decks while the rest of the decks play along in perfect time. Multitrack recording does just that. It permits the ability of recording each instrument on a separate track while maintaining a synchronized relationship with other tracks. This is the essence of a multitrack recorder. It simply records each track as a separate entity that can be manipulated, rerecorded, or erased without affecting the other tracks.

Selecting Device Order

The **Multitrack Device Preference Order** is set from the **Options>Device Order** in the same way as the **Edit View** devices were selected. The difference is that **Edit View** uses only one device to record or play back a single track. **Multitrack View** can use as many devices as are present in the system; however, the preferred order in which Audition uses the cards must be set. The **Device Order** controls which tracks are assigned to a device when opening a session. Setting the order is simple.

1. Press **F12** or select **View>Multitracks View** if not already in the **Multitrack View** mode.

2. Select **Options>Device Order**.

3. Click the **Playback Devices** tab and highlight any devices in the left-hand list that will be used for playback when in **Multitrack View** mode.

4. Press the **Use** button to move any devices that should be used for playback and the **Remove** button to disable any devices.

5. Click the **Recording Devices** tab and press the **Use** and **Remove** buttons to configure the devices to be used for recording.

6. Highlight the device and use the **Move Up** and **Move Down** buttons to place the devices in the desired order.

7. Click **OK**.

Full Duplex: Multitrack recording requires at least one sound card that is capable of both input and output simultaneously. This is called full-duplex sound. If the computer contains only one sound card that is only half-duplex, tracks will need to be recorded in **Edit View** before insertion into **Multitrack View**. Systems equipped with at least two half-duplex cards can still record in multitrack by selecting one sound card for the input of the track used for recording.

Enabling **Adjust to zero-DC when recording** is recommended to remove DC bias during recording. The option is accessed from **Options** > **Device Properties** > **Wave In** tab. See page 39 for a discussion of DC offset.

 Device-specific playback and recording settings can be configured with the **Options** > **Device Proper-ties** > **Wave In** and **Wave Out** tabs. Consult your device documentation for more information.

Adjusting Monitor Volume

The overall monitor volume is adjusted the same way for both **Edit View** and **Multitrack View**. See "Adjusting Monitor Volume" on page 90 earlier in this chapter for information on volume controls. Adjustment of individual track volume and channel is done through volume and panning controls on each track. Each track can be muted, or the track can be soloed. These individual track controls are available through the **Track Properties** and **Track Console** windows.

Setting Recording Levels

Input level control is not available directly through Audition. Recording input levels are set through **Options>Windows Recording Mixer,** a third-party control panel supplied with the device, or a compatible workstation controller. The input adjustments and recording levels are handled the same way as in **Edit View** mode.

Working with Multitrack Level Meters

Level metering and options are the same in **Edit View** and **Multitrack View** with one major difference. The level meters can be displayed for all available devices and will show both input and output levels. To enable monitoring levels on multi-ple devices, right-click on the level meters and select **Show Meters for All Devices** from the pop-up menu. But beware; there is a significant performance hit when monitoring meters on multiple devices.

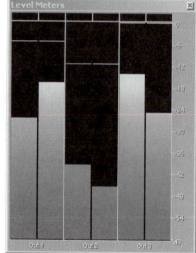

Recording a Single Track

Before beginning the session, make sure that you have plugged in a microphone or another input device and that your monitoring system volume is at a comfortable listening level. If not already in **Multitrack View** mode, press **F12** to switch workspaces.

5.17 Level meters set to monitor three stereo output devices

1. Select **Ctrl+N** or **File>New Session**.

2. Select the sampling rate for the session files and click **OK**.

5.18 *Input and output devices, track configuration, and arming the track for recording are among settings controlled with the Track Properties window.*

5.19 *Audition provides alternate ways to access most options. Right-clicking on the track waveform presents a pop-up menu offering access to the same options available via the Track Properties window. (right)*

3. Press **Alt+4** to open the **Track Properties** window and click on the **Track 1** tab if more than one tab is shown.

4. Enter a descriptive name for the track in the **Title** field.

5. Select the desired playback device from the **Output** pop-up menu.

6. Select the device to be used for input from the **Record** pop-up menu.

7. Choose **Left Only, Right Only,** or **Stereo** to select the track channel configuration and the recording resolution from the pop up menus.

8. Click the **Record** button to arm the track for recording.

9. Select **F10** or double-click on the level meters to monitor the source input levels. This will allow setting maximum recording levels without starting the recording.

10. Make sure that **Option>Show Levels** on **Play and Record** is enabled. Checking this option allows the level meters to display levels during recording and playback.

11. Select **Options>Windows Recording Mixer** or your sound card or device's mixer.

12. Enable the **Select** checkbox of the desired input.

13. Adjust the volume fader on the selected device until the level meters are within an acceptable range.

14. Press **F10** to disable the **Monitor Record Level,** and click on the clip indicators to clear the level meters.

15. Press the **Record** button or **Ctrl**+spacebar to initiate the recording.

16. Once the performance is complete, press the spacebar or click the **Stop** button to end the recording.

17. Click the **Play** button to audition the recording.

18. Select **File>Save Session** to save the session and recording to the hard drive or hit the **Home** key to return the cursor to the start. Reset the level meters and press the **Record** button to record the track again. Note that recording again will erase the previous recording.

 Right-click on a clip and select **Lock in Time** to prevent you from inadvertently moving the clip. A padlock icon will appear in the lower-right corner of the clip.

 The **Lock for Play Only** option disables the record capability for the track. Even though the track may be armed, it will not record. This is a good habit to get into when working in **Multitrack View**. Right-click on the clip to access this option.

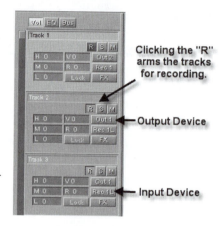

Clicking the "R" arms the tracks for recording.

Output Device

Input Device

5.20 *Multiple tracks armed for recording*

Recording Multiple Tracks

Recording multiple tracks simultaneously is as easy as recording a single track in **Multitrack View**. Configure the input and output for each track and arm the tracks. Individual volume and panning controls are available on the track controls for each track. The number of tracks that can be used at one time depends upon your computer, hardware, and settings. See page 21 in Chapter 2 for information on optimizing your system.

 The metronome can be sent only to an output and should not record on the tracks. If the metronome or another track is being recorded on a new track, check the **Windows Recording Mixer** or the mixer control panel for the sound device and make sure that **Wave Out Mix** or another similar input is not selected.

 Creating session templates for different recording setups can get you rolling quickly. The session templates retain settings such as input and output devices for each track. Save the templates with descriptive file names for each setup and set the most frequently used session as the default session. To prevent someone from accidentally saving changes to the session templates, find the session template file, right-click, select **Properties**, and change the file attributes to **Read Only**.

Latency and Offset

What's this multitrack latency? Not all sound cards are created equal. Some sound cards lag slightly during the record process. Although the latency may be so small to be negligible, this problem can be corrected through the **Multitrack Latency** field on the **Device Properties Wave In** tab.

The latency value is entered in milliseconds. The offset can be determined by playing a sound with a sharp attack from one track while recording it on another. The latency is the value of the offset between the two tracks. The following method can be used to find the latency value.

1. Set **Display Time Format** to **Decimal**.

2. Select **Insert > Audio** and insert the *Latency Test.wav* file into **Track 1**. (This file can be found in the *Chapter 05-Audio* directory on the CD that accompanies this book.)

3. Mute the audio monitors using the volume control.

4. Connect a patch cable from the output of the sound card to the input.

5. Select the desired input and output device for each track.

6. Arm **Track 2** and press **Ctrl+spacebar** or click the **Record** button.

7. After **Track 2** has been recorded, zoom into the beginning of the tone.

8. Highlight the segment from the beginning of the tone on **Track 2** to the beginning of the tone of **Track 1**.

9. Enter the value found in the **View-Length of the Selection/View Controls** into the **Multitrack Latency** field of the sound card or device.

Punch In Recording

Punch in recording in **Multitrack View** allows rerecording of a selected segment. For example, the vocalist's performance was perfect except for one phrase that was a little flat. One option would be to record the phrase again on another track and "fix it in the mix." The other option would be to use the Punch In feature and replace that phrase on the track it was originally recorded.

The **Punch In** feature is quick and easy to use. It offers the option of recording and saving multiple takes; however, you must enable the **Allow Multiple Takes** option.

The steps involved in using **Punch In** are simple:

1. Select **Edit>Allow Multiple Takes** or right-click on the track and choose **Allow Multiple Takes** from the menu.

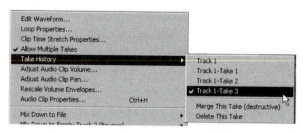
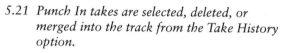

5.21 *Punch In takes are selected, deleted, or merged into the track from the Take History option.*

5.22 *The Record button changes to the infinity symbol when looping in record mode.*

2. Highlight the segment to be recorded. This is done by clicking on the track at the location the recording should begin and dragging to the location that the recording should end.

3. Select **Edit>Punch In,** and the record mode on the track will arm.

4. Move the cursor far enough before the point that the recording will begin to give the talent time to get ready.

5. Click the **Record** button.

6. Stop the transport by pressing the spacebar or the **Stop** button.

Allow Multiple Takes permits recording with **Punch In** until the take is acceptable. To continue recording takes, repeat steps 4 though 6. As each take is recorded, the take name will appear in the **Organizer** window. When satisfied that a usable take has been recorded, right-click on the track and highlight the **Take History** option. A submenu lists all the takes. Select a take to audition it in context with the rest of the track and then use the **Merge This Take (destructive)** menu item to insert the selected take into the track. Merging the take is destructive and cannot be completely reversed.

 The system sound card and devices will determine the options for providing a cue mix (headphone) during multitrack recording. The most efficient and flexible system should include a mixer or surface controller.

Looped Record

Audition also has two other recording options available by right-clicking the **Record** button. **Loop While Recording (View or Sel)** and **Loop While Recording (Entire or Sel).** These options differ from the **Continuous Linear Record** that we have been using by continuously looping while recording. The options loop the current viewable track segment or the entire track respectively. Selection of the **Allow Multiple Takes** will record each loop.

 If you are both the engineer and talent and want to record yourself, consider using the looping record options and **Allow Multiple Takes**.

MICROPHONES

There are a multitude of microphones available on the market, but they all share one common purpose: converting acoustical energy into electromagnetic energy. As mentioned earlier, each model of microphone has characteristics that affect the way it sounds or colors the natural sound. Each type of microphone has specific strengths and weaknesses. Using the most expensive is not necessarily the best choice.

Types of Microphones

Microphones can be grouped into three basics types: dynamic, ribbon, and condenser.

Dynamic

Dynamic microphones or "moving coil" microphones tend to be the least expensive, most level-tolerant, and least sensitive. The mechanics of the dynamic microphone are simple. A thin diaphragm is attached to a coil that surrounds a magnet. As sound waves compress the diaphragm, the coil moves and generates voltage waveforms that mimic the acoustic sound waves. This voltage is converted to a digital signal by the sound card or audio interface (see Figure 5.23).

Ribbon

Ribbon microphones are the least-used type of microphone. Ribbon microphones tend to be moderately sensitive and generally return more of the high frequencies than dynamic mikes, but this varies depending upon the brand and model. The mechanics are similar to a dynamic microphone, but instead of using a diaphragm and coil, a very thin piece of metal is suspended within a magnetic field. Sound waves cause vibration of the metal, which in turn generates voltage that is converted to a digital signal by the analog to digital converter in the same manner as the dynamic microphone (see Figure 5.24).

Condenser

Condenser microphones are considered the premium microphones by most recording engineers (see Figure 5.25). Condenser mikes are very sensitive and tend to be more accurate than other types of mikes. The mechanics are significantly different from dynamic or ribbon mikes. Condensers use a metallic diaphragm parallel to another metallic plate. As the sound waves enter the microphone, the vibration of the diaphragm varies the distance between the diaphragm and the plate. As the electrically charged diaphragm vibrates and moves closer to the plate, electrons jump across the gap to the metallic plate, creating a

> Condenser microphones tend be the first choice for many engineers, but they require a power source. Many condenser microphones use a method called phantom powering, which uses a power source from the mixing board or console.

5.23   The Shure SM57 is a dynamic microphone. It is an excellent choice for snare drum, kick drum, percussion, and even vocals. The SM57 can handle high signal levels and is exceptionally durable. Although the sound quality may fall short of a large capsule condenser microphone, it is a great utility microphone that should be in every studio arsenal. © 2004 by Shure Incorporated, used with permission. (left)

5.24   The RCA-77DB, a ribbon microphone that is an excellent choice for brass. Photograph courtesy of Darrin Warner. (lower left)

5.25   The AKG C 451 B is a small-capsule condenser microphone. Typical uses include overhead drums, percussion, and acoustic guitar. It handles transients extremely well and adds little coloration to the sound. ©2004 by AKG Acoustics, used with permission. (right)

measurable voltage. Unfortunately, the voltage is too low and requires an external power supply or battery to amplify the voltage to a usable level. Condenser microphones are classified as either small-capsule or large-capsule.

Preamps

Microphones require a boost in signal before converting the waveform to digital audio. Sound cards or audio interfaces with mic inputs contain a preamp that increases the microphone signal. If the sound card does have a mic input, an external preamp is required when using a microphone. Most mixing consoles have built-in preamps. See Chapter 1 for an in-depth discussion of this topic.

Many of the workstation controllers such as the Tascam US-224 and US-428 eliminate the need for a sound card or preamp and provide additional features for controlling Audition (see Figure 5.26). Appendix A on page 293 offers more information on Audition-compatible workstation controllers.

5.26 *Tascam US-428 Workstation Controller. © 2004 by Tascam, used with permission.*

Miking Techniques

Selecting the right microphone for the job is only the beginning. You should consider the microphone's pick-up pattern, frequency response, and placement. Microphone placement can have as much or more effect on the sound than the type of microphone that is used.

Polar Patterns

A microphone's directionality is shown by the polar pattern or pick-up pattern. There are four basic types of pick-up pattern: omnidirectional, bidirectional, cardioid, and hypercardioid. Many microphones permit changing the patterns with a switch. Omnidirectional microphones pick up sound from all directions around the microphone. Cardioid and hypercardioid microphones are less sensitive to sound from the side and rear. Bidirectional microphones pick up audio from the back of the microphone equally but reject sound from the sides.

Frequency Response

The frequency response of a microphone affects how the microphone will hear the sound. The response is typically graphed by the microphone manufacturer and shows how well the microphone works at specific frequencies. Understanding the microphone's personality will help you match it to the instrument (see Figure 5.28).

Placement

Most microphones should be placed about four inches from the instrument, but use your ear to help find the sweet spot. Don't be afraid to try some different positions until you find the

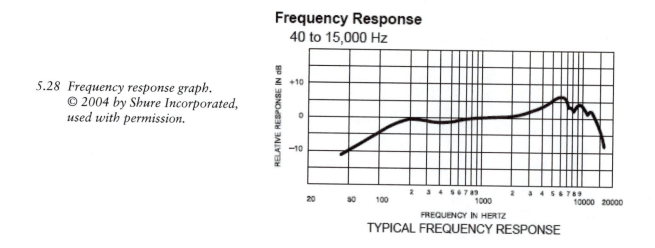

Frequency Response
40 to 15,000 Hz

5.28 *Frequency response graph.*
© 2004 by Shure Incorporated,
used with permission.

TYPICAL FREQUENCY RESPONSE

placement location that works for you. Remember to consider the frequency response and pickup pattern when selecting and placing the microphone. When recording multiple players or vocalists, place them across from each other or in a manner to allow the pickup pattern of the microphone to reject and reduce leakage from the other instruments or vocals. Strategic placement of baffling or other acoustically absorbent materials around the players can also help reduce leakage.

Polar Pattern

Unidirectional (cardioid), rotationally symmetrical about microphone axis, uniform with frequency.

5.27 *Microphone polar*
patterns. © 2004 by Shure
Incorporated, used with
permission.

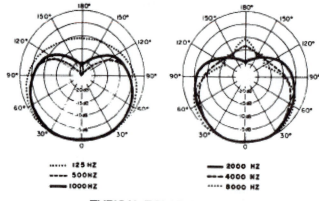

TYPICAL POLAR PATTERNS

Microphone placement will vary according to the microphone, talent, and desired sound, but there are some typical starting locations. These are only starting points. Don't be afraid to try something new or unusual. You might surprise yourself and the producer at the same time.

The best results are usually obtained on vocals or narratives by placing the microphone 3–4 inches away and slightly off to the side of the talent's mouth. A kick drum records well with the front head removed and the microphone placed inside the drum about 4–6 inches from the head and off to the side. Try the snare drum mic about 2 inches above the top head just barely in from the rim. Overhead left and right drum mikes should be balanced to obtain the best mix of cymbals and full tom-tom sounds. Depending upon the drummer, it may be necessary to add additional mikes, but beware of the potential phase shift and frequency cancellation. Try using a separate hi-hat mic a few inches above the hi-hat. Pianos tend to sound full yet crisp when microphones are placed 6–8 inches over the low- and high-end ranges of the soundboard. Acoustic guitars are inclined to bark when the microphone is placed too close to the sound hole. A good starting point is 6–8 inches away and off to the side of the hole. Adding another microphone over the fret board can produce a nice stereo effect. Smaller string instruments need room for the sound to expand, with mic placement 5–10 feet above the string section, but instruments such as the cello or upright bass usually sound better with close microphone placement similar to the acoustic guitar placement. Instruments such as the saxophone or trumpet sound good with microphones placed about six inches away and slightly off to the side of the bell. Instruments such as the French horn benefit from allowing the sound to swell and bounce off walls or windows.

Remember, these are simply suggestions to get started. Use you imagination, be creative, and don't be afraid to try something different.

> Douglas Spotted Eagle once pointed out that "a microphone was like a grenade; the closer it is…the better it works." That statement is very true for a number of reasons, including a phenomenon called the proximity effect. The proximity effect is the increased sensitivity to low-end frequencies that occurs as a microphone gets closer to the sound source.

TIP!! Monitoring through a good studio-quality set of headphones while adjusting mic placement can help find the sweet spot.

Difficult Situations

If you haven't already, you will run into some difficult voices or instruments to record. Many problems are easily solved with a microphone adjustment, a word to the talent, or a little processing or EQ. Other problems are not quite so easy to resolve.

Excessive sibilance can be a noticeable problem when recording vocals. Sibilance occurs on the S and F sounds. Because these sounds are predominately high frequencies, they tend to quickly overload the electronics and cause distortion. Because high frequencies are directional, try moving the microphone off to the side of the mouth. If this does not reduce the sibilance to an acceptable level, try using another microphone such as a dynamic mic that is not as sensitive to those frequencies. The last resort should be signal processing called *de-essing*. A de-esser acts a high-frequency limiter that triggers when the high-frequencies exceed a particular threshold. It is not recommended that de-essing be applied during the recording because any processing-generated artifacts due to incorrect settings would be uncorrectable.

Plosives, or microphone pops that occur when the talent sings or says a word with a P sound, can usually be taken care of with a wind screen. Repositioning the microphone a few inches to the left or right of the talent's mouth should resolve problems the wind screen doesn't fix. Other options include switching microphones or enabling a low-end roll off filter on the microphone.

Low-end filters (also called high-pass filters) can help resolve other issues related to low frequencies such as the rumble caused by air-conditioning systems. Of course, the best way is to turn the A/C off, but this is not possible in many instances, especially when doing location recordings.

There are too many potential situations to discuss, but if you understand the fundamentals, most difficulties can be reduced if not completely eliminated with a little common sense and ingenuity.

Microphone Suggestions

Every human hears audio slightly differently. Our tastes are based on personality, environment, and previous experience. The following is a list of the microphones and their uses that I have found to be my preference, but of course, microphone choice varies depending on the particular instrument, talent, arrangement, studio, and last but not least: availability.

Table 5.3   Author's preferred microphones and usage

Brand/Model	Type	Usage
AKG C414	Condenser	Vocals, narration, strings
AKG C451	Condenser	Overhead drums, acoustic guitar, strings
AKG D12	Dynamic	Kick drum
Neumann U-87	Condenser	Vocals, piano, strings, narration
Neumann U47	Condenser	Vocals, narration

Table 5.3   Author's preferred microphones and usage (Continued)

Brand/Model	Type	Usage
Neumann M147	Condenser	Vocals, narration
Sennheiser 421 II	Dynamic	Piano, saxophone, guitar amp, vocals, narration
Sennheiser 441	Dynamic	Voice, but can be used for music. CD-ROM and multimedia content. Internet usage when bandwidth is not an issue.
Shure SM57	Dynamic	Kick drum, snare drum, live or scratch vocals, guitar amp
RCA 77DX	Ribbon	Brass
RCA 44BX	Ribbon	Brass

Appendix B on page 297 of this book includes a listing of many microphone manufacturers and their contact information. Many of these manufactures have a host of technical information, product guides, and tips freely available on their web sites.

Recording Techniques

Miking techniques are only part of the equation to getting the best recording. The following are a couple of techniques that are widely used.

Overdubbing

Overdubbing has been used in music production for years. Although it would be much more efficient to record everything at the same time, it is typically not possible. Usually the rhythm tracks such as drums, bass, piano, and rhythm guitar were tracked together. After a good solid take of those instruments had been recorded, individual tracks such as lead guitar, solos, and synth pads were added.

This technique allowed more focus on each stage of the recording and reduced the chances of one of the tracks being less than acceptable. With the changes in technology and MIDI, overdubbing is almost the de facto method of recording. Many tracks are added one at a time to the final composition. Audition lends itself to this style of production.

Doubling

A single voice without effects or echo can sound stark naked. Adding echo, flanging, phasing, and other processing effects can help give the voice a unique or richer sound, but one of the techniques that gives vocals the desired quality is doubling or multing. Having a vocalist sing in unison with themselves can add a characteristic to the sound that is almost impossible to achieve any other way. As the vocalist sings along with their own voice, there will be slight variations in timing, pitch, and quality. It is not unusual to combine a number of these doubled tracks in the mix along with reverb, EQ, and signal processing to get the right vocal sound. The doubling technique can also work well for harmonies and other instruments such as guitars, but just as with vocals, the performance needs to be tight or the end result will just sound sloppy and cloud the arrangement.

Chapter 6

Making the Cut

WHAT IS EDITING?

It is rare that the first take or even the 10th take of a recording is perfect. Perhaps the talent made a few mistakes reading the script, or the producer likes the first part of one take and wants to combine it with another take. Even if the take is perfect, there is usually some unintentional noise or dead time that needs to be removed. The process of correcting mistakes and deciding what will be removed is called *editing*. During editing, the audio elements are modified, combined, and assembled into the final sequence. Editing is also often used to define the composition or sometimes to create the composition of musical projects. Sometimes new compositions are inspired as a result of hearing the project from a different viewpoint.

Editing Techniques

Audition provides a wide range of methods to edit and assemble digital audio. The **Edit View** mode is the editing workhorse of Audition and is used to edit a single mono or stereo waveform. **Multitrack View** is used to composite or layer tracks in a linear timeline. Although **Multitrack View** provides the ability to split, delete, and move segments of a track, **Edit View** offers tools to fine tune the edits and polish the waveform for use in **Multitrack View**. Both workspaces offer unique advantages; however, there are distinct differences in how the modifications are saved. **Edit View** employs a technique called *destructive editing* that destroys the original recording, but **Multitrack View** simply stores a list of changes in the session file and does not affect the recordings.

Destructive and Nondestructive Editing

Digital audio and computers have changed the methods of audio editing. In the past, magnetic tape was the medium of choice, and editing was done with a razor blade and metal splicing block. During the editing process, any unwanted segments were bladed out and usually thrown away or added to an outtake reel. This process was destructive since it altered the original recording. It could be very difficult if not impossible to return the master to its original form before the editing.

Audition is able to employ both destructive and nondestructive methods. Audition does not alter the original audio files when editing or assembling tracks in **Multitrack View**. Audition maintains a list of the locations and modifications as a set of instructions for the session. When a session is played back, Audition makes those changes in real time as the track or tracks play.

Edit View handles editing in a different way using both nondestructive and destructive methods. Instead of editing the original file, modifications made in **Edit View** change a temporary copy of the audio file. The original file is not changed until the file or track is saved. This method permits using the **Undo** command to reverse edits or changes while editing the track yet also provides the ability to save the file once editing is complete.

> **TIP!!** Changes made in **Edit View** cannot be reversed once the files are saved and closed. Make a backup copy of the original files before beginning the editing. Backup copies can be saved to another location, preferably on another drive, or using another filename. Doing so will always allow you to go back and make changes if necessary.

Splicing

Digital audio has brought about another change in editing techniques. The razor-blade method required cutting the tape at one of two diagonal angles and splicing the tape back together. Those were the only choices.

6.1 *Magnetic tape could be cut only at one of two angles.*

In addition to a simple splice, Audition offers several other types of edits. The crossfade cut smooths out the tougher edits by feathering the transition between the two segments (see Figure 6.2). **Trim** removes audio on both sides of the selected audio. The **Mix Paste** option can overlap, modulate, and even the invert the signal phase.

We'll discuss these editing techniques and others during this chapter. To understand how to edit and become proficient, you will need to recognize good editing points such as the beginning of words, beats, and sounds. The beginning of percussive sounds such as a drum are easy

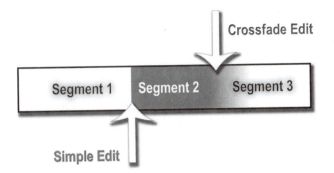

6.2   *Segment 1 is spliced to Segment 2 using a simple edit. The audio of Segment 1 ends abruptly at the edit, and the Segment 2 audio starts instantly at the splice point. Segment 2 begins fading out as Segment 3 fades in using a crossfade on the splice.*

to spot, whereas words or sounds with a slow attack are not as obvious and are more difficult to locate (see Figure 6.3).

EDITING IN EDIT VIEW

We are going to do some basic voice and music editing. Although there are definite things you should not do when editing that will be obvious to your ear, there is no set procedure for editing. There are several ways to accomplish the same result. I will present a couple of examples that use various methods and shortcuts to help familiarize you with the available tools, but it will be up to you to chose the techniques and tools that work best for you. Audition offers a host of features for creating loops, effects, and mixing. We will use some of those features while exploring the editing tools. In-depth discussions of those features are presented in the chapters that follow this one.

Before beginning to edit, we need to discuss the setup and use of one very important feature. It's an ability that would be great to have in our daily lives, the ability to undo mistakes or redo actions.

Undo/Redo

The **Undo/Redo** commands are located under the **Edit** menu. **Undo** and **Redo** commands allow reversing the previous edit or applying the edit or change again. This feature is enabled

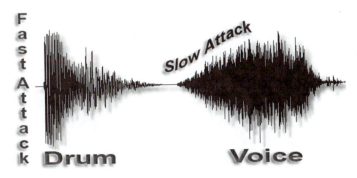

6.3   *The attack or envelope of a drum and a word beginning with the letter S*

when a checkmark appears to the left of the **Enable Undo/Redo** option. It is recommended that this option be enabled. Disabling this feature may be desired when working with large files (45 minutes or more) or if free drive space is low.

Undo/Redo can also be enabled by pressing **F4** and selecting **Enable Undo** checkbox on the **Settings>System** tab. The minimum number of undo levels is set on this tab. The maximum number of undo levels is determined by the available drive space for temp files. The **Purge Undo** button deletes the temporary undo files and is used to free drive space, but once clicked, it prevents you from reverting to previous edits.

The **Undo** and **Redo** commands can be selected from **Edit>Undo** and **Edit>Redo,** but the fastest method might be pressing **Ctrl+Z** for **Undo** and **Ctrl+Shift+Z** to **Redo.**

![Undo settings panel with Enable Undo checkbox checked, value 5, Levels (minimum), and Purge Undo button]

6.4 Undo/Redo settings are set on the System tab of the Settings dialog box

> **TIP!!** Use the **Undo/Redo** command to quickly compare the audio before and after an edit or make a comparison of the audio with or without an effect.

Preroll and Postroll

When making an edit, it should be habit to review the edit to confirm that it was performed as intended. Audition makes this review process easier with the preroll and postroll options by playing a predetermined amount of time before and after the edit. This option allows you to preview an edit before making it with the **Play Preroll and Postroll (Skip Selection)** function. Three other options are available that allow playback of different combinations of the preroll, selection, and postroll.

The amount of time that will be played back before the selection called preroll and the amount of time after the selection called postroll is determined through the **Preroll and Postroll Options** dialog box. It can be selected by right-clicking on the **Play** button or from the **Options** menu.

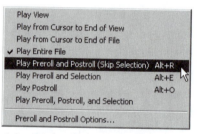

6.5 Right-click on the Play button or choose a shortcut to select a Preroll/Postroll function.

Selecting Segments

Edits are applied based on the segment of the waveform selected. Selected segments are highlighted. The entire waveform can be selected by pressing **Ctrl+A** or **Edit>Select Entire Wave.** You can also right-click on the waveform and choose **Select Entire Wave** from the pop-up menu, but the fastest way may be double-clicking the waveform. If no selection is made, any

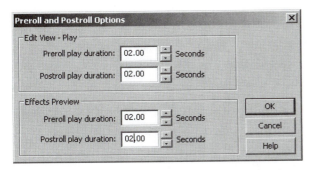

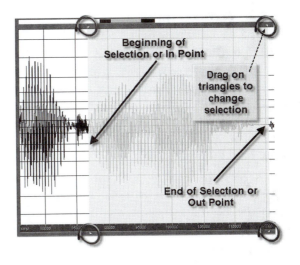

6.6 *The Preroll and Postroll Options dialog box (above)*

6.7 *Selection in Edit View (right)*

change or effect will be applied only to the segment of the waveform currently visible. This behavior can be changed so that the entire waveform is affected by changing the **Default Selection Range** to **Entire Wave** on the **General** tab of the **Settings** window.

Selection of segments other than the entire waveform or visible waveform is quick and painless, and the starting and ending points of a segment are easily changed. There are a number of keyboard shortcuts to vary the selection area in addition to using a pointing device. Segment selection begins with placing the cursor over the desired location on the waveform and clicking the left mouse button. Continue holding the mouse down and drag to the left or right, until the desired segment is highlighted. The beginning and ending points (or as some editors refer to them, the in and out points) of the segment will have triangles called handles at the top and bottom of the waveform. The selection area can be shortened or lengthened by left-clicking and dragging on any of these handles. The selection area can also be modified using **Shift+Left Arrow** and **Shift+Right Arrow** to move the ending point of the selection left or right respectively. **Shift+Home** and **Shift+End** also useful in making selections by creating selections for the cursor to the beginning or ending of the waveform.

You may want to consider creating the shortcut keys **Ctrl+Shift+Left Arrow** and **Ctrl+Shift+Right Arrow** to enable keyboard adjustment of the left side of the selection. Adding shortcuts is discussed in detail in Chapter 12 on page 271.

Selecting only the left or right channel of a stereo waveform is accomplished by moving the cursor toward the top or bottom of the waveform until an **L** or **R** appears next to the cursor. Click on the waveform, and the opposite channel will dim. The shortcuts **Ctrl+L**, **Ctrl+R**, and **Ctrl+B** provides another method of selecting left, right, or both channels as does the **Edit>Edit Channel** submenu option.

> **TIP!!** If no selection is made and an effect or modification is made to a waveform, only the visible segment of the waveform will be affected. To change this behavior so that the entire waveform is affected, press **F4** and click the **Entire Wave** radio button under the **Default Selection Range**.

The **Selection/View Controls** provide another method of making a selection or altering the current selection. The **Selection View Controls** consist of six fields organized in three columns and displays values in the format set via **View>Display Time Format.** The top row, labeled **Sel**, contains the beginning point, end point, and length of the current selection. The bottom row, labeled **View**, shows the beginning location, ending location, and length of the current visible waveform.

6.8 *Selection/View Controls show numeric values of beginning and end points of both current selection and view.*

Entering the value into one of the control fields can change the current visible waveform or selection. The control always shows current values regardless of how the view or selection is changed.

Cut

Let's begin making some edits. The first type of edit is called a cut. We are going to remove a few words from a recording. To make this edit, we will need to locate the beginning of a couple words. Figure 6.9 provides an illustration of a few of the words under the waveform.

> **TIP!!** It is a good practice to never edit the original recording. Because changes made in **Edit View** are destructive, start with a copy of the original or use the **Save As** command instead of the **Save** command to preserve the original file. This practice uses more drive space, but the ability to go back to the original can be a lifesaver.

Make sure that Audition is open and in the **Edit View** mode. The CD that accompanies this book contains a file named *First Edit.wav.* The file is a recording of the following text, "Selec-

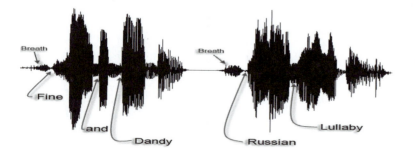

6.9 *Segment of First Edit.wav showing words under the waveform.*

tions on the DVD include Jeepers Creepers. Fine and Dandy. Russian Lullaby." We will be removing the words, "Fine and Dandy," so that the text reads, "Selections on the DVD include Jeepers Creepers. Russian Lullaby." Let's make the cut.

Using the Cut Command

1. Select **File>Open** and locate the *First Edit.wav* in the *Chapter 06-Audio* directory on the CD that accompanies this book.

2. Right-click on the time display window and select **SMPTE 30 fps** from the pop-up menu.

3. Right-click on the **Play** button and select **Play from Cursor** to **End of View**.

4. Press the spacebar or click the **Play** button and listen to the audio while noting the location of the word "Fine."

 Click the **Play** button and alternate between **Rewind** or **Fast Forward** by pressing the **J** and **K** keys to help locate the word.

5. Click on the waveform in the approximate location that the word "Fine" occurred, and press the spacebar.

6. Repeat Step 5, moving the cursor closer to the first occurrence of the word "Fine" until the audio starts with "Fine and Dandy." You can also use the scroll wheel if your mouse has one to magnify the waveform.

7. When the beginning of the word "Fine" is found, click and drag the cursor from that point to the beginning of the word "Russian." Don't worry about being exact. We'll fix that in a minute.

8. Press the spacebar or click the **Play** button. If you hear any other words than *"Fine and Dandy,"* left-click on one of the triangles above or below the waveform and drag to change the selection area and play it again. Repeat this step until only those words are heard.

9. Use the **Play Preroll and Postroll (Skip Selection)** function by pressing **Alt+R** to audition the edit without actually making it. When satisfied with the preview, select **Crtl+X** or **Edit>Cut** to remove the phrase.

10. Press the **Home** key and click the **Play** button.

    Remember, if the edit does not sound right, use **Ctrl+Z** to undo the edit and try it again.

 The inflection, a change in loudness or pitch of the voice, can make or break an edit. If an edit does not sound good because of an inflection, see if the words are repeated anywhere else in the recording. If they are, try using them.

Breathless

Removing breaths or other noises between words can often make the time between words too short and results in a recording that sounds unnatural. Inserting digital silence can work if the room noise or room ambience is masked by a music track or sound effects, but if there is nothing to hide the sudden loss of room noise, the edit will be obvious. It is a good practice to record about a minute of room tone immediately after recording the talent. The ambience can be used to replace long noises and makes for undetectable edits. Be careful not to remove all the breath sounds. The recording will sound artificial and tend to bother the listeners even if they don't know why. Instead, try a combination of removing some breaths and lowering the volume of other breaths.

Delete

The **Delete** command is executed directly from the **Delete** button on the keyboard. It can also be called from **Edit>Delete Selection**. **Cut** and **Delete** are essentially the same with one small difference. The **Cut** command places the selection on a clipboard as it removes it from the current waveform. **Delete** only removes the selection. It does not place it on a clipboard.

The **Delete** command works well for removing mouth or paper noises in narration recordings.

> **TIP!!** Any selection can be replaced with silence by right-clicking on the waveform and selecting the **Silence** option from the pop-up menu.

Trim

The **Trim** function is called by pressing **Ctrl+T** or selecting **Edit>Trim**. The **Trim** command is great for cleaning up noise at the head and tail of recordings. Let's use the file edited in the previous tutorial and trim the recording to remove noise before and after the phrase.

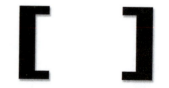

6.10 Left and right bracket keys are used to chose the selection's beginning and ending points as the waveforms plays. Some editors may be more familiar with this process, referred to as setting the in and out points on the fly.

Using the Trim Command

1. Select **Ctrl+O** and locate the *Trim Edit.wav* in the *Chapter 06-Audio* directory on the CD that accompanies this book.

2. Right-click on the **Play** button and select **Play from Cursor to End of File**.

3. Press the spacebar or click the **Play** button and listen for the word "selections."

4. Press the **Home** key to return the cursor to the head of the track and repeat Step 3, but this time, while watching the cursor play across the waveform press the left-bracket ([) key on the keyboard just before the word "selections" occurs and press the right-bracket (]) key right after you hear the last word, "lullaby." Don't worry about being exact. We will fix that shortly.

5. Press **Alt+Home** or click the **Zoom In** to **Left Edge** button to see a magnified view of the waveform.

6. Use **Zoom In to Left Edge of Selection** button or **Alt+Home** to continue zooming in until the start of the word "selections" is very apparent as shown in Figure 6.12.

7. Drag the triangle handle at the top or bottom of the waveform to adjust the selection so that all of the word "selections" is highlighted.

8. Press the **Zoom In to Right Edge of Selection** or **Alt+End** to view the end point of the selection.

9. Use the **Zoom In Horizontally** button or press the minus (–) key until the right end of the word "lullaby" is visible and adjust the selection with the triangle handle until the highlight covers the end of the last word.

10. Press **Ctrl+T** or select **Edit>Trim** to remove the areas of the waveform that were not highlighted.

11. Press the spacebar to audition the result.

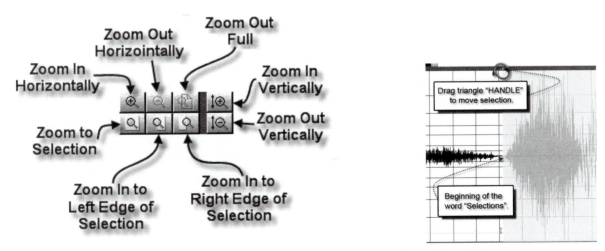

6.11 *Zoom buttons adjust the horizontal and vertical view of the waveform (above left)*

6.12 *Use the triangle-shaped handle to place the cursor at the beginning of the word. (above right)*

The wheel on a scrollable mouse permits quick zooming in and out of the waveform. Another method is to use the minus sign (-) key and the equal sign (=) key to zoom horizontally. Using the **Alt** modifier key with these keys causes the waveform display to zoom vertically.

Copy

Selecting **Edit>Copy** will copy the selection to one of the five internal clipboards or the Windows system clipboard. The desired clipboard is chosen with the **Edit>Set Current Clipboard** menu option. Clipboard 1 through Clipboard 5 are only available to Audition; however, audio can be transferred to many other Microsoft Windows applications if the Windows clipboard is set as the current clipboard before the **Copy** command is executed. Clipboard content remains in memory until Audition is closed, although you can disable deletion of the clipboards on exiting the application.

Copy to New

Selecting **Edit>Copy** to **New** copies the data to a clipboard and to a new waveform display.

Paste

The **Paste** command is similar to most word processing and spreadsheet applications. Selecting **Ctrl+V** or **Edit>Paste** inserts the content of the currently selected clipboard into the waveform at the current cursor location. Audition will automatically convert the clipboard content to match the format of the waveform into which the content is being pasted.

 You can adjust the amplitude of a selection by choosing **Effect** > **Amplitude** > **Amplify/Fade** and changing the Amplification slider. Fading the audio in or out can be done from the **Fade** tab of this control as well as choosing **Fade In** or **Fade Out** from the **Favorites** menu.

6.13 *Audition provides six clipboards for storing temporary content.*

Set Current Clipboard	▶	Clipboard 1	Ctrl+1
Copy	Ctrl+C	Clipboard 2 (empty)	Ctrl+2
Cut	Ctrl+X	Clipboard 3 (empty)	Ctrl+3
Paste	Ctrl+V	✔ Clipboard 4	Ctrl+4
Paste to New	Ctrl+Shift+N	Clipboard 5 (empty)	Ctrl+5
Mix Paste...	Ctrl+Shift+V	Windows' (empty)	Ctrl+6
Copy to New			

Paste to New

Select **Edit>Paste to New** to open a new waveform display and paste the content of the active clipboard into the new waveform. Activate a clipboard by selecting **Edit>Set Current Clipboard** or **Ctrl+1** through **Ctrl+6**.

Mix Paste

Mix Paste is an expanded version of the **Paste** function and is selected while holding down the **Shift** key and pressing the same keyboard shortcut as **Paste**. It can also be activated by choosing **Edit>Mix Paste**, which opens a dialog box that presents a number of options.

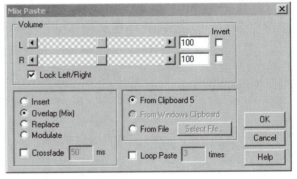

Volume

The **Volume** section of the **Mix Paste** dialog box permits level adjustment of the signal that will be pasted into the waveform. Channel sliders and corresponding numeric fields allow individual adjustment of left and right

6.14 The Mix Paste dialog box

channels expressed as a percentage of the original volume. The **Lock Left/Right** checkbox groups the channel volumes together and forces the same level for both. Phase for one or both channels can be flipped with the **Invert** checkbox. See Chapter 1 on page 5 for a discussion on phase.

Insert

Selecting this option inserts the data at the current cursor location much in the same way as pasting text into the middle of a sentence. This is sometimes referred to as a *ripple edit*. If a segment of the waveform is selected and **Insert** is chosen, the data will replace the selection. If the clipboard content is longer than the selection, Audition will ripple the waveform by forcing all content to the right of the selection to move to the right.

Overlap (Mix): The **Overlap** option combines the waveform and contents of the clipboard using the volume set in the **Mix Paste** dialog box. This is used to mix the signals much like the results obtained by mixing the signals using a traditional mixing console.

Replace: This option replaces the waveform with the clipboard content. The amount of waveform replaced is equal to the duration of the data pasted into the waveform.

Modulate: The **Modulate** option modulates the waveform using the amplitude of the clipboard content by multiplying the two signals. This is an option that requires some experimentation.

Crossfade: Enabling the **Crossfade** checkbox can make the edit transition sound smoother by fading the beginning and ending of the clipboard content. The duration of the fade is entered in milliseconds. For most voice edits, 30-50 milliseconds is a good value.

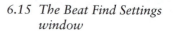 Crossfades are typically a good idea on edits. Not only does the crossfade feather the transition, crossfading ensures that there will not be a click or pop caused by an abrupt change in level at the edit.

Loop Paste: Enabling the **Loop Paste** checkbox causes the content to be pasted into the waveform as many times as you specify. The source of the paste can be a clipboard or file. A clipboard can be selected before choosing the **Mix Paste** command by holding down the **Control** key and pressing the clipboard number or selecting **Edit>Set Current Clipboard**. Selecting the **From File** radio button and clicking the **Select File** button opens a dialog box allowing selection of a file as the source for the **Loop Paste** instead of a clipboard.

Find Beats

Audition has an exceptional ability to accurately locate musical beats. Select **Edit>Find Beats>Find Next Beat (Left Side)** to activate the function. The cursor will move to the next beat. Once the desired beginning point is found, Select **Edit>Find Beats>Find Next Beat (Right Side)** to locate the desired end point. The **Beat Find Settings** window is accessed from **Edit>Find Beats>Beat Settings**. The **Decibel Rise** field sets the increase in level, and the **Rise Time** field sets the attack time required for Audition to consider a transient signal as a beat. Increase the **Decibel Rise** value if too many beats are found, and decrease it if not all the beats are found. The **Rise Time** value works with the **Decibel Rise** value and may need to be increased or decreased depending upon the musical style and attack of each beat. In other words, percussive instruments with a sharp attack reach the **Decibel Rise** threshold quickly whereas woodwind instruments tend to take longer to attain the same threshold.

There are a number of ways the **Find Beats** function can be used to speed up the production process, but we'll leave that to your imagination. Right now, let's look at how this feature can be used to quickly remove several measures from a music track.

6.15 The Beat Find Settings window

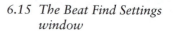 Turning off the **Snapping** options is recommended for more accurate results when using the **Find Beats** or **Auto-Cue** command. Select **Edit > Snapping** to disable the options.

Using the Find Beats Command

1. Start Audition in the **Edit View** workspace, press **Ctrl+0** and locate the *Find Beats.wav* in the *Chapter 06-Audio* directory on the CD that accompanies this book.

2. Right-click on the **Time** window and select **Bars and Beats** from the pop-up menu. Confirm that the **Snapping** options are not enabled.

3. Press and hold the **Shift** key and push the left-bracket ([) key. The cursor will move ahead one beat each time the key is pressed. Continue until the cursor even with the **Cue Mark** labeled **Beginning**. The **Cue Mark** is at approximately 6:04.04 on the timeline.

4. Press and hold the **Shift** key and continue pushing the right-bracket (]) key until the cursor is even with the **Cue Mark** labeled **End**. Notice that the cursor is jumping along the waveform to locations that Audition is considering beats based on the **Beat Settings** of **Decibel Rise** and **Rise Time** along the waveform to locations that Audition is considering beats based on the **Beat Settings** of **Decibel Rise** and **Rise Time**.

5. Press **Alt+R** to preview the edit and execute the edit using the **Delete** key.

6. Press the **Home** key and review the edit.

   Here is an optional exercise before closing this tutorial file.

1. Select **Ctrl+Z** to undo the edit, **Ctrl+C** to copy the selection to the clipboard, and then **Ctrl+Shift+V** to open the **Mix Paste** window.

2. Enable the **Loop Paste** checkbox, type **3** in the **Times** field, and click **OK**.

3. Press the **Home** key and listen.

   Think about this application for scoring industrial and corporate videos.

 Find Beats is an easy way to extend sound tracks. Use **Find Beats** to locate the measures you want to repeat and copy them to the clipboard. Then use the **Find Beats** to locate the insertion point and **Mix Paste** to insert them. The **Loop Paste** function can be used to fill longer segments.

Zero Crossings

Abrupt changes in amplitude can cause an audible click or pop. The **Zero Crossing** function provides the means of automatically moving edit points to the closest point where the waveform has a zero value. Select **Edit>Zero Crossings** to adjust the selection points. The **Zero Crossing** option provides six different options that allow moving both selection points, the left selection point, or the right selection point. The option names describe the function.

Delete Silence

The **Delete Silence** command is accessed by selecting **Edit>Delete Silence**. This function is useful for removing dead time between words and sentences or music tracks. Any audio signal

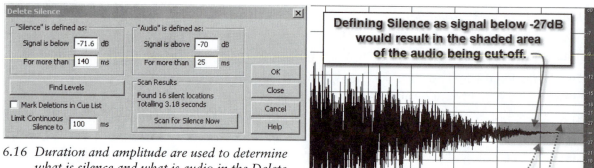

6.16 *Duration and amplitude are used to determine what is silence and what is audio in the Delete Silence dialog box. (above)*

6.17 *Setting Delete Silence thresholds too high can delete more than silence. This shaded area in this illustration shows that the ending of a sound would be deleted with incorrect settings. (above right)*

level that falls within the range defined as "Silence" is deleted. The thresholds that define these ranges are set in the **Delete Silence** dialog box.

Find Levels

The **Find Levels** button scans the selection and automatically calculates and populates the amplitude and duration fields. These values are good starting points; however, they may require some adjustment to achieve the desired result. Increasing the amplitude values will increase the amount of silence deleted. Decreasing the amplitude values decreases the amount of silence deleted and reduces the likelihood of the losing the beginnings and endings of words or music.

Mark Deletions in Cue List

Checking the checkbox adds each location that silence was removed to the cue list where silence was removed.

Limit Continuous Silence to

This value determines the minimum length of silence that will be removed. This setting prevents removing too much time between words. 100 milliseconds is the default value, however 125-150 typically works better on narration.

Scan for Silence Now

The **Scan for Silence Now** button activates a search for silence and displays the scan results in the window. These results state the number of silent locations and the total duration of silence that will be removed.

> **TIP!!** Delete Silence can be a big time-saver when doing commercial production. For example, the copy for a :60 radio spot is still two seconds too long, the client refuses to delete any more copy, and the talent just can't read any faster. Adjusting the **Delete Silence** parameters until the **Scan Results** equal two seconds can save a lot of time that would have been spent manually editing out the silence to achieve the same result.

Auto-Cue

The **Auto-Cue** function provides an automatic method of selecting segments of audio such as musical phrases, beats, and even sections of a narration. Depending upon the chosen option, the selections may be added to the **Cue List**. **Auto-Cue** and the options are selected from **Edit>Auto-Cue**.

Adjust Selection to Phrase

This option adjusts the selection boundaries on each end of the current selection, disregarding any audio that is below the amplitude threshold value in the **Auto-Cue** settings.

 Press **F8** to add the selection to the **Cue List**.

Find Phrases and Mark

Find Phrases and Mark scans the current selection and adds each separate phrase of audio to the cue list. A separate segment or phrase of audio is created each time the audio signal falls below the amplitude and exceeds the duration settings in the **Auto-Cue** settings.

Find Beats and Mark

Find Beats and Mark scans the current selection and adds beat cues to the cue list for every beat found.

Auto-Cue Settings

The **Auto-Cue Settings** window sets the amplitude thresholds and durations that determine whether the audio will be considered valid audio or silence. The **Find Levels** button makes a reasonably good attempt to guess the optimum settings, but some adjustment may be

Zero Crossings	▶
Find Beats	▶
Auto-Cue	▶
Snapping	▶
Group Waveform Normalize...	
Adjust Sample Rate...	
Convert Sample Type... F11	

Adjust Selection to Phrase
Find Phrases and Mark
Find Beats and Mark...
Auto-Cue Settings...
Trim Digital Silence

6.18 Auto-Cue options

required. If words sound chopped, lower the required amplitude threshold so more audio is considered valid. Increase the silence amplitude to remove more silence.

Trim Digital Silence

This option removes digital silence from the head and tail of the file.

Snapping

The **Snapping** option enables the selection point to jump to a particular type of time location much like a magnet. Using **Snapping** enables quick and accurate placement according to the **Snapping** option and **Time Display** format. Select **Edit>Snapping** or right-click on the **Horizontal Ruler** to chose the **Snapping** type. Four types of **Snapping** options are available in **Edit View**.

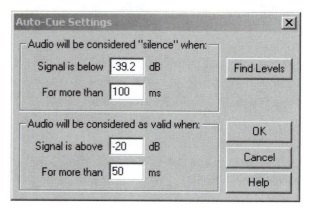

6.19 The Auto-Cue Settings dialog box

Snap to Cues

Snap to Cues allows the selection to snap to **Cue** points listed in the **Cue List**. All options except **Snap to Ruler (Coarse)** and **Snap to Ruler (Fine)** can be selected at the same time.

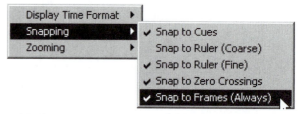

6.20 Snapping Options available in Edit View.

Snap to Ruler (Coarse)/(Fine)

Snap to Ruler (Coarse) allows the selection to snap to major ruler divisions such as **SMPTE**, **Decimal**, and **Samples**. **Snap to Ruler (Fine)** allows snapping at more precise locations. Both **Coarse** and **Fine** cannot be enabled at the same time.

Snap to Zero Crossings

Snap to Zero Crossings allows the selection to jump to the nearest point with zero amplitude. This option prevents clicks and pops caused by sudden increases in amplitude.

Snap to Frames (Always)

This option should be used when mastering for compact disc. The audio will always snap to a frame boundary and avoids clicks and pops caused when the audio begins in the middle of a frame.

TIP!! Don't forget about the toolbar buttons. Options such as **Snapping to Cues** can be toggled on and off quickly from the toolbars. Placing the mouse over the button for a second or two will bring up a tool tip to identify the button function.

Sample Level Editing

Audition has another editing feature that deserves discussion. **Edit View** provides the ability to edit at the smallest division of digital audio: the sample. This means that a waveform with a 192kHz sampling rate could be edited to an accuracy of 1/192,000th of a second. This provides the ability to make a slightly cleaner edit than the 1/30th of a second resolution available when editing video.

To edit at the sample level, **Zoom In Horizontally** button or the equal sign key (=) until the waveform zooms in and small black squares or handles called nodes appear on the waveform. Each of the squares is a sample point. Click and drag to select one or more samples. The amplitude of a sample can also be adjusted with the mouse or entered as a number value by right-clicking on the handle.

The Marquee Selection Tool

Until now, we have been making all edits with the time selection tool. In fact, most other digital audio editing applications use a combination of time-based tools and filters. Audition 1.5 ups the ante and begins the revolution of truly bringing digital audio to the desktop publishing world with the introduction of the **Marquee Selection** tool.

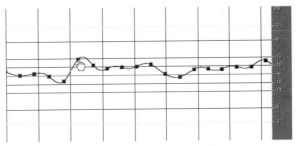

6.21 *The cursor changes to a hand allowing amplitude adjustment of individual samples.*

Many users may be familiar with the **Marquee** tool in Adobe Photoshop and other such image-editing applications. The operation is essentially the same. Just click and drag to make a selection. The **Marquee Selection** tool is available only in the **Spectral View**; however, it provides the ability to remove noise or to apply effects to specific frequencies. Although these functions can be accomplished using the traditional tools, the **Marquee Selection** tool is easy to use and fast to set up. It offers some interesting potential for creative minds.

TIP!! F9 toggles between **Waveform** and **Spectral View**. Pressing the **M** key once in **Spectral View** selects the new **Marquee** tool. Pressing the **S** key returns to the standard **Time Selection** tool.

Insert in Multitrack

Once the editing is complete and the file is saved, the waveform can be moved into **Multitrack View** for layering and mixing. There are a number of ways to move the file. Press **Ctrl+M**, select **Edit>Insert in Multitrack,** or right-click on the waveform and choose **Insert in Multitrack** from the pop-up menu.

EDITING IN MULTITRACK VIEW

The **Multitrack View** workspace has a number of editing features. One major advantage to using **Multitrack View** is that editing is nondestructive. Instead of working directly with waveforms, **Multitrack View** uses clips placed into any of the available 128 tracks. Any changes made in **Multitrack View** are stored as instructions in the session (.ses) file, and the audio files are not modified. It is very similar to an Edit Decision List (EDL) used by many audio and video editing systems.

Clips

Multitrack View displays a graphic representation of the file called a clip. A clip can represent an audio file, MIDI file, or a video file. They can be moved, copied, edited, and repeated or looped. Effects can be added, volume adjustments made, and the mix of signal in each channel can be adjusted with the pan control. The clip is a virtual waveform and functions, for all practical purposes, just as if it were the actual file.

There are differences in the way some of the commands affect selected clips in **Multitrack View**. For example, the **Cut** command in **Edit View** removes the selection and splices the audio together. The **Cut** command in **Multitrack View** removes the content and leaves a gap equivalent to the deleted selection. The main difference to remember is that none of the commands are destructive with the exception of the **Merge** command.

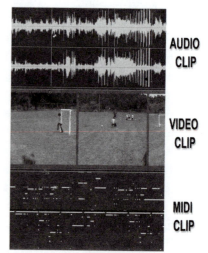

AUDIO CLIP

VIDEO CLIP

MIDI CLIP

6.22 Three types of files shown as clips in Multitrack View

Selections

Making selections in **Multitrack View** works much like in the **Edit View** mode. Selected segments of the waveform will appear highlighted; however, pressing **Ctrl+A** or **Edit>Select All Clips** selects every clip in **Multitrack View**. **Edit>Select All Clips in Track n,** with **n** being the currently selected clip, selects all clips in that track. A selection area can be shortened or lengthened by left-clicking and dragging on any of the triangle selection handles.

Multitrack View handles editing with ease, but some tracks may require the tools available in **Edit View**. For example, editing the left channel of a stereo recording without affecting the right channel is not possible in **Multitrack View**. No problem. Double-click on the track, and Audition will change back to the **Edit View** mode with the track open in the waveform display and ready for editing. Once the changes are made, press **F12** to return to the **Multitrack View**.

Tools

Let's take a look at the tools available for working with clips. How you use the tools depends upon your own workflow and way you are used to working.

Three tools are provided. The **Hybrid** tool, **Time Selection** tool, and **Move/Copy** tool. The main difference between the tools is the how the mouse buttons react. The **Hybrid** is the easiest tool to use, because it functions like the time selection tool and also allows moving clips like the **Move/Copy** tool with the right mouse button. The tools are accessed via **Edit>Tools** or single key shortcuts; **R** for the **Hybrid** tool, **S** for the **Time Selection** tool, and **V** for the **Move/Copy** tool.

Working with Clips

Now that you're familiar with some of the editing techniques and tools in **Edit View**, we'll begin working with clips in **Multitrack View**.

If Audition is already open, select **Close All** to close all the open files. Open Audition and switch to **Multitrack View,** if necessary, by pressing **F12**. Select **Ctrl+I** and locate the file named *First Edit.wav* in the *Chapter 06-Audio* directory of the CD that accompanies this book. The filename will appear in the **Organizer** window on the left of the screen.

It is assumed that by now the device ordering preference has been set up. If not, see the section in Chapter 5 or select **Options>Device Order** and make sure that the **Playback Devices** tab shows your sound card or device at the top of the list on the right.

Take the time to name files with a descriptive name. Using a naming scheme such as *Gtr_Solo_07* for a guitar solo with the number used to identify the take or some nomenclature that works for you can save you a lot of time and grief. If you find yourself searching the **Organizer** List for the right file, turn on the **Auto-Play** button in the **Organizer** window. It will automatically play a file when highlighted in the Organizer window.

Now that the files are open, let's begin with the basic editing commands.

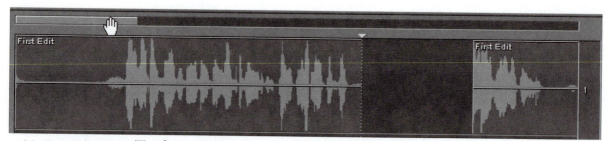

6.23 *First Edit clip in* **Track 1** *of the Multitrack display. The gap is left after using the Cut command to delete the highlighted selection. Notice the cursor shape when the cursor is over the end of the horizontal position bar.*

Cut

The **Cut** command in **Multitrack View** removes the selection segment of the clip or clips. Unlike the **Cut** command in **Edit View**, it does not remove the gap left when the selection is removed, nor does it place the content on the clipboard. The next tutorial will demonstrate the differences between the two modes. We will make the same edit as we did in the **Edit View** tutorial.

Using the Cut Command

1. Right-click on the time display window and select **SMPTE 30 fps**.
2. Click and drag the *First Edit.wav* file from the **Organizer** window into **Track 1**.
3. Right-click and drag the clip in **Track 1** all the way to the left. This positions the clip at the beginning of the timeline.
4. Place the cursor on the right end of the horizontal position bar. The cursor will change into a magnifying glass with two arrows above. Click and drag to the left until the waveform fills the entire track.
5. Position the cursor on the word "Fine" and drag the cursor until just before the word "Russian."
6. Press the spacebar to audition the selection that will be removed.
7. Use **Alt+Home** to zoom into the left edge of the selection and drag the yellow triangle handle to adjust the left selection edge.
8. Use **Alt+ End** to zoom into the right edge of the selection and drag the yellow triangle handle to adjust the right selection edge.
9. Click the **Zoom Out Full** button and press select **Edit>Cut**.
10. Right-click on the clip on the right and drag it to the left until the edges of the clips touch. A white vertical snapping line appears when the clips are perfectly adjacent to each other.

If you prefer using **Edit View** to select segments, double-click on the clip or select **File > Edit Waveform**, and the waveform will be displayed in **Edit View**. Make the selection and press **F12**. The segment highlighted in **Edit View** is now the same selection in **Multitrack Options > Synchronize Clips with Edit View** must be enabled for this to function properly.

Highlighting the desired selection to be deleted and pressing the **Delete** key accomplishes the same thing as the **Cut** command.

Undo

Ctrl+Z selects the **Undo** command. The **Undo** levels are determined by available drive space and can be turned on or off in the **System** tab of the **Settings** dialog box. It is highly recommended to leave this feature on unless working with extremely long files.

Full

The **Full** command restores any segments that have been removed and returns a clip to its original form just as if the clip were freshly dragged into the track. Other segments of the original clip may also be open in the track. The next tutorial will demonstrate how other clips may coexist after the **Full** command is issued.

Using the Full Command

1. If the last tutorial titled "Using the Cut Command" is still open and no changes have been made since the tutorial was completed, press **Ctrl+Z** to undo moving the clip. Otherwise, select **File>Open Session** and choose *Full Command.ses* from the *Chapter 06-Audio* directory on the CD that accompanies this book.

2. Right-click on the second clip and select **Full** from the pop-up menu.

It's that simple…but wait. Right-click on the clip and slide it slightly to the right. Now play it back. You should hear some digital delay. To see what happened, right-click on the clip and drag it down to **Track 2**. Notice that the first clip is still on **Track 1**. When the second clip was

Multitrack Recording

Multitrack recording provides an alternative to editing multiple takes together by making a composite track or comping. The technique can be applied to anything, but it's usually done on vocals. The idea is to record multiple takes of a vocal on separate tracks, select the best sections of each track, and bounce those sections down to a single track. This technique is frequently repeated many times before a final version is completed.

restored with the **Full** command, it restored that clip to its original form. The first clip was not modified and left exactly where it was. This can be a source of aggravation if you are not aware of this course of action. The next command could be used to delete the extra clip.

Check for Hidden Clips

Pressing **Shift+F5** or selecting **Edit>Check for Hidden Clips** will bring any hidden clips into view.

Remove Clips

The **Remove Clips** command does exactly what its name implies. The command is selected from the **Edit** menu or by right-clicking on a clip and selecting the command from the pop-up menu.

 To remove all the clips in a track at once, right-click between the clips or at the end of the track and choose **Select All Clips in Track**. Then right-click on a clip and select **Remove Clips**.

Destroy Clips

The **Destroy Clips** command removes any instances of the clips and closes the file. A warning is presented noting that the action cannot be reversed. The command is selected from the **Edit** menu or by right-clicking on a clip and selecting the command from the pop-up menu.

Enable Clip Time Stretching

Enabling this option permits a clip to be stretched or shortened by dragging the edge of the clip. The method used to stretch the clip is set by the **Clip Time Stretch Properties** dialog box.

Clip Time Stretch Properties

When **Enable Time Stretching** is checked, any clip can be lengthened or shortened nondestructively by dragging the left or right edge of the clip. The stretch does not alter the original file, and the clip can be restored to the original length at any time. A watch icon appears near the cursor when positioned near the edge. Stretch percentage and extended clip time show as a tool tip when dragging the edge of the clip. This is a very handy tool for stretching sound effects or a music track to fit a segment of video.

 Stretching a clip that is loop-enabled will override the **Follow Session Tempo** command.

To enable time stretching, select **View>Enable Clip Time Stretching** or right-click on the clip, select **Clip Time Stretch Properties** and check **Enable Time Stretching**. You can also quickly enable time stretching on a clip by holding down the **Control** key and dragging the edge of the clip. There are four methods of time stretching available. **Time-scale Stretch** is the default. Right-clicking on the clip provides the ability to select the stretching method. The dialog also allows enabling or disabling of time stretching, the percentage of stretch, transposing pitch, and the parameters used in the stretching method.

Time-scale Stretch : **Time-scale Stretch** expands or contracts the duration of the clip without altering the pitch. Three quality levels are available; higher levels require more processing time. The **Frame Size** value is the number of splices per beat used when time scaling the clip. Splices are slices of audio inserted or removed to alter the time scale. Higher frame values produce results that are more accurate but that introduce artifacts that are more audible. Audition attempts to determine the best values. **Frame Overlapping** is expressed as a percentage and determines how much the frames overlap. Overlapping helps smooth the splices but causes the scaling to sound electronic at higher values. The recommended **Frame Overlapping** value is 15–25 percent.

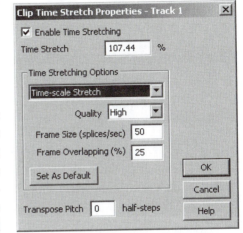

6.24 *The Clip Time Stretch Properties dialog box*

Resample (affects pitch): **Resample** alters the pitch proportionately. Three levels of quality are selectable; higher levels require more processing time.

Beat Splice: Beats are used to determine how to the expand or contract the clip. The **Auto-Find Beats** values set the sensitivity used to determine what constitutes a beat. This method works the best on extremely percussive and rhythmic tracks such as drums and is not recommended for use on voice or instruments with sustained notes.

Hybrid: The Hybrid method uses the current time scale stretching settings when the tempo is slowed down and the Beat Splice method when the tempo is sped up.

Insert/Delete Time

This command affects every track in the session. The command is selected either from the **Edit** menu or from the pop-up menu that appears when right-clicking on an empty spot on a track. The available options of the **Insert/Delete Time** dialog box vary according the cursor location.

Placing the cursor over any track will insert the amount of time entered at the cursor location and move everything to the right of the cursor by the same amount of time. The time should be entered in the current time display format.

Deleting time works much like the **Delete** command in **Edit View** by deleting the highlighted selection and moving everything to the right of the selection to the left, filling the deleted segment.

6.25 *Insert/Delete Time dialog box*

Let's try the same edit we have done before using the **Insert/Delete Time** command.

Using the Inset/Delete Time Command

1. If any files or sessions are open, select **File>Close All**.

2. Select **File>Open Session** and choose *Delete Command.ses* from the *Chapter 06-Audio* directory on the CD that accompanies this book.

3. Right-click on the horizontal ruler and select **Snapping>Snap to Clips**.

4. Click and drag from the right edge of the first clip to the left edge of the second clip to highlight the area between the clips. Notice that the cursor snaps to the edge of the clip.

5. Right-click anywhere on the highlighted selection and choose **Insert/Delete Time** from the pop-up menu.

6. Click the **Delete Selected Time** radio button next to and click **OK**.

7. Click the **Rewind** button on the transport controls until the cursor is a few seconds from the end of the first clip, and click the **Play** button.

Trim

The **Trim** command removes everything except the selection. Use this command to remove unwanted noise or other audio at the head and tail of the clip or track.

Adjust Boundaries

The **Adjust Boundaries** command is similar to the **Trim** command in that it can be used to shorten the clip, but it also provides the ability to redefine the clip's boundaries. Using this command will define the clip as the highlighted area as long as the original clip is long enough.

Enable Clip Edge Dragging

The **View** menu holds an option that could be used in place of commands such as **Adjust Boundaries, Cut,** or **Trim** in many instances. This feature is called **Clip Edge Dragging.** When enabled, it allows the clip to be shortened or lengthened up to its original length by dragging the edge of the clip.

Split

The **Split** command cuts or divides the clip in two at the current cursor location. Select **Ctrl+K, Edit>Split,** or right-click on the clip to access this function.

Merge/Rejoin Split

This command rejoins two clips that have been split. The clips have to be adjacent before this option will become available. This option can also be used with Punch In recording to merge the desired take into the file. It is the same as selecting **Edit>Take History>Merge This Take.** The **Merge** function is one of the few destructive editing functions in **Multitrack View.**

Align Left

Align Left will align all selected clips to the left edge of the last clip highlighted. Note that the left edge of all highlighted clips will be aligned with this command, even if there is more than one clip on the track. As with most of the other editing commands, it is found under the **Edit** menu and on the pop-up menu accessed by right-clicking on the clip.

 To highlight multiple clips without highlighting all clips, hold down the **Control** key while left-clicking on the desired clips. All selected clips can be moved simultaneously by right-clicking and dragging on one of the highlighted clips.

Align Right

Align Right is identical to the align left command except that the right edge of the selected clips will align to the right edge of the last clip selected.

Convert to Unique Copy

Effects or changes in **Edit View** are destructive and will change all copies of the same clip in a session unless the clip copies are unique. Highlighting a clip and selecting **Edit>Convert to Unique Copy** creates a duplicate of the original file. You can also hold the **Control** key and right-click and drag the clip to another track to make a unique copy.

 Holding the **Shift** key while right-clicking and dragging a clip to another location will create another clip or virtual image of the file. Any changes made to the original file will be reflected in all of these virtual images in the session.

Group Clips

Groups of clips will frequently compliment each other and need to retain a direct time relationship. For example, the clip on **Track 1** is an acoustic guitar and **Track 2** contains a clip with the vocal. If these clips are moved, they need to shift together, or the resulting music will not be so pleasing to the ear. Grouping the clips causes all clips to move as a group when any member clip is moved.

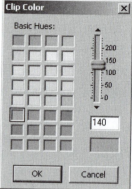

Press the **Control** key and left-click on the clips to be included in the group. Once all the intended clips are highlighted, press **Crtl+G** or select E**dit>Group Clips.**

Group Color: Each group of clips can have a unique color in the display area. To select the color, highlight the group, select **Edit>Group Color,** and select the color from the color palette.

Clip Color

Clip Color is the same as **Group Color** except it affects only a single clip. To select a clip color, highlight the clip and select **Edit>Clip Color** or right-click on the clip and choose **Clip Color.**

6.26 *The Clip Color dialog box*

Insert Menu

The **Insert** menu permits opening various file sources directly into a track. Of particular interest is the ability to import supported video formats and MIDI files. Up to 10 open files will appear as menu choices.

Empty Audio Clip (stereo): This option will insert an empty audio file into the currently highlighted selection. There are several variations of this option that are self-explanatory.

Audio: This option opens audio files directly into a track and places the clip at the current cursor location.

 You can open multiple audio files directly into individual tracks using **Insert > Audio**.

MIDI from File: MIDI files are placed into tracks. Only one MIDI file can be imported at a time; however, multiple MIDI tracks are not limited.

Video from File: Choose this option to import an a supported video file. Audition supports using one video track per session, and the video track will appear as a filmstrip in the selected track. Audio will be separated from the video file and reside as an independent track in the session. Moving the video or audio clips separately will result in a loss of the sync relationship between them.

Selecting **Window>Video** opens a window that displays video. This window can be docked and resized and moved to a convenient location on the screen. Right-clicking on the **Video** window offers playback size and quality options.

 Audition is tightly integrated with newer Adobe video applications such as Premiere Pro and After Effects as part of the Adobe Video Collection. This ability to communicate between applications makes it possible to open the original mixing session from these applications and make changes to the mix with the new mixdown version updated in the video application. Chapter 10 includes a discussion of this capability called the Adobe Workflow.

Audio from Video File: Choosing this option imports only the audio from a supported video file.

File/Cue List: The **File/Cue List** opens a window listing all open files and cues within those files. Highlighting a file places the file as a clip on the currently selected track at the cursor location.

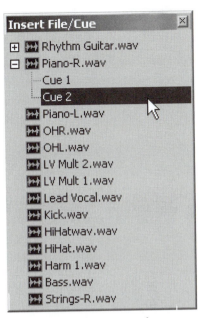

6.27 *Insert File/Cue window. Clicking on a file or cue inserts it into the track.*

Audio Clip Properties

The **Audio Clip Properties** window provides access to a number of controls including volume, pan, **Clip Color**, and **Mute**. We'll discuss those controls features in more detail during Chapter 10, which covers mixing.

Filename/Path: This field displays the current filename of the original file. Changing the name will change the original filename upon saving. Note that **Filename/Path** is not the same as the track name set in the **Track Properties** window. **Filename/Path** is directly below the filename and displays the location of the original file.

Lock in Time: Enable **Lock in Time** once the clip is placed at the desired location. A small padlock icon will appear in the left-hand corner of the clip, and the horizontal movement of the clip will be disabled. This prevents you from

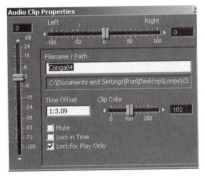

6.28 *Audio Clip Properties window*

 The **Lock in Time** toolbar button is a quick way to lock a clip.

accidentally changing the time relationship of the clip to the other tracks and still allows moving the clip vertically to another track.

Lock for Play Only: The **Lock for Play Only** should be enabled as soon as recording is completed. Enabling this feature prevents recording over the clip even if the track is armed for record.

Time Offset: The **Time Offset** shows the location of the left edge of the clip. The offset is measured from the beginning of the timeline. Entering offset values can be used for placing clips at precise locations.

> Lock your files in place as soon as you are sure of the desired placement. Moving a track accidentally by even a frame or two can have disastrous effects on the end result, not to mention the time spent trying to determine why things just don't sound quite right.

Let's discuss one other topic before ending this chapter and use several of the features we've just covered in a tutorial.

Crossfades

Crossfades are used to smooth the transition between edits. The concept behind crossfades is to fade one segment out as another is fading in. The duration of the crossfade can be only milliseconds or as long as the track allows, but typical crossfades are fairly quick so as to not draw too much attention to the transition.

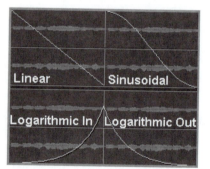

6.29 *Linear, sinusoidal, and logarithmic fades can be chosen for clip transitions.*

The **Crossfade** function is selected from the **Edit** menu or by right-clicking on the waveform and selecting it from the pop-up menu. The **Crossfades** submenu offers several types of crossfades: linear, sinusoidal, logarithmic in, and logarithmic out.

The **Crossfade** function works best when the clips are on separate tracks. You can create a crossfade with both clips on the same tracks, but it takes a little more finesse, and with the 128 available tracks, it hardly worth it.

Using the Crossfade Command

Clear all waveforms and sessions by selecting **Close All** before beginning this tutorial.

1. Select **Ctrl+O** and navigate to the *Chapter 06-Audio* directory of the CD that accompanies this book.

2. Highlight the *Crossfade.ses* file. Notice the **Component Files** list on the right listing the files that are associated with this session. Click **OK**.

3. Right-click anywhere in **Track 1**, choose **Insert>Audio**, and open the *Crossfade_Track 1.wav*.

4. Right-click the clip in **Track 1** and drag it left so the clip begins at 0:00.000. Press **Ctrl+H** and enable the **Lock in Time** option. Right-click on the clip in **Track 2** and select **Lock in Time** from the pop up menu. This will disable changing the time relationship between the two clips.

5. Click and drag from the beginning of the clip on **Track 2** to the end of the clip in **Track 1**.

6. Hold the **Control** key and left-click each clip. The clips should appear brighter. This selects or gives the focus to both clips.

7. Right-click on either clip and choose **Crossfade>Linear**. The green lines represent the volume envelopes or fades.

Play the track back and listen to the transition. Take some time to experiment. Select **Ctrl+Z** to undo the crossfade and try the **Sinusoidal** crossfade. Select the first few seconds of **Track 1** and try the **Logarithmic** in crossfade. Then try the **Linear** crossfade on the last few seconds of **Track 2**.

The Art of Timing

Editing is an art form. The right timing combined with creative transitions and clever editing have made for some wonderful commercial soundtracks. It takes time and practice to master the craft. Audition has made the technique of editing simple, but at the same time, it opens the doors to a new world of ways to edit, layer, and composite audio that were unheard of a few years ago. The next chapter will introduce some new ways to use Audition.

Chapter 7

On-Cues, Loops, and Sounds

ON-CUES

As you've seen, Audition is a robust multitrack recording and editing application, but recording and editing are just the beginning of what Audition can do. Audition also provides the ability to create cues, loops, and even original sounds. We'll begin this chapter by discussing cues, the cue list, and the play list. We'll also work through some tutorials using the **Delete Silence** and **Auto-Cue** functions to create cues.

What Is a Cue?

In theatrical terms, when something is on cue, it occurs when it is supposed to occur. In Audition, a *cue* is a point that denotes a particular location such as the beginning of a musical phrase, a track, or an anomaly.

There are four types of cue marks available in Audition. Each type can be a single point within the waveform or a *range* with a start point and an endpoint. The types are as follows:

Basic: marks a point or range for reference. The *basic cue* is a great way to mark a pop or an edit for review for editing later. Basic cues can be used as stop and start points in the playlist.

Beat: marks a musical beat.

Track: marks the point that will begin a track on a compact disc.

Index: marks points within a CD track.

141

Cues are not limited to marking only one location point. A cue can identify a segment of the audio with a beginning point and an ending point. When the cue notes both the beginning and ending points, the cue is said to contain a range. The beginning cue mark or point appears as a small red triangle called a *cue handle* above and below the waveform. When two or more cue points are merged together to form a range, the ending cue handle turns blue, and both cue handles turn to point to each other as shown in Figure 7.1.

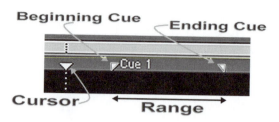

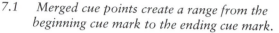

7.1   *Merged cue points create a range from the beginning cue mark to the ending cue mark.*

Before we discuss creating, placing, and modifying cues and ranges, let's look at the **Cue List** window.

Cue List Window

The **Cue List** window enables management of cues. Adding, deleting, merging, sorting, and modifying cues and ranges can be done from the window. The window is displayed by pressing **Alt+8** or selecting **Window>Cue List**.

Column Bar: runs along the top of the **Cue List** window. Sort cues by clicking on any of the headings. The sequence of the headings can be rearranged by dragging the heading horizontally.

Edit Cue Info: brings up the cue information and allows you to edit the **Begin, End, Length, Label, Description,** and **Type** fields.

Auto-Play: automatically plays the highlighted cue when enabled.

Add: adds cues to the cue list.

Label	Begin	End	Length	Type	Description
Cue 1	00:00:02:12		00:00:00:00	Basic	
Cue 2	00:00:04:16	00:00:06:27	00:00:02:11	Basic	
Cue 4	00:00:09:23		00:00:00:00	Beat	
Cue 5	00:00:12:01		00:00:00:00	Track	
Cue 6	00:00:13:16		00:00:00:00	Index	

Begin 00:00:02:12   Type Basic
End
Length 00:00:00:00
Label Cue 1
Desc

Edit Cue Info   Auto-Play
Add   Del   Merge   Batch

7.2   *The Cue List window shows the four different types of cues. Cue 2 has an end time and is called a range. Cue information can be edited directly in the Cue List window.*

Del: deletes a cue from the cue list.

Merge: creates a cue range from the highlighted cues.

Batch: displays the **Batch Process Cue Ranges** dialog box in preparation to save the cue ranges to discrete files. Batch processing is discussed in Chapter 12.

Manual Cue Placement

There are a number of ways to create or place cue marks. Let's look at some of the different methods.

Cueing from the Keyboard

The quickest and easiest way to place a basic cue mark is to locate the cursor at the desired location on the waveform or clip and press **F8**. Note that the cue handle and label may be hidden by the cursor.

Placing cue marks from the keyboard is not limited to the basic type. Placing track marks for compact disc is just as easy. Press **Shift+F8** to place a track cue. The cue label will appear with the abbreviation "trk" in parentheses. Index points are placed by pressing **Ctrl+F8** and the abbreviation "idx" will appear in parentheses alongside the cue label.

 Throw away the old paper log sheets. Locations can be marked with cues during recording or playback and stored with the file as metadata. The cues can be named and noted in the label and description fields of the **Cue List** window without affected the recording or playback. Once the cue information is noted, press **Alt + 1** to set the cursor focus back to the main display and your ready to mark the next location. This can be a hugh time saver during editing or production, but don't forget to check the **Save extra non-audio information** box when saving the file, or all the cues will be lost.

Cueing from the mouse

Placing cue points with the mouse is almost as easy as from the keyboard. Locate the cursor at the desired spot and right-click on the yellow triangle, called the cursor handle. A pop-up menu presents the options: **Insert in Cue List, Insert CD Track Marker,** and **Insert CD Index Marker.** Select the desired cue type.

Auto-Cue Placement

We briefly discussed the **Auto-Cue** function in Chapter 6 on page 125 on editing. Now we're going to put Audition to work for us using the **Delete Silence** and **Auto-Cue** functions.

Using Delete Silence to Place Cues

In the first tutorial, we're going to make cues from a wave file. The trick here is that we are going to do it "automatically." Make sure that Audition is opened and in the **Edit View** workspace. Close any open files or sessions using the **File>Close All** command.

1. Select **File>Open** and locate the *Numbered Phrases.wav* in the *Chapter 07-Audio* directory on the CD that accompanies this book.

2. Press **Alt+8** to open the **Cue List** window.

3. Drag the **Cue List** window by the title bar and dock it above the waveform display. This will keep the window visible without overlapping the waveform display.

4. Select **Edit>Delete Silence** and make sure that **Mark Deletions in Cue List** is checked and the **Limit Continuous Silence to vale** is 150 milliseconds.

5. Press the **Scan for Silence Now** button and note the number of silent locations and total seconds of silence. This is the amount of time that will be deleted from the waveform length shown in **Selection/View Controls**.

6. Press the **Find Levels** button. Notice that the signal will be considered as silence any time the signal falls below −63.5dB for more than 140 milliseconds.

7. Click **OK**.

The **Delete Silence** function has removed the dead time between phrases and marked the beginning of each phrase with a basic cue mark. To verify this, highlight the first cue in the **Cue List** window and click the **Play** button. Click the **Auto-Play** button in the **Cue List** window and highlight any of the cues.

Using Auto-Cue to Place Cues

In the next tutorial we're going to create the same six cues; however, we are going to leave the dead time intact and make each cue a range. Audition should be open and in the **Edit View** mode. Close any open files or sessions using the **File>Close** All command.

1. Select **File>Open** and locate the *Numbered Phrases.wav* in the *Chapter 07-Audio* directory on the CD that accompanies this book.

2. If the **Cue List** window if not already open, press **Alt+8** to open the **Cue List** window and dock it above the waveform display.

3. Select **Edit>Auto-Cue>Auto-Cue Settings**.

4. Click the **Find Levels** button. Notice that only signal above −58.8dB for a duration of at least 25 milliseconds will be considered as valid audio. Click **OK**.

5. Select **Edit>Auto-Cue>Find Phrases and Mark**.

Choosing the **Find Phrases and Mark** option uses the values determined by the **Find Levels** function to locate the beginning and ending of each phrase. Since the function located both a

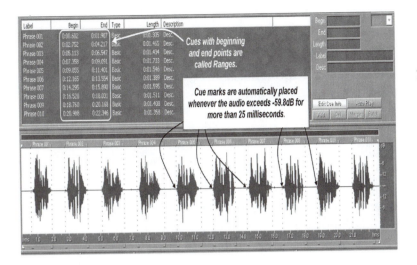

7.3   Cues can be modified from either the Cue List window or the waveform display. Using the Find Phrases and Mark function creates a range for each segment of audio.

start and end point, the cue points were merged into a range. Note that unlike cues, ranges display an **End** time value in the **Cue List** window.

> Placing cues can be very helpful when working with narratives or long programs. Placing cues and labeling them can help locate segments quickly.

Creating Ranges

We've just seen how ranges can be created automatically, but what if we want to create a range from other cues? It's simple, but there are some limits. Only two ranges can be merged at a time. Cues are not held to that rule. You can combine as many cues as you want at one time.

The **Cue List** window makes it simple to create or merge cues. Highlight the cues that will be combined by dragging over them or holding down the **Shift** key and highlighting the desired cues. Use the **Control** key to select nonsequential cues or to deselect cues. Click the **Merge** button in the **Cue List** window. The new cue range will retain the properties of the first cue point and inherit an end time. The later cue point will cease to exist as a cue.

Let's look at another way to create a range.

Using Adjust Selection to Phrase

We are going to work with the *Numbered Phrases.wav* file once again. Audition should be in the **Edit View** mode. Close any open files or sessions using the **File>Close All** command.

1. If the **Cue List** window if not already open, press **Alt+8** to open the **Cue List** window and dock it above the waveform display.

2. Right-click in the **Organizer** window, choose **Import**, and locate the *Numbered Phrases.wav* in the *Chapter 07-Audio* directory. Drag the *Numbered Phrases.wav* from the **Organizer** window into the **Waveform Display**.

3. Highlight one of the phrases in the waveform. It doesn't matter which one, and you do not need to be careful how close your selection is to the phrase as long as the selection does not include any other phrase.

4. Select **Edit>Auto-Cue>Adjust Selection to Phrase**. The selection area should have contracted around the phrase.

5. Press F8.

The **Cue List** window should now show a range labeled **Cue 1**. You can create a range from a selected area any time by pressing F8 or one of the other cue mark placement keys.

> **TIP!!** Files and individual cues can be placed into tracks quickly and easily using the **Insert > File/Cue List** command in **Multitrack View**.

Modifying Cues and Ranges

Cues can be modified through the **Cue List** window or in the **Waveform Display** area. To change cues in the **Cue List** window, press the **Edit Cue Info** button and enter the changes in the appropriate fields. Changing the length will alter the end point but not the beginning. A dropdown menu permits changing the cue type. Highlight the **Label** and **Description** fields and type the information to change them. Clicking the **Add or Del** buttons will add or delete highlighted cues respectively.

Unless the exact time location or length is known, moving cues in the waveform display may be easier. To resize the cue, place the cursor over the cue handle. When the cursor shape changes to a hand, hold the left mouse button down and drag to the desired position. You can also right-click on the cue handle to access other options from a pop-up menu. These options include opening the **Cue List** window, changing the cue type, and deleting the cue. The menu is contextual, meaning that if the cue is a range, an option will be present to change the range into a cue point. If the cue is not a range, the option **Make Range** will be shown.

 Cue marks will not be saved if the **Save extra non-audio information** is disabled when saving the file.

Play List Window

Audition has another useful tool for the inventive mind. The **Play List** window offers the ability to sequence cues and even loop cues. Once an acceptable sequence is settled on, the sequence can be inserted into a track in **Multitrack View** by selecting **Edit>Insert Play List in Multitrack.**

The **Play List** window is nondestructive, meaning that any changes made have no effect on the original files or cues.

Show Cue List/Insert Cue(s): opens the **Cue List** window if not already open and toggles to the **Insert Cue** function, allowing addition of the currently highlighted cue in the **Cue List** window.

Remove: removes the currently highlighted cue from the **Play List** window.

Loops: repeats the currently selected cue by the value entered to the right.

Play/Stop: toggles between playing the sequence and stopping playback beginning with the currently highlighted cue.

Autocue: automatically plays the cue following the highlighted cue.

Move Up: moves the highlighted cue up or earlier in the playback sequence.

Move Down: moves the highlighted cue down or later in the playback sequence.

Total Time: displays the total time of the sequence including loops.

7.4   *The Play List window is similar to a jukebox for cues with a few more features.*

Using the Playlist

This tutorial demonstrates inserting and looping cues in the playlist. It will also provide some hands-on adjustment of the cue range and finish with inserting the playlist into the **Multitrack View.**

Close any open files or sessions using the **File>Close All** command and, if necessary, press F12 to return to **Edit View.**

1. Select **File>Open** and locate the file named *Play List Cues.wav* in the *Chapter 07-Audio* directory on the CD that accompanies this book.

2. If the **Cue List** window if not already open, click the **Show Cue List** button on the toolbar or press **Alt+8** to open the Cue List window and dock it above the waveform display.

3. Click the next button on the toolbar, **Show Play List**, or choose **Window>Play List** and dock the window below the **Cue List** window.

4. Double-click between the **Cue 2** and **Cue 3** labels on the waveform display to highlight **Cue 2.**

5. Click the **Play Looped** button on the transport controls, and Cue 2 will play repeatedly.

6. Stop the transport and press **Alt+Home** four times to magnify the waveform. Click once on the waveform the deselect the cue range.

7. Use the cursor to move the red beginning **Cue** handle to the left so it is closer to the beat. Double-click between the cue handles and press the **Play Looped** button again.

8. Make some drastic changes and listen to the results. Then make the loop transition as smooth as possible.

9. Highlight Cue 2 in the Cue List window and click the **Insert Cues(s)** button in the **Play List** window.

10. Highlight the word **End** in the **Play List** window to position the next cue insertion. Cues are inserted above the highlighted selection in the **Play List** window.

11. Highlight **Cue 1** in the **Cue List** window and Insert it into the playlist.

12. Highlight **Cue 2** in the **Cue List** window and Insert it into the playlist.

13. Insert **Cue 3** into the playlist.

14. Insert the cue labeled **Fade** into the playlist.

15. Highlight **Cue 1** in the playlist, press **Alt+L**, and enter **3** into the **Loops** field.

16. Right-click on the **Horizontal Ruler** and select **Zooming>Zoom Full**.

17. Highlight the top cue in the **Play List** window and press the **Play** button. Notice the cursor as it travels across the waveform display and plays each cue according to the sequence in the Play List window.

18. Select **Edit>Insert Play List into Multitrack** and hit the **F12** function key to view the sequence in **Multitrack View**.

The sequence is now ready to mixdown or combine with other tracks in **Multitrack View**. That was a very simple demo of the power Audition offers to quickly create custom music scores by sequencing and repeating cues. We'll take an even close look at repeating sound bytes in the next section.

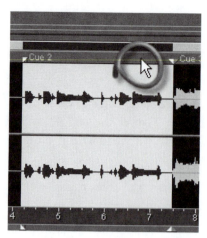

7.5   *Double-click between cue labels to select the cue range.*

7.6   *Transport controls*

7.7   *Zoom controls*

LOOPS

The last 10 years have brought enormous changes to music production techniques. The days of having to spend tens of thousands of dollars on acoustically tuned studios are over, having been replaced by prerecorded instrument samples readily available on CD at the local music store. Sample libraries are available for almost every conceivable instrument and sound, and more are marketed everyday.

Let's not get confused by the terminology used in audio production. When talking about a sample in the context of sampling rates, a sample is an interval at which a measurement of the signal amplitude is recorded. In the context of the musical instruments and loops, a sample is a recording of a musical note, chord, or other sound. For example, a recording of middle C on a Steinway grand piano from the attack of the hammer on the string until the note decays is a sample of the Steinway piano. The sample recording can be used in a hardware device or software application called a *sampler*, which is very similar to a synthesizer. When middle C is played on the sampler, the sample of the piano is played back exactly as it was recorded. However, when a higher note is played, the sample of the piano is played back at a higher playback sampling rate, raising the pitch of the note proportionately. Hitting a lower note on the sampler causes the piano sample to play back at a lower playback sampling rate, lowering the pitch proportionately.

What Is a Loop?

It didn't take long for musicians to realize that they could not only use digital samples to create music, but they could also create digital musical phrases that can be easily repeated. These musical phrases are called *loops*. Loops can be any duration: one note, one bar, two bars, four bars, twelve bars, or even nonmusical lengths. They can be mixed and matched in a modular fashion much like a set of building blocks. The loop content can be as simple as a single snare drum or a complete orchestra.

 Sony's ACID is a popular software application for creating and working with loops. Audition can also use the ACID loop format.

Loops and Looping

Loops and looping techniques are great for creating "original" music compositions. At one time, this was referred to as sample posing (composing with samples). In fact, there are many

7.8   *Bar 1 was looped or repeated four times. The audio content for Bars 1–4 is identical.*

music construction libraries or loopkits available for this purpose. Other practical ways to use loops is in creating music beds for TV and radio commercials and scoring video productions. The loops can be built from samples or from an existing collection of the loops called *loop libraries*. Using looping for these types of projects allows creative freedom not readily available from traditional prerecorded or needle-drop music libraries. For example, the loop tempo can be tailored to a segment, instrumentation can be changed to vary the mood, or the key can be changed to smooth a musical transition. Presto. Custom scoring without the hassle or the cost.

To demonstrate this more effectively, let's open and work with a couple of the loops bundled with Audition.

> **TIP!!** Audition is packaged as a two-disc set. The second CD contains thousands of royalty-free loops.

Using Loops

In this tutorial, we're going to create a short music segment using a drum, bass, and guitar loops. Make sure Audition is opened and in the **Multitrack View** mode. Close any open files or sessions using the **File>Close All** command.

1. Select **File>Import** and locate the *Chapter 07-Audio* directory on the CD that accompanies this book. Hold down the **Control** key and highlight the *DblBDrum07.cel*, *DeepBass3.cel*, *DeepBass4.cel*, and *GuitSlow10.cel*.

2. Press the **Enter** key, and all four files will open into the **Organizer** window.

3. Right-click on the **Time Display** window and select **Bar and Beats**.

4. Right-click on the **Horizontal Ruler** and select the **Snap to Ruler (Course)**, **Snap to Clips**, and **Snap to Endpoints** options. Snapping will help align the edges of the clips.

5. Left-click and drag the *DblBDrum07.cel* to **Track 1**.

> **TIP!!** The first track placed in the **Multitrack View** dictates the session tempo. Additional loops placed into tracks will adjust to match the session tempo. Although this can be changed in the **Session Properties** control, it is usually much easier to place the track with the desired tempo first.

6. Right-click on the clip in **Track 1** and drag it all the way to the left. This will ensure that the track starts on the first beat of the session.

7. Move the cursor over the right edge of the clip until the cursor shape changes into the shape shown in Figure 7.9 and drag until the right-edge is even with beat 1 of measure 9 shown as 9:1 on the **Horizontal Ruler**. The drum loop is now eight bars in length. Notice the vertical dotted line on the clip indicating each time the loop repeats.

8. Hit the **Home** key to move the cursor to the beginning and press the spacebar to audition the track.

Using loops is that simple. Of course, looping can be much more complex. Let's add a bass line and lead guitar. We are also going to use some of the clip-editing techniques discussed in Chapter 6.

 Should you have any problems completing this exercise, the tutorial is saved along with the loop files as a session file named *Using Loops.ses*.

Before continuing, press **Alt+2** to open the **Mixers** window and enter −3 into the field at the top of the Master **Fader**. This reduces or attenuates the overall level by 3dB.

9. Drag and drop the *DeepBass3.cel* file on **Track 2**. Right-click and slide the clip to the beginning as we did with the drum loop in **Track 1**.

10. Extend the loop so that the right-edge lines up with **Bar 5.1** on the horizontal ruler.

11. Drag and drop *DeepBass4.cel* onto **Track 2** behind the other clip and move it so that the clip begins at Bar 5:1.

12. Click the **V** key to activate the **Move/Copy** tool. Right-click and drag the first clip in **Track 2** to **Bar 6:1** and choose **Copy Reference Here**. Shorten the loop by dragging the right edge back to **Bar 9:1** and then press the **R** key to change back to the **Hybrid** tool.

13. Click on the clip in **Track 1** to highlight it and use the yellow triangle handle to move the cursor to **Bar 5:1**.

14. Right-click and select **Split** from the pop-up menu. The clip in **Track 1** is now split into two clips.

15. Move the cursor to **Bar 6:1** and press **Ctrl+K** to split the clip again.

16. Click on the middle clip on **Track 1** and hit the **Delete** key to remove it.

17. Drop the *GuitSlow10.cel* on **Track 3** at **Bar5:1**. Press the **Home** key and then the spacebar to play the track.

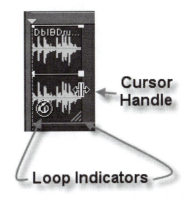

7.9 *Loop-enabled clips display a circular arrow within a circle on the left corner and three diagonal lines on the right corner.*

7.10 *The Mixers window*

The tracks sound very plain, but it demonstrates the looping concept. We'll discuss ways to add dimension later on. For now, let's move on to creating a loop.

Creating a Loop

In this tutorial, we are going to create a loop from an existing track, determine the tempo, configure the loop properties, and save the loop as an Audition loop or CEL file.

1. In **Edit View**, select **Ctrl+O** and locate the file named *Drum Intro.wav* in the *Chapter 07-Audio* directory on the CD that accompanies this book.

2. Set the time display to **Bars and Beats** and turn all **Snapping** options off. The **Find Beats** function tends to be more accurate when the **Snapping** options are off.

3. Find the first beat by pressing **Shift+[**.

4. Find the first beat of the next measure by pressing **Shift+]** until the end of the selection is parallel to **Bar 2.1** on the horizontal ruler. Don't worry if it's not exact; we'll fix that in a minute.

5. Click the **Play Looped** button on the transport controls. The highlighted selection will now loop.

6. Press **Alt+Home** about three times to zoom in on the beginning of the selection. Drag the triangle selection handle close the beginning of the beat and then use the **Shift+H** and **Shift+J** keys to move the selection as close the beat as possible.

> You can also hold down the **Shift** key and drag the cursor to make shorten or lengthen the selection, however you should make certain that the **Snap to Zero Crossings** is enabled to avoid potential clicks or pops.

7. Press **Alt+End** to zoom in on the end of the selection. Drag the triangle selection handle close the beginning of the next beat, and then use the **Shift+K** and **Shift+L** keys to fine tune the selection.

Using the **Shift** key modifier and the **G, H, J,** and **K** keys to move the selection to the closest **Zero Crossing** may not be necessary, but a pop or click can result at the loop transition if the amplitudes are not equal. In other words, both ends of the loop need to cross zero amplitude at the edit point. Making this part of your routine will ensure that you have good, clean loops.

In order to take advantage of the looping features, the loop tempo must be determined and set along with other metadata in the **Wave Properties>Loop Info** tab. Keep the tutorial files open and use them as you work through the following **Edit Tempo** and **Wave Properties** sections.

Edit Tempo

The **Edit Tempo** function automatically calculates the waveform tempo based on user input. **Edit Tempo** can also change the relative position of the waveform on the timeline.

Extract from Selection: allows you to enter the number of **Beats Highlighted** or **Bars Highlighted** in the currently displayed waveform. Clicking the **Extract** button calculates and displays the Beats per Minute in the **Tempo** section of the window.

Offset: The **Current Beat At** field permits entering a bar and beat number that changes or offsets the current selection on the horizontal ruler. For example, entering **9:1** would show the current selection beginning at measure 9 in the waveform display. The **Reset 1:1 to Cursor** button sets the selection at the beginning of measure 1 on the horizontal ruler. **Song Start** shows the number of milliseconds from the beginning of the track to the beginning of the selection.

7.11 Edit Tempo window

Tempo: displays the tempo in beats per minute (BPM). Calculation of the BPM requires that the correct time signature is entered in the **Beats per Bar** and **Beat Length** fields. The **Ticks per Beat** value determines the number of divisions or ticks per beat. Acceptable values are 2-3,600, and the tick values are reflected in the **Display Time Format**.

Let's continue the tutorial using the **Edit Tempo** function.

8. Right-click on the **Time Display** and select **Edit Tempo** to open the **Edit Tempo** window.

9. Select **Beats Highlighted** and enter **4**, or select **Bars Highlighted** and enter **1**. Click the **Extract** button. The tempo will display **116.98 BPM**. Close the **Edit Tempo** window.

10. Right-click on the waveform and select **Copy to New**. The action copies the selection to a new waveform and displays the new waveform name in the **Organizer** window as *Drum Intro (2).wav*.

There is one more step involved before we can save the finished loop. The settings that define the file as a loop have to be changed in the **Wave Properties** settings. We'll take a look at these settings before continuing with the tutorial.

Wave Properties

The **Loop Info** tab of the **Wave Properties** window stores the settings, or metadata, that determine how the file will behave when used in **Multitrack View**. The metadata includes the number of beats in the loop, the tempo, key and stretching method along with file format information and other user-entered data. The **Wave Properties** window can be selected from View>**Wave Properties** or the keyboard shortcut **Ctrl+P.**

Loop: enables clip looping in **Multitrack View.**

One Shot: causes the file to play once and end when used in **Multitrack View.** Selecting One Shot does not prevent a clip from looping in **Multitrack View;** however, that would require modifying the settings of the clip.

Number of Beats: Entering the number of beats allows Audition to calculate the tempo.

Tempo: permits the user to enter the tempo in beats per minute or calculates tempo automatically based on waveform length and number of beats.

Key: sets the waveform's key. The key is used as a reference for use in **Multitrack View.** The first loop added to a session will determine the **Session** key unless manually entered or changed in **Session Properties.** As additional loops are added to the session, Audition will attempt to match the key of the session.

Find Nearest: analyzes the waveform and attempts a best guess at the key. It is best to enter the key if known; however, Audition usually makes a good guess.

Tempo Matching-Stretch Method

Five options are available that determine how the loop behaves when the loop has to be shortened or lengthened to fit the session tempo.

Fixed Length (no stretching): Repeats the file as a loop. No action will be taken. The loop will remain at the same length, tempo, and pitch regardless of the **Session Properties** settings.

Time-scale Stretch: expands or contracts the loop to match the session tempo. Three quality levels are available; higher levels require more processing time. The **Frames** value is the

7.12 *The Loop Info tab of the Wave Properties window*

number of splices per beat used when time-scaling the loop. Splices are slices of audio inserted or removed to alter the time scale. Higher frame values produce more accurate results but also introduce artifacts that are more audible. The default is 32, but higher rates may produce better results. **Frame Overlapping** is expressed as a percentage and determines the how much of the frames overlap. Overlapping helps smooth the splices but causes the scaling to sound electronic at higher values. The recommended **Frame Overlap** is 15–25 percent.

Resample (affects pitch): resamples the loop at one of three user-defined quality levels. Higher levels require more processing time. This option will alter the pitch depending on the amount of stretching.

Beat Splice: uses beat cues to determine how to the expand or contract the loop. The **Auto-Find Beats** option locates the beats in the file using the same algorithm as the Find Beats function. **Beat Splice** looks for transients that exceed a particular level within a certain duration. This method works the best on extremely percussive and rhythmic tracks such as drums. The **Use File Beat Markers** radio button is enabled only when the waveform has beat cues present.

Hybrid: uses the current **Time-Scale Stretching** settings when the tempo is slowed down and the **Beat Splice** method when the tempo is sped up.

Let's finish the tutorial by setting the **Loop Info** tab information and saving the file as an Audition loop file.

11. Press **Ctrl+P** and choose the **Loop Info** tab.

12. Click on the **Loop** radio button and enter **4** in the **Number of Beats** field.

13. Enter **117** in the **Tempo** field.

14. Choose **Hybrid** as the **Stretch Method**. **Hybrid** is usually the best choice for drum tracks.

15. Select **File>Save Copy As** and select *Audition Loop.cel* from the **Save as Type** pop-up menu.

16. Click the **Option** button and select the desired compression options. The most commonly used settings are the **MP3** radio button with **–320 Kbps, 44100 Hz, Stereo (8.8.1)** in the pop-up menu. You may want to add a preset for recalling frequently used settings.

Once a loop file is saved, it retains the loop settings and can be included as part of any number of future sessions and music construction libraries.

 Audition ships with thousands of royalty-free loops. Feel free to experiment with these loops or use them in your production. Please note the licensing restrictions. There are also some demo loops from some other publishers on the CD that accompanies this book, and Appendix B on page 297 contains a listing of many music loop–related web sites.

Loop Properties

The **Audio Clip Looping** dialog box is accessed by right-clicking on the desired clip. It is available only in **Multitrack View** and allows you to change the loop behavior of any audio file.

Looping: enables one of three looping methods.

Simple Looping (No gaps): loops the audio continuously without any space or gaps between each loop and does not alter the tempo or pitch of the loop. This is the easiest method to use.

Repeat every ___ seconds: causes the loop to begin an iteration every X seconds as determined by the value entered in the **Seconds** field. The tempo will not be altered.

Repeat every ___ beats: causes the loop to complete within the number of beats as determined by the value entered in the **Beats** field. The file will be stretched.

Follow session tempo: causes the loop to stretch to the tempo of the session. Enabling **Time Stretching** in the **Clip Stretch Properties** window or disabling this checkbox will force the loop to ignore the session tempo.

Lock position to tempo: forces the beginning of the loop to remain locked to the measure and beat regardless of the amount of stretching. Disabling this feature allows the loop to move when stretched. This option should be enabled for most music composing.

Transpose Pitch: allows transposing the pitch of the loop in half-step increments. Positive values raise the pitch; negative numbers lower the pitch.

Adjust ALL loop-enabled clips that use this wave: determines whether the loop property settings affect only the current clip or all clips in the session that use the same original audio file. For example, with this option disabled, a clip referencing an original bass synthesizer loop file

7.13 Audition Loop format options are set using MP3 or mp3PRO settings.

7.14 *The Wave Clip Looping dialog box.*

might be copied and have its pitch transposed by a half-step. The first clip would remain at the original pitch, but the pitch of the second clip would be one half-step higher. Enabling this option would transpose both the first clip and the copied clip by one half-step.

> **TIP!!** Presets are found throughout Audition. Using presets for frequently used or favorite settings can speed up production and can help prevent you from forgetting to change an option or using the wrong setting.

The Loop File Format

Loop files can be stored in virtually any format supported by Audition; however, there are advantages to saving the loops as Windows PCM (.wav) files, or Audition loop files. These two formats can store properties used to control loop behavior such as the number of beats in the loop, the tempo, key, and the tempo-matching method. Without this metadata, the loop file is simply an audio file trimmed to the exact loop length.

> **TIP!!** If the **Save extra non-audio information** checkbox is not checked when saving the file, the loop-properties data will not be saved with the file.

One of the main reasons loops have become more popular is the ability to exchange samples and loops over the Internet. Saving files in a standard Windows PCM file can yield a rather unwieldy file size and can be an obstacle for users with slower modems. Audition provides the Audition loop file to address this issue. The Audition loop file contains the .cel extension. The .cel file is a modified version of the popular mp3 format that stores the loop properties. In addition to the loop information, the .cel format contains data describing where audio data starts. Audition uses the data to trim any silence added to the audio by the mp3 format.

Looping Techniques

As you have seen, creating loops is relatively easy in Audition, but as with any craft, there are always techniques that can improve the work. Creating loops is no different, so here are a few ideas to consider when developing your loop libraries.

Loops can be easily built from samples, and the samples don't have to be traditional instruments. Whether working with samples or loops, make sure the crossfades are smooth and clean, but be careful not to clip off the attack. Loops can be built from the bottom up. Lay down some drum tracks, add the bass line, and layer with pads, melody, and solos. If the loop needs a laid-back feel, group the drum clips and shift them back by about 5–10 milliseconds. Shift the drums ahead for a more on-top-of-the-beat or pushed feel. Make the loops interesting by varying the arrangement, and try to keep them short. Shorter loops are easier to mix and match. Mix a number of different versions that can be combined later. Drop the melody on one version, and try half-time or doubling the tempo on another version. Varying the envelope of an instrument can give the loop a more interesting sound. Transposing can also add an unusual flare to the loop.

These are a just a few ideas. Creativity and experimentation are the key to creating a good collection of loops. Audition makes creating loops easy, but there is one caveat. It can be addictive.

SOUNDS

We've seen that Audition can record, edit, and loop audio, but Audition also has some very useful tools for creating sound. The tools are found on the Generate menu in **Edit View** mode and are divided into four options: **Silence**, **DTMF Signals**, **Noise**, and **Tones**.

Silence

The **Silence** option generates digital silence equal to the value entered in the seconds field. The field accepts values as small as 1/1,000th of a second. The silence is inserted at the cursor point, and waveform content to the right of the cursor is shifted or rippled to the right.

7.15 *Generate Silence dialog box*

> Using silence is an easy method to insert clean space into a waveform; however, inserting the ambience from the original recording may be less objectionable depending upon the ambient level. For example, inserting silence into a recording with an audible air handler rumble can sound unnatural and draw the listener's attention to the absence of sound. Recording and saving at least 30 seconds of room or location ambience during each recording session is a good practice. You may not usually need it, but you'll have it in case it's needed.

DTMF Signals

This is the tool to use when that client wants to drop the sound of a touch-tone phone into the radio spot. The acronym DTMF stands for Dual Tone Multi-Frequency. DTMF is the system used by touch-tone phones to transmit the number dialed. In fact, you can dial the phone by using this option. Enter the telephone number in the **Dial String** field and click the **Preview** button with the phone next to the monitor. This tool can be customized, but the default settings should serve all but very specialized needs. Consult the Audition user's guide if more detailed information is required.

7.16 *Generate DTMF Signals dialog box*

7.17 The Generate Noise dialog box

Noise

Noise is typically something an engineer attempts to minimize or remove from a recording, but there are specific uses for noise. Audition is capable of generating three types or colors of noise: white noise, pink noise, and brown noise. Specific colors of noise can be used to measure frequency response of audio components and to create ambience or other effects.

Selecting **Generate>Noise** inserts the noise specified in the **Generate Noise** dialog box at the cursor, replacing the selection and rippling any audio to the right. The dialog box presents several options.

Color: selects the type of noise used.

White: contains all frequencies in the available spectrum at the same relative level. It sounds like hiss.

Pink: contains less high-frequency content. The relative level drops 3dB per octave, or in other words, every time the frequency doubles. Pink noise tends to sound more like rain.

Brown: contains even less high-frequency content with a relative level drop of 6dB per octave. Thunder is a good example of brown noise.

Style: determines the noise source and relationship for each channel.

Spatial Stereo: produces a stereo effect with more depth by centering a noise source while delaying separate noises to the left and right channels.

Independent Channels: generates the noise for each channel separately creating a quasi-stereo waveform.

Mono: uses the same noise on both channels.

Inverse: uses the same noise for both channels; however, the phase of one channel is placed 180° out of phase.

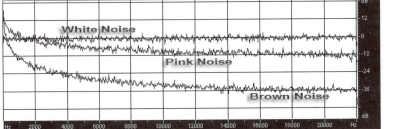

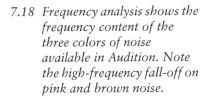

7.18 Frequency analysis shows the frequency content of the three colors of noise available in Audition. Note the high-frequency fall-off on pink and brown noise.

Intensity: determines the quality of the noise. Increasing the value causes the sound to have an overdriven quality. Increasing the value will increase the level.

Duration: determines the length of the generated noise. Values are accurate to 1/1,000th of a second.

Tones

The **Generate Tones** dialog box is loaded with options for generating sounds. **Select Generate>Tones** to open the **General Tones** dialog box. The dialog box presents two tabs that are both initially labeled **Locked**.

When the tabs are locked, the settings on the first tab will control the tone for the entire duration of the sound. Unchecking the **Lock to these settings only** checkbox unlocks the tabs, and the tab labels change to **Initial Settings** and **Final Settings**. In this mode the tone begins with the settings on the **Initial Settings** tab and transforms to the settings on the **Final Settings** tab.

The **Generate Tones** function presents two options available in many of the Audition effects: the **Presets List** and the real-time **Preview** button. The **Presets List** enables you to save favorite or frequently used settings. Presets are easily added or deleted. Click the **Add** button and enter a name for the preset, and the current settings will be saved with that name. To delete a preset, highlight the preset name and click the **Del** button. The **Preview** button allows you to audition the tone with the current settings in real time.

Unless you have experience working with analog synthesizers and oscillators, it will probably take some experimentation and patience to achieve the desired sound using the **Generate Tones** function.

Base Frequency (0): sets the primary or fundamental frequency used for tone generation. For example, to generate a 1kHz tone, enter **1000**.

Modulate By: determines the range that the base frequency is modulated. For example, entering **5** in this field causes a base frequency of 100Hz to oscillate between 95Hz and 105Hz.

7.19 *The Generate Tones dialog box*

Modulation Frequency: sets the number of times per second or speed that the base frequency is modulated by the value entered in the **Modulate By** field.

Frequency Components: control five harmonics of the base frequency. The base frequency is multiplied by value of the field below each of the faders, and the faders determine the percentage of the harmonic added to the overall signal.

Phasing: permits adjustment of the tone phase properties.

Start Phase: determines the starting phase.

Phase Difference: allows variation of the phase relationship between left and right channels. Entering **180** will place the channels out of phase, and a value of 0 will be in phase.

Change Rate: sets the number of times per second that the phase relationship between left and right channels will rotate by 360°.

Flavor: selects the waveform shape. Selection choices are **Sine, Triangle/Saw tooth, Square,** and **Inverse Sine**. Selecting different waveform shapes can drastically alter the sound. The **Sine** option sounds the smoothest, and **Square** adds a harsh quality.

Flavor Characteristic: permits fine-tuning of the waveform selected in the **Flavor** pop-up menu.

dB Volume: provides separate control of the left and right channel levels.

DC Offset: A direct current (DC) offset can be entered here. Expressed as a percentage, this will move the waveform in a positive or negative direction from zero.

Modulate: Enabling the **Modulate** checkbox causes modulation of the selected waveform segment in **Edit View**.

DeModulate: Enabling the **DeModulate** checkbox demodulates the selected waveform segment in **Edit View**.

Overlap (mix): Enabling the overlap checkbox mixes the waveform segment selected in **Edit View** with the generated tone.

Duration: determines the length of the generated tone. If a segment is selected, the time of the selection will appear in this field.

Copy from Initial Settings: appears only on the second tab and copies the values on the initial tab to the final tab for modification. This feature saves time when creating effects that retain some of the initial settings.

Log Sweep: enables a logarithmic sweep providing a smoother transition through the frequency sweep.

It is probably more convenient and faster to use a hardware or software synthesizer; however, Audition does provide tools for generating original sounds and even music. If you haven't experienced analog synthesizers, do yourself a favor and just do some experimenting with these functions. The **Noise and Tones** options can be used to create sound effects such as a blizzard, laser guns, R2D2, earthquakes, and endless number of sound effects limited only by time and your imagination. Using these tools in combination with some of the effects and filters can produce some unique sounds that may just be the right touch for your project. We'll use these tools in the next chapter as we learn how to use the **Effects** options.

Audition ships with a script collection that demonstrates several examples of using the Generate function to build custom sounds. To see the examples, select **Options > Scripts** and then press the **Open/New Collection** button. Locate the file called *scratch.scp* in the *Scripts* directory. The path should be: *C:\Program Files\Adobe\Audition 1.5\Scripts\sounds from scratch.scp*. Open the file, highlight a script from the list, and click the **Run Script** button.

Chapter 8

Audio Props and Effects

WHAT IS AN EFFECT?

The earliest recordings were live performances recorded with a single microphone that captured the performance as well as the acoustical characteristics of the venue. As recording technology evolved and moved into studios designed for recording, it became a standard practice to use multiple microphones and place them closer to the instruments. Although this tighter miking technique provided more control over the sound of the instruments, the acoustic qualities of the room were diminished.

To replace the natural echo lost by tight miking, a number of devices and techniques were introduced to simulate the different room acoustics. The earliest effects added a delay or echo to the signal to mimic the effect of the natural sound reflections. Through the years, electronic devices were developed to affect, filter, or manipulate the analog audio signal. With the introduction of digital signal processors (DSPs), the array of available effects quickly expanded to include signal

8.1   *Programming code or routines are embedded into integrated circuits called digital signal processors (DSP). ©2004 by Motorola, used with permission.*

165

> ### *History Lesson*
>
> One early effect was the Cooper Time Cube. The magic of this effect was created by using a garden hose with a small speaker on one end and a microphone on the other end. As the audio played through the speaker, the microphone on the other end of the hose picked up the delayed audio.
>
> Another popular effect that used a similar concept was the EMT chamber. Instead of a hose, a large metal plate was suspended by springs in a box. The length of the echo was controlled by tightening the springs securing the metal plate. The tighter the springs, the less the plate could vibrate, and therefore the shorter the echo. Many studio control rooms were equipped with remote controls to adjust tension of the springs.
>
> An even simpler method of creating an echo effect was to place a microphone and speaker in another room with desirable acoustics. This is still a relatively simple alternative to digital effects and can provide a unique quality for a particular project.

processors developed to control almost every attribute of audio production. Today, there are a multitude of effects readily available in Audition or as third-party software plug-ins.

WHY USE EFFECTS?

Effects have taken on a much broader definition since the advent of DSPs and digital audio workstations (DAWs). In addition to the traditional effects such as echo, phasing, and flanging, the term *effects* or **FX** now includes signal processing such as equalization, limiting, time compression, pitch bending, and noise reduction. In fact, Audition includes more than 40 DSP-based effects, or *transforms*, as they are sometimes called. These effects provide the tools to compress or limit the dynamic range of a recording; alter the frequency response by adding or removing specific frequency ranges; squeeze or stretch the duration; remove hiss, pops, and other noise; adjust levels; add echo; and a number of other functions to tweak the track or mix.

Note   In audio, the terms *effect* and *filter* have traditionally had specific and different definitions. Because Audition has chosen to group all signal-processing terms under the umbrella of *effects,* we will substitute the word *effect* in most cases. However, *filter* has typically been used in the context of equalizing, and *effect* has been used in the context of signal processing, such as flanging, delay, or echo.

The use of effects can have a huge impact on the final product. For example, some notes of a bass guitar may be hidden or masked by other instruments. Using compression can reduce the dynamic range of the bass, making the notes more audible. A de-esser effect can make a sibilant voice less noticeable, and the right echo effect can place an instrument on the stage by suggesting a sense of depth. Equalization can be used to remove a muddy or dark quality of a voice or to add some presence to a guitar. Some of the more popular effects are the noise-reduction effects enabling painless removal of clicks, ticks, and hiss from old but precious vinyl recordings. Video editors and production engineers can use limiting to remove excessive peaks on a voiceover, use the filters to reduce a hum or other background noise, and add that reverb many of the car dealerships like to use on their radio spots.

Although the effects can sound really sweet, the old cliché "less is more" is apropos. The overuse of effects may not only degrade the sound quality but also become tiresome. To produce the maximum impact, use effects sparingly and judiciously.

These are hundreds of ways to use effects and as many options used to apply them. Unfortunately, there is no standard formula. Applying effects is as subjective as composing music, and the results depend upon the waveform. There are some starting points, and you will find some standard settings that suit your taste and workflow. Don't reinvent the wheel; try the presets and then modify them.

Before beginning the discussion of the individual effects, it will help to understand the properties common to many of the effects.

Presets

The **Presets** control saves time by storing effect settings for instant recall and can serve as a good starting point for adding an effect. Highlighting any effect in the list changes the effect settings to the setting stored with the preset's name. Click the **Add** button and name the preset to store a custom preset. Highlighting an effect and clicking the **Del** button will delete a preset.

8.2   *Computers running Windows XP in multiuser mode store the presets in a hidden directory in the user's Documents and Settings directory.*

Take advantage of this control and store settings that appeal to you. Give the presets a descriptive name and use caution when deleting presets, as multiple occurrences of the same name are allowed, and the wrong settings could be deleted.

It is also a good idea to make a backup of your settings if you have made a number of custom presets or want to use you presets on another machine. The presets are stored in the *AUDITION.INI* file found in the Audition program directory on single-user machines or the *C:\Documents and Setting\(User's Logon Name)\Application Data\Adobe\Audition\1.5* on

C:\Documents and Settings\Ron\Application Data\Adobe\Audition\1.5

| File | Edit | View | Favorites | Tools | Help |

Back ▾ Search Folders

Address C:\Documents and Settings\Ron\Application Data\Adobe\Audition\1.5\AUDITION.INI Go

| Name ▲ | Size | Type | Date Modified |

8.3 *Computers running Windows XP in multiuser mode store the presets in a hidden directory in the user's Documents and Settings directory.*

multiuser machines. Copy this file to backup the presets or replace the existing file to install your presets.

If you cannot find the *AUDITION.INI* file, try using the Microsoft Windows search tool available in the **Start** menu. The file may be in a hidden directory, so you may have to use the advanced search options to locate hidden file and folders.

Note Audition effects, or transforms, are stored in the Audition program directory and are recognized by the .xfm extension.

Graph Controls

A graph control is available in many of the effects. The graph control provides a visual method of setting the effect parameters. Different graphs are used by different effects, and some effects contain a graph control for each channel, but they all share the same basic mode of operation. Click and drag a square or node to the desired position on the graph. Additional nodes can be placed by clicking anywhere on the graph. Nodes can be deleted by dragging them into another node or off the graph control. Parameters can also be adjusted by right-clicking on a node and entering the numeric values(s).

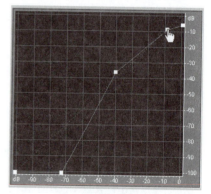

8.4 *Graph controls are used to set effect parameters by dragging the node or square to the desired plot on the graph.*

A cursor data field is displayed under many of the graph controls and displays the X- and Y-axis information under the current cursor location.

Two other controls usually accompany a graph control. The **Flat** button restores the graph control parameters to the default state, and the **Spline Curves** checkbox adjusts the position of the nodes to create a curve and results in a smooth transition as the effect parameters are changed from node to node.

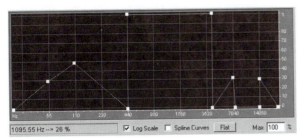

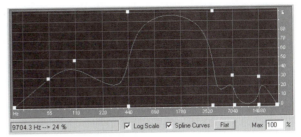

8.5　*Graph control with Spline Curves checkbox disabled*

8.6　*Graph control with Spline Curves checkbox enabled*

Preview

Most of the effects available in **Edit View** feature the ability to preview the effect and any parameter changes in real time without applying the effect. Once the **Preview** button is clicked, the selected segment (or the entire waveform) is played back in a loop, and any changes to the current preset or effect parameters are heard instantly. The **Preview** button label changes to **Stop** while the effect is in **Preview** mode.

Checking the **Bypass** checkbox allows you to audition the selection without the effect. The ability to hear how the settings are changing the effect and to bypass the effect during the preview is a terrific aid in setting up an effect.

8.7　*Graph control parameters can be set to specific values by right-clicking on a node and entering the desired numeric values.*

8.8　*Cursor Data field*

Enable Preroll and Postroll Preview

It is often useful to hear the transitions into and out of the selection on which an effect is being applied. Checking allows playback of not only the selected waveform, but a preset duration of time before and/or after the affected selection. The duration times are set in the **Effects Preview** section of the **Preroll and Postroll Options**.

8.9　*The Preview button allows the audition adjustment of effect settings, and the Bypass checkbox disables the effect during Preview mode. (left)*

8.10　*The Preroll and Postroll Options dialog box (right)*

The rest of this chapter deals with the specifics of each effect and suggests some applications. Documenting all the options and potential applications would require at least another book, so experiment with the effects. Take the time to get familiar with them. Try each of the options with extreme changes in values to hear how the effect changes the audio. The only effect that is incorrect is the one you don't like. Don't be afraid to try something; however, you may want to make certain the monitor volume is low before going crazy.

USING EFFECTS IN EDIT VIEW

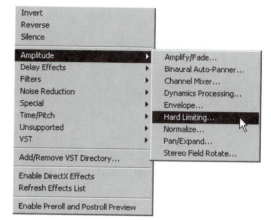

All of the effects in Audition with the exception of three can be applied in the **Edit View** mode. The **Preview** button allows you to audition the effect before applying it. You should note that effects applied in the **Edit View** are destructive and that reversing the effect may not be possible even with the **Undo** option. Once the file is saved, the effect is permanently applied to the audio file.

Audition groups the available effects in the **Effects** menu into categories. Each of these categories appears as a submenu item. The first three effects, **Invert**, **Reverse**, and **Silence**, have no subcategories or option settings. Additional submenus may appear depending on whether any third-party plug-ins have been added to your system.

8.11 Effects are grouped by function under the Effects menu.

To apply an effect, select the segment of the waveform to which the effect is to be applied and choose the desired effect from the **Effects** menu. A dialog box will appear containing the effect parameters and any other effect options. Adjust the settings and click the **Preview** button to review the effect. Once the settings are satisfactory, click **OK** to apply the effect.

> **Ctrl + Z** will undo most effects provided that **Edit > Enable Undo/Redo** is turned on and the file has not been saved since the effect was applied.

The **Effects** tab within the **Organizer** window provides another method of selecting effects. The effects can be organized using the **Group By Category** and **Group Real-Time Effects** buttons at the bottom of the **Organizer** window. Effect groups are expanded by clicking the plus sign to the left of the group or category and collapsed by clicking the minus sign. The **Generate** menu options **DTMF Signals**, **Noise**, **Tones**, and **Silence** are also available in the **Effects** tab.

To apply an effect using the **Organizer** window, double-click on the effect name. The effect dialog box will appear allowing effect adjustment.

> TIP!! The default selection range in Audition is the currently viewable waveform. Some engineers prefer to change the default on the **Settings > General** tab to **Entire Wave** instead of **View** to ensure that the effect is applied to the whole waveform when no selection is made.

8.12 *The Effects tab of the Organizer window is a quick method of selecting an effect.*

Invert

The **Invert** effect reverses the phase of the selected waveform by 180°. It is a simple solution for correcting out-of-phase channels of a stereo mix or correcting a track that was recorded with a microphone that was wired out of phase.

Using Invert

To **Invert** the phase of a single channel:

1. Open any stereo waveform in **Edit View**.

2. Move the cursor toward the top or bottom of the waveform until the letter **L** or **R** is displayed beside the cursor and click.

3. Select **Effects>Invert**. The phase of the highlighted channel will be inverted, and the dimmed channel will remain unaffected.

Reverse

The **Reverse** effect flips the selected waveform so that the waveform plays backwards.

Silence

Apply the **Silence** effect to reduce the level of the waveform selection to digital silence. Applying the **Silence** effect retains the time relationships of the waveform before and/or after the selection

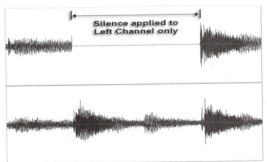

8.13 *The Silence effect attenuates the amplitude to infinity but does not alter the waveform position in time.*

and mutes the audio during the selection. Use **Silence** to add length to a waveform before adding an effect such as a long delay. This will extend the waveform and prevent the effect ending abruptly.

> Use **Generate** > **Silence** to insert silence and ripple or move the current waveform.

Amplitude

The **Amplitude** category contains nine effects used to control signal level. Several of the amplitude effects change the volume over the duration of the selected waveform.

Although some of the amplitude effects, such as **Normalize** and **Channel Mixer,** adjust the amplitude by a constant value, other effects such as **Dynamics Processing** change the amplitude of the output based on a ratio of the input to output signal amplitude. For example, a ratio of 20:1 changes the output by 1dB for every 20dB of input signal that exceeds the threshold. This type of amplitude processing can divided into three methods: compression, limiting, and expansion.

Compression is applied to a waveform to reduce or compress the dynamic range by increasing the output gain when input signals fall below a certain threshold. Compression is used to maintain a relatively consistent level and eliminate fluctuations in level that might allow an instrument or voice to be masked or hidden by elements of the soundtrack. For example, some words of a narration may be unintelligible when mixed with music. Using compression on the voice boosts the words with the lower levels and makes them rise above the music level. Compression is also used to reduce the dynamic range of a voice allowing it to sit better within a multitrack mix. A typical voice setting is around 3:1.

Limiting reduces the level of output gain as input signal exceeds a threshold. Limiting is merely hard compression and has traditionally been used to prevent overload or clipping. Limiting a voice or instrument that has a good dynamic range can help the track fit into the mix or squeeze a little more average level out of a final mix. The **Hard Limiting** effect in Audition provides just this function.

Expansion is the opposite of compression and decreases the output gain of input signals that fall below a threshold. The net effect of expansion is an increased dynamic range.

There are many other ways to use dynamics processing. Combining amplitude processing with functions such as filtering can provide effects that engage limiting only on specific frequency bands. One such effect is a **De-esser** and is often used to reduce sibilance on a vocal. Extreme attenuation on signals that fall below the threshold can effectively turn off or gate the sound. Such effects, called **Noise Gates,** are sometimes used to remove unwanted noise between musical notes or words.

Amplify/Fade

The **Constant Amplification** tab of the **Amplify/Fade** effect boosts or attenuates the selected waveform by a uniform amount. Amplitude changes are made with the slider control or by entering the desired value expressed as a negative or positive number. Clicking on the slider control enables changes in increments of one-tenth of one decibel using the arrow keys. Disabling **View all settings in dB** shows the values as a percentage rather than decibels. By default, the left and right channels of stereo waveforms are adjusted together, however disabling the **Lock Left/Right** checkbox allows individual channel adjustment (see Figure 8.14).

The **Fade** tab allows you to apply a fade in or fade out of the selected waveform and displays a pair of slider controls for the initial amplification and the final amplification. Radio buttons determine whether the rate of fade or slope is a **Linear Fade** or **Logarithmic Fade**.

Click the **Calculate Now** button to normalize the selection. The normalization function scans the selection, locates the sample with the highest peak value, and places the difference between the peak level and 0dBFS in the **Amplification** fields. A maximum peak value can also be entered in the **Peak Level** field to change the normalization reference level. For example, this feature can be used when outputting to analog or video formats that cannot accept levels recorded at 0dBFS.

Enabling the **DC Bias Adjust** checkbox permits removal of any direct current signal that may affect the amplitude or result in clicks or pops. Select the **Differential** radio button and click the **Find Zero Now** button to automatically determine the DC bias adjustment values or select the **Absolute** radio button to enter a DC offset value that will be used as a constant offset throughout the waveform.

Binaural Auto-Panner

The **Binaural Auto-Panner** dialog box (formerly named the Brainwave Synchronizer) is a unique plug-in. Renamed and moved to the **Amplify** category of effects, the **Binaural Auto-Panner** effect delays opposite channels to simulate a circular panning effect. The graph control

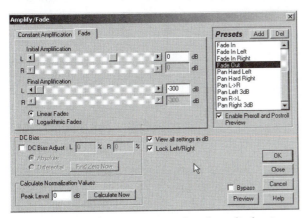

8.14 *Preset fades can be stored and applied using the Fade tab of the Amplify/Fade dialog box.*

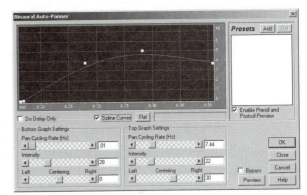

8.15 *The Binaural Auto-Panner dialog box*

Vocal Removers

There are a number of applications or black boxes on the market that claim to have the ability to remove vocals from a stereo mix. Once the tracks are mixed together, it is difficult if not impossible to remove a vocal without removing other components. There are techniques to lessen the damage, but they all primarily use the same method of inverting the phase of one channel and applying some equalization. The level of success depends completely upon the song content.

The **Center Channel Extractor** effect in Audition provides one of the best tools for attempting vocal elimination. Again, the level of success depends on the audio content and the amount of removal deemed acceptable.

curve sets the frequency or cyclical speed of the panning effect over the *X*-axis or duration of the selected waveform. The **Bottom** and **Top Pan Cycling Rate** sliders work in tandem to adjust the *Y*-axis or frequency of the graph control. The **Intensity** sliders vary the width of the panning, and the centering sliders determine the origination point of the pan.

This effect has been touted by many to have the ability to synchronize brainwaves, and many web sites contain information and recordings supporting this claim. Accurate or not, it would be unfair to dispute these theories without sufficient study; however, this effect can add an interesting dimension to the stereo image when applied to the appropriate instrument.

Channel Mixer

The Channel Mixer dialog box provides a method of mixing various combinations of left- and right-channel content. Channel content is determined by adjusting the sliders or entering a percentage of the original left and right channels in the **New Left Channel** and **New Right Channel** sections. Clicking the slider button enables adjustment with the arrow keys in increments of 1dB. You can enter values that exceed 100, but that can result in distortion if that waveform is already at full level. The **Invert** checkbox flips the new channel phase. Inverting both channels at the same time will have no net affect because both channels will remain in relative phase.

The **Channel Mixer** dialog box has a stock preset named **Vocal Cut**. Let's try the classic request, "Can you take the vocals out of this song?" Make sure that Audition is in the **Edit View** mode.

1. Press **Ctrl+O** and locate the file named *Vocal Cut Example.wav* in *Chapter 08-Audio* directory on the CD that accompanies this book.

2. Select the **Effects** tab in the **Organizer** window, and click on the plus sign to the right of the Amplitude group to expand the effects group.

3. Double-click on the **Channel Mixer** effect.

4. Highlight **Vocal Cut** in the **Presets** list and click the **Preview** button to audition the result.

5. Click the **Bypass** checkbox on and off while the selection loops and then try some other adjustments and notice the difference in low-end or bass content and the fullness of the sound.

Dynamics Processing

Dynamics Processing affects the dynamic range of a signal. The effect is versatile and provides functions to compress, limit, and expand the signal. Optional parameters enable the effect to act as a noise gate or de-esser.

Four tabs offer control of the effect settings. The **Graphic** and **Traditional** tabs adjust the input-to-output ratios and threshold levels.

The **Graphic** tab displays a graph control using nodes to make ratio changes. Input amplitude is displayed on the X-axis, and output amplitude on the Y-axis. The dotted diagonal line represents a ratio of 1:1, meaning that the input amplitude will be exactly equal to the output amplitude. Moving a node changes the parameters and updates the result in the display areas under the Presets List as well as the cursor data field below the graph. Right-clicking on the node allows entering precise numeric values. The **Invert** button will invert the graph; however, the nodes have to be at (0,0) and (100,100), and each successive node between must increase in amplitude.

The **Traditional** tab allows multiple processing settings. The highest selected radio button determines the number of available processing settings and enables editing of the **Ratio** and **Threshold** fields. A pop-up menu sets one of three types of processing: **Flat, Compress,** or **Expand.** An **Output Compensation** (gain) field is also available to adjust the overall amplitude.

The **Attack/Release** tab controls the attack and release times and gain control. The input level feeding the effect is set in the **Input Gain** field, and the final output level of the effect is adjusted in the **Output Gain** field. Level detection can be set for either **Peak** or **RMS** (Root Means Square). **RMS** is recommended. Output channels can be processed separately or jointly by enabling the **Joint Channels** checkbox, which causes the effect to be applied to both chan-

8.16 *The Channel Mixer dialog box*

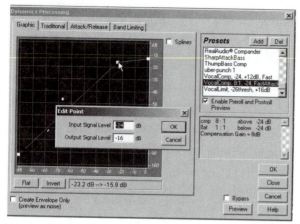

8.17 *Dynamics Processing displayed with the Graphic tab shows an 8:1 compression ratio with a threshold of –24dB.*

8.18 *Dynamics Processing effect displayed with the Traditional tab shows the parameters set on the Graphic tab in Figure 8.17.*

nels equally even when the threshold occurs only on one channel. Enable this feature when working with stereo tracks such as overhead drum mikes or piano to avoid shift of the stereo image.

The **Attack Time** fields are expressed in milliseconds and determine the time required for the effect to react to amplitudes that exceed the thresholds, and **Release Time** determines the time required for the effect to return the amplitude to the normal level. The attack time is how quickly the effect reacts and takes action, and the release time is how quickly the effect lets go and stops altering the signal. The **Lookahead Time** field sets the time the effect scans the upcoming signal, causing the attack to begin before the threshold is reached.

> **TIP!!** Attack and release times can have a drastic impact on the result of the sound. Fast attacks on transient sound such as drums can steal the initial attack of the drum and result in a bland sound. Short release times can cause an instrument or voice to have a "pumping" sound as the effect turns on and off.

The **Band Limiting** tab contains only two fields, the **Low Cutoff** and **High Cutoff** fields. Values entered in these fields determine the range or band of frequencies that will be affected by the effect. A frequent use of this is feature is de-essing.

The presets included with Audition are not only a good starting point for using this effect and building your own, but also a way to help familiarize you with the effect parameters. While experimenting with this effect, try enabling the **Create Envelope Only (preview as noise)** checkbox and vary the effect settings. The waveform is substituted with noises, but it will preview the setting changes in real time.

8.19 *Dynamics Processing options in the Attack/ Release tab*

8.20 *Dynamics Processing effect displayed with the Band Limiting tab*

Envelope

The **Envelope** effect provides a method of adjusting the shape or envelope of a waveform by placing nodes on the graph control. The duration of the effect is determined by the waveform selection and displayed on the X-axis, and the amplitude is set as a percentage of the waveform's original amplitude in the **Amplification** field and displayed on the Y-axis.

The **Envelope** effect can be a handy as well as creative tool for placing long fades on tracks. A small bump or short, gentle increase in level toward the end of the fade can be a tasteful effect. Visual adjustment of the attack and release are also useful for trimming sound effects or shaping a sound generated in Audition.

Hard Limiting

Hard Limiting prevents the amplitude from exceeding the value in the **Limit Max Amplitude to** field. It is recommended that this value is set to –0.1 to avoid clipping in 16-bit mode, but a value of –0.5 is safer. The overall amplitude of the waveform can be adjusted before limiting by entering a value in the **Boost Input by** field. The **Lookahead Time** and **Release Time** field values determine the attack and release of the effect. Recommended value ranges are listed next to the fields; however, each waveform is unique, and critical listening should be used when previewing the effect. The **Link Left and Right** checkbox forces equal adjustment of stereo channels. The stereo image of tracks recorded in stereo such as drum tracks, piano, or mixdowns can be destroyed if each channel is limited independently. Clicking the **Gather Statistics Now** button displays minimum and maximum amplitudes and the percentage of clipped samples if limiting were not applied using the current settings.

In Figure 8.22, the values in the **Left** column show the peaks before limiting, and the values in the **Right** column show the signal after limiting. No increase in amplitude was applied in

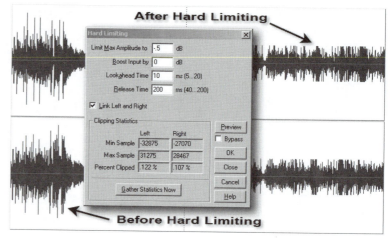

8.22 The Hard Limiting dialog box

order to show the effects of limiting. Notice that the waveform peaks appear uniform after limiting, almost like a new haircut.

Normalize

The **Normalize** function is one of the greatest features introduced with digital audio. Selecting **Normalize** scans the selected waveform and locates the sample with the greatest value. The value of the sample is subtracted from the value of digital zero, and the amplitude of the entire

---

Envelope

One of the key components of sound is the envelope. It is what helps distinguish one sound from another. The envelope is composed of four basic elements; Attack, Decay, Sustain, and Release and is commonly referred to by the acronym ADSR. The attack of a sound typically provides the sound's identity. For example, a gunshot or percussion instrument have very fast attacks, but a siren starts slowly as the rotor begins spinning. Decay follows the attack as the sound begins to fade. A drum has a quick decay, but a woodwind instrument generates a longer decay. As the decay reaches a relatively constant level, it is described as sustain. The last segment of the envelope is called the release as the sustained sounds begins to diminish. Figure 8.21 shows the components of a simple ADSR envelope; however, the envelope of a sound is usually much more complex than this example.

8.21 Create Envelope dialog box

selection is increased by that amount. The result is a waveform boosted to the maximum level obtainable without causing clipping or distortion.

The **Normalize** function offers four options. The default setting will normalize the waveform referenced to 0dBFS; however, alternate values can be set by enabling the **Normalize to** checkbox and entering the desired value. **Disabling the Decibels Format** checkbox displays the **Normalize to** field value as a percentage of the maximum achievable level. **Normalize L/R Equally** should remain enabled unless there is a specific requirement to normalize channels individually. Disabling this option can result in an unbalanced stereo mix.

8.23 The Normalize dialog box

Normalization should be one of the last effects applied to a waveform.

Pan/Expand

The **Pan/Expand** effect is used to manipulate the stereo image by adding the left and right channels to simulate the presence of a center channel and using the difference between the channels to expand or narrow the stereo image. The waveform selection determines the *X*-axis or duration of the effect of both graph controls. The node position on *Y*-axis of the **Center Channel Pan** graph determines the placement of the center channel in the stereo image. The node position on *Y*-axis of the **Stereo Expand** graph determines the amplitude of the left minus right channel with 100 percent as the normal state.

Pan/Expand has its applications, and it can be very cool, but using it on a stereo mix is simply introducing phase inconsistencies that can negate hours of hard work and care in creating the final mix. This is an effect that requires experimentation and judicious use.

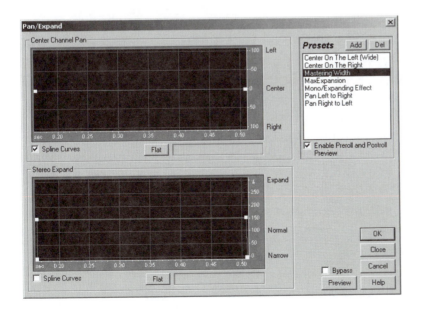

8.24 The Pan/Expand dialog box

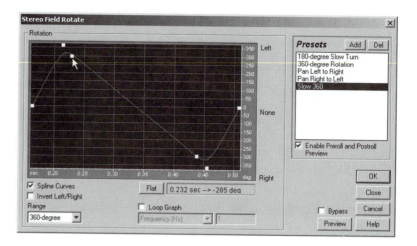

*8.25 The Stereo Field Rotate
dialog box*

Stereo Field Rotate

The **Stereo Field Rotate** effect rotates the stereo image by 45°, 90°, 180°, or 360° through the **Range** pop-up menu or any value up to 360° by adjusting the *Y*-axis position of the node. The *Y*-axis scale reflects the selected range. The *X*-axis displays the duration of the waveform selection unless the **Loop Graph** checkbox is enabled. When the **Loop Graph** checkbox is enabled, the effect is looped for the duration of the selected waveform, and the loop length is set in from the pop-up menu and numeric field under the **Loop Graph** checkbox. The loop length duration value can be entered in seconds, frequency, tempo, or total cycles depending upon the pop-up menu selection.

Again, this effect requires experimentation and should be used carefully to preserve the stereo image.

Delay Effects

The **Delay Effects** category includes effects or transforms that use methods of delaying the signal to simulate reflected sound waves such as the echo heard in a large hall or the reverberation in a gymnasium. These effects are frequently called **Echo** and **Reverb**. The difference between echo and reverb is subtle. Echo is usually referred to as distinct and recognizable repetitions of the original sound, and reverberation is generally considered as a repetition of the original sound repeated so closely in time that a single echo or repetition of the original sound is not discernible.

Other effects in this category use small amounts of delay time to phase-cancel the signal or some components of the signal at given intervals, causing an artificial or robotic sound. These effects are called **Chorusing, Flanging,** and **Phasing.**

The attack or shape of the waveform will affect most transforms or effects, but as a general guideline, delays less than 15 milliseconds are useful for phasing effects where the ear perceives the original signal and the delayed signal as a single entity. Delays of 15 to about 35 milliseconds cause flanging or chorusing effects where the ear can begin to distinguish discrete sounds. Delays greater than 35 milliseconds generate echo or repeated sounds that are softer in amplitude but recognizable as individual sounds.

Chorus

The **Chorus** effect has become one of the more popular delay-based effects for musical applications and can be used to add a subtle texture to the mix or sci-fi sounds with extreme parameters. As the name implies, the effect attempts to simulate multiple voices or variations of the source signal as heard in a chorus by applying changes to the timing, intonation, and vibrato of the voices.

The **Thickness** field sets the numbers of voices used in the effect. Adding voices will add a thicker quality to the source just as adding people to a choir; however, as the number of voices increases, the quality and clarity of the source can be compromised. One of the qualities of a chorus is the slight time differences and pitch variations between singers. The **Max Delay** field limits the amount of delay time variation the effect uses to simulate this quality. As with the **Thickness** setting, higher values will affect the tightness and quality of the effect. The **Delay Rate** controls the modulation of the delay and results in variations of each voice as the pitch of the sample is increased or decreased over time. A higher **Delay Rate** value increases the amount of pitch variation. Feedback controls the amount of affected signal routed back into

8.26 *The Chorus dialog box*

the effect. This functions in the same way as microphone feedback, and although the effect can be unusual, the ringing is generally not found in anything other than a sci-fi effect. The **Spread** amount adds an additional delay to each voice. Again, high values are analogous to a poorly rehearsed choir. **Vibrato Depth** and **Vibrato Rate** set the amplitude variation over time.

The **Average Left & Right** checkbox controls whether the channels are averaged before applying the effect. The stereo image remains intact if the checkbox is disabled. Use of **Add Binaural Cues** is not recommended unless the output is intended only for headphone listening. The **Narrow Field/Wide Field** slider affects the placement of the chorus effect in the stereo image.

The output balance between the **Dry Out** (original unaffected signal) and the **Wet Out** (chorused signal) is adjusted by the corresponding sliders. The original signal without the effects can be heard during preview by selecting the **Bypass** checkbox. Enabling the **Highest Quality (but slow)** checkbox applies the effect in a high-quality mode; however, the effect can burden the CPU.

Delay

The **Delay** effect is the simplest effect in the **Delay Effects** group. It creates a single echo of the selected waveform. The time between the original sound and the delayed signal is controlled with a separate **Delay** slider for each channel. One of the channel controls is dimmed when the effect is applied to single channel or mono selection. Delay values can also be entered directly into the field next to the **Delay** slider with the time format displayed in beats, milliseconds, or samples according to the current time display format. Use this feature to create a delay that coincides with the tempo. The maximum delay value is 500 milliseconds. The delay effect also provides the ability to invert the phase of each channel by enabling the **Invert** checkbox.

 If you don't make sure that the waveform is long enough to accommodate any delay-based effects, the effect may end abruptly. If the waveform is too short, press the **End** key and select **Generate > Silence** to add more length or dead time to the waveform before applying the effect.

8.27 The Delay dialog box

8.28 *This Dynamic Delay effect shows a smooth increase in the amount of delay to about 10 milliseconds while the amount of feedback increases to 80 percent with a bump between 2 and 3 seconds into the waveform.*

Dynamic Delay

The **Dynamic Delay** effect allows the amount of delay and effect feedback to vary over the duration of the waveform. The X-axis of both the delay and feedback graph controls display the duration of the selection. The Y-axis of the delay graph displays the time in milliseconds, and the Y-axis of the feedback graph shows the percentage of the effect being returned and mixed into the effect. The slider control adjusts the ratio of original versus delayed signal, and the Invert checkbox reverses the signal phase.

Enabling the **Loop Graphs** checkbox changes the duration of the effect based on the **Frequency**, **Period**, and **Total Cycles** fields. The graphs are updated to reflect the loop length. Entering a positive value into the **Stereo Curve Delay** causes the right channel to be delayed by the same value while entering a negative number delays the left channel.

Echo

The **Echo** effect is a simple but powerful tool. The options are few, but they're more than adequate for most audio and video postproduction work.

Individual channel sliders control the rate of decay, length of delay, and initial echo volume. The amplitude of each consecutive echo is set to the decay percentage of the previous echo. For example, if the decay value is 90, the amplitude of the first repeat or echo of the sound would be at 90 percent. The amplitude of the next echo would be at 90 percent of the amplitude of the previous echo and so forth until the echo fades out. A value of 100 percent results in endless echo, because the echo will never decay. The delay values determine the time between each echo and the initial echo volume adjusts the volume of the echo in relation to the original sound. The **Lock Left/Right** checkbox forces the channel controls to function in tandem and prevents separate adjustment of individual channels. Enabling **Echo Bounce**

8.29 *Echo effect provides an eight-band filter to help simulate room acoustics on the echo.*

swaps the echo in the left and right channels on each successive repeat. **Echo Bounce** is not an obvious effect in stereo unless the parameters of one channel are altered. Otherwise, even though the same effect is bouncing between channels, the result is same sound in both channels.

In addition to the decay, delay, and amplitude settings, the **Echo** effect allows equalization or filtering of the echo. An eight-band subtractive filter provides the ability to attenuate the preset frequency bands by up to 15dB. Reducing low frequencies can help approximate an acoustic environment with hard surfaces, and reducing high frequencies emulates a room with absorbent materials. The same filter is applied to each successive echo, so any changes to equalization become apparent quickly.

The **Continue echo beyond selection** checkbox allows the echo to be extended past the selected waveform without adding the effect to the next segment. It is not unusual for a broadcast producer to request an echo effect on a single word or a few words in a radio spot. The **Continue echo beyond selection** is an easy way to accomplish this effect. Select the word in the waveform, set the desired echo settings (hopefully you will have created a few presets for just such occasions), and apply the effect with the checkbox enabled. The echo will continue under the next sentence without affecting that sentence. Keep in mind that this is a destructive effect in **Edit View**.

8.30 The Echo Chamber dialog box

Echo Chamber

The **Echo Chamber** provides a number of variables to simulate the acoustics of a room; however, developing and applying this effect, especially as the room size is increased, requires some patience.

The concept behind the effect is to build a virtual room by entering the desired room dimensions in the **Room Size** fields. Values in the **Damping Factors** fields determine the reflectivity of the walls, ceiling, and floor. A value of zero is completely absorbent, and a value of one is completely reflective. The **Damping Frequency** field limits the maximum frequency that will be reflected. Increasing the **Damping Factors** and **Damping Frequency** values creates a live room with harder, more-reflective surfaces such as bare concrete or tile, and lower values absorb more of the high frequencies and deaden the room.

The effect also allows placement of a virtual stereo sound source and stereo microphones. The **Signal Source and Microphone Placement** matrix allows you to position the source and microphones relative to the left wall, back wall, and ceiling. Increasing the distance between the source and microphone(s) will increase the audibility of the effect. The computations required to simulate a stereo source and pickup can be a substantial load on the CPU. Enabling the **Mix Left/Right Into Single Source** loses the stereo miking effect, but it also cuts the processing time by 50 percent.

When customizing the **Echo Chamber** effect, begin with a lower **Echoes** value and compensate with higher **Intensity** value. This will reduce the CPU load and make the preview available sooner. Once the settings are in the ballpark, increase the **Echoes** value to around 20,000 and the **Intensity** value to 15 percent. Preview the effect and increase the **Echoes** values if the echo is not satisfactory.

In the analog domain, flanging was created by feeding the same audio to two different tape machines and pressing on one of the tape flanges to slow the tape. Because the signals were combined, the delayed signal from the slowed machine caused a continuously varying phase cancellation. Hence the term "flange."

8.31 The Flanger dialog box

Flanger

The **Flanger** effect is a great effect when used sparingly. Although flanging was not the technique used to create the Star Wars light saber sound, it could have been. In fact, flanging and phasing effects are excellent tools to create electronic and sci-fi sound effects.

Setting the **Original-Expanded** slider at 50 percent combines equal amounts of the original source and the effect, but interesting effects can result when the proportion is varied. The **Initial Mix Delay and Final Mix Delay** controls determine when flanging will begin and end in relation to the original. **Stereo Phasing** is used to rotate the delay setting of the left and right channels. For example, a value of zero starts both channels at the same **Initial Mix Delay** value. Entering a value of 180 starts one channel at the **Initial Mix Delay** value and the other channel at the **Final Mix Delay** value. The amount of effect returned is determined as a percentage using the **Feedback** slider. The **Rate** section controls the rate at which the effect cycles. Entering a value in any one of the three fields automatically updates the corresponding values of the other fields. The **Mode** section contains three checkboxes that can alter the effect significantly. Take the time to experiment with them.

Full Reverb

The **Full Reverb** effect is versatile; however, it is also the most processor-dependent and complex of the reverb effects. Although the **Preview** function works, a delay will occur while the processing occurs.

Three tabs control various parameters and divide the parameters into groups by function. The balance between **Original Signal (dry)**, **Early Reflections**, and the **Reverb (wet)** are set by slider controls. The **Combine Source Left and Right** checkbox should be enabled to reduce processing time or when using a mono source.

8.32 The General Reverb tab of the Full Reverb dialog box

The **General Reverb** tab uses sliders to adjust the basic characteristics of the reverb (see Figure 8.32). The **Total Length** slider sets the time the reverb effect takes to decay or fade out. The **Attack Time** slider adjusts the time required for the reverb to climax. The **Diffusion** and **Perception** sliders affect the quality and smoothness of the reverb.

The **Early Reflections** tab controls the construction of a simulated room. The **Room Size** slider is measured in cubic meters; width and depth are determined by the **Dimension** slider. Display of the simulated room dimensions, reverb length, and attack time are instantly updated below the sliders.

The **Left/Right Location** slider positions the source in the stereo image. Enabling the **Include Direct** checkbox delays the **Original Signal** to match the direction of the early reflections. This affects the apparent origin of the source in the stereo image. The **High-Pass Cutoff**

8.33 The Early Reflections tab of the Full Reverb dialog box

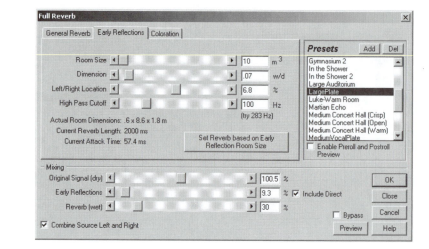

8.34 *The Coloration tab of the Full Reverb dialog box*

slider rolls off unwanted low frequencies, and a suggested setting may be displayed below the field as the room parameters are changed.

The **Set Reverb based on Early Reflection Room Size** button allows automatic calculation of the reverb parameters based on the settings in Early Reflections tab.

The **Coloration** tab provides basic equalization control with **Low Shelf**, **Mid Band**, and **High Shelf** sliders. The vertical sliders control boost and cut, and the **Q** field accepts a numeric value to set the **Mid Band Q** or width of the frequencies affected surrounding the center frequency. The equalization can also be adjusted by dragging the dots on the graph. The **ms** field affects the time for the reverb to decay following the coloration curve.

Multitap Delay

The **Multitap Delay** dialog box can look intimidating upon first view, but the effect is rather simple to set up. This is not to say that setup cannot become very complex. After all, the effect supports 10 delay units, each with stereo imaging, filtering, delay, and offset options. It is worth spending a few minutes getting familiar with this effect, particularly for music production. A couple of the stock effects provide good starting points.

Up to a total of 10 delay units can be used simultaneously. Delay units are added or removed with the **Add New and Remove** buttons. They are listed in numeric order with the parameters displayed for each unit. Highlighting a delay unit changes the color of the device's name to red and enables the options for that unit. The **Offset** slider determines the number of milliseconds before the effect starts, and the **Delay** slider controls the length of the delay. The **Feedback** slider controls the amount of the effect returned. Enabling the **Allpass Feedback** checkbox reduces any DC component that may occur. The **Low-Cut** and **High-Cut** filters settings are retained for each delay unit, and each can be assigned placement in the stereo image with the radio buttons.

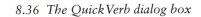

8.35 Multitap Delay dialog box

QuickVerb

The **QuickVerb** effect uses an algorithm that requires less processing than the other built-in reverb effects. As with all other effects, values are controlled with the sliders or entering the value directly into the field beside the slider. The unit of measurement for **Room Size** is not specified, but numbers well over 100 can be used. The **Decay** value is expressed in milliseconds; higher values result in a longer trail out of the reverberation. The **Diffusion** slider varies the smoothness of the echo, and the **High** and **Low Cutoff** sliders filter frequencies above and below the control values respectively.

Use this effect for board mixes as you lay tracks or even rough mixes, but **Reverb** and **Full Reverb** are better choices for use on final mixes.

8.36 The QuickVerb dialog box

8.37 The Reverb dialog box

Reverb

Reverb provides usable presets right out of the box. The algorithm is different than **Quick-Verb** and requires more CPU power. Although the **Preview** mode functions, real-time adjustments during preview are disabled. The **Bypass** function works during **Preview**, but some patience may be required depending upon the CPU speed and the effect settings.

In addition to the **Mixing** sliders that allow balancing the **Original Signal** (dry) with the **Reverb Signal** (wet), four other sliders are provided. The top slider sets the time the reverberation will take to fade out. Smaller values simulate smaller rooms. The next slider determines the reverberation attack time—in other words, how quickly the reverb will achieve its maximum amplitude. Decreasing the **High-Frequency Absorption Time** value reduces the time required to attenuate high-frequency reverb content. Increase this value to liven the room. The **Perception** slider adjusts the smoothness of the reverb with lower values sounding smoother. The **Combine Source Left and Right** checkbox can be enabled to mono the source and reduce the processing requirements.

Studio Reverb

The **Studio Reverb** effect is a compromise between **QuickVerb** and **Full Reverb**, offering real-time processing in **Edit View** and **Multitrack View**. Although **Studio Reverb** offers more control over the effects settings than **QuickVerb** and the sound quality is better, it is not quite up to par with the sound quality achieved using **Reverb** or **Full Reverb**.

The **Room Size** slider determines the size of the room, with higher values increasing the room size. **Decay** sets the duration for the reverb to fade out, and larger values in the **Early Reflection** field increase the amount of echo. The **Stereo Width** slider controls the effect allocation between left and right channels, with a value of one being mono. **Low and High Cut** filters affect only the reverb signal.

The **Damping** slider is used to attenuate higher frequencies over time, with higher values offering a warmer, more muffled sound. The **Diffusion** slider imitates a room with hard surfaces; higher values create a room with more absorption. **Wet and Dry** sliders control the balance of reverb or **Wet** signal to the original or **Dry** signal. It's usually a good idea to keep the combined percentage of **Wet** and **Dry** signals to 100 percent or less.

Sweeping Phaser

The **Sweeping Phaser** effect brings back those glory days of the 70s and provides another tool for improving poor vocal performances and creating sound effects.

8.38 *The Studio Reverb dialog box*

The **Center Frequency** slider sets the center of the frequency sweep. The **Depth** slider controls the width of the sweep from the center frequency. The **Sweeping Rate** slider adjusts the duration of the sweep cycle and can be entered in Hertz or cycles, in milliseconds, or in beats per minute to match a tempo. The effect offers a choice of **Sinusoidal** or **Triangular** sweep modes. **Sinusoidal** is a softer sweep. **Logarithmic** or linear sweeps are also selectable. **Linear Frequency Sweep** provides a smoother sweep. A **Low Pass** filter can be selected, although **Band Pass** is typically used. Selecting the **Low Pass** filter will prevent the effect from being

8.39 *The Sweeping Phaser dialog box*

applied to any frequencies above the center frequency. Adjustment of the effect parameters can cause significant variations in overall amplitude, so the **Master Gain** field is provided to compensate for gain changes.

DirectX

Third-party DirectX plug-ins appear under this submenu. There are some requirements to enable new DirectX plug-ins. See "Third-Party Plug-Ins " on page 213 toward the end of this chapter for more information.

Filters

Filters are used to remove or equalize bands or frequencies from the waveform. Eight equalization-based filters, each with a specific specialty, are included in this group.

Center Channel Extractor

The **Center Channel Extractor** effect can be used with varying degrees of success to boost or attenuate frequencies common to both left and right channels. For example, many recordings have the lead vocal panned center. Because the vocal is centered, equal amounts of the frequency content are present in both channels, and the **Center Channel Extractor** effect would be effective on the vocal. This is another vocal eliminator effect; however, it tends to work better than most.

This filter has a number of controls. Most applications will require the **Get Audio Phased At** control to be set to **Center**; however, surround-sound audio can be extracted by setting the pop-up menu to **Surround**. The custom setting permits entry of specific phase and panning settings. A preset **Frequency Range** determines the frequencies that are affected and can be chosen from a pop-up menu, or a range can be entered by selecting **Custom**. The **Center Channel Level** slider and **Volume Boost Mode** sliders checkbox enable adjustment of the effect balance,

8.40 The Center Channel Extractor dialog box

and the **Crossover** slider alters the separation between center channel information and the mix. Higher **Phase Discrimination** values tend to be more effective for center channel extraction, and lower values tend to be more effective for center channel attenuation. Lower values in the **Amplitude Discrimination** field cause the effect to be more dependent on the amplitude of the signal than phase, and higher values cause the opposite. The default **FFT Size** value is 8192, although higher values may result in better results. The **Overlays** field sets the number of FFT samples that are overlapped. Values of 3–9 are recommended. The **Interval Size** and **Window Width** values perform the same task. Interval sizes of 10–50 milliseconds or window widths of 30–100 percent typically produce acceptable results.

Play with this filter and the settings. The results will vary according to the waveform's stereo content, but it offers a good chance of returning usable results.

Dynamic EQ

The **Dynamic EQ** filter applies changes in EQ over the duration of the selected waveform. When the **Loop Graph** checkbox is enabled, the available values in the pop-up menu for duration are a fixed **Period, Frequency, Tempo,** or **Total Cycles.** Graph controls on the **Frequency, Gain,** and **Q (bandwidth)** tabs are used to adjust respective parameters.

> ***Filter Types:*** There are primarily two types of digital filters in use today. The Finite Impulse Response (FIR) and Infinite Impulse Response (IIR). IIR filter is more efficient and claims to produce superior results; however, it is harder to implement and less stable.

> **TIP!!** Equalization will frequently affect the amplitude of a waveform. Make sure you leave headroom for level increases when applying filters.

FFT Filter

The **FFT** (Fast Fourier Transform) **Filter** can handle many tough equalization tasks as well as the simple ones. The stocks presets can be handy for postproduction work and are good starting points for customizing your own presets (see Figure 8.44).

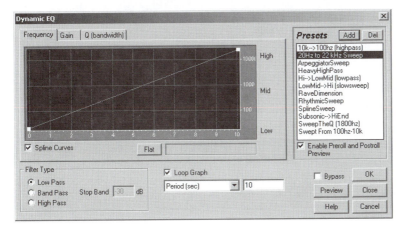

8.41 *The Frequency tab in the Dynamic EQ dialog box with a dynamic sweep from 20Hz to 22kHz over a duration of 10 seconds*

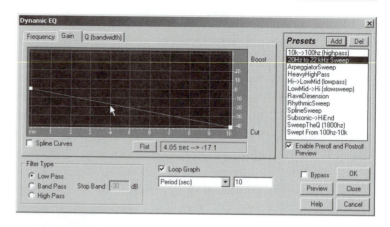

8.42 *The Gain tab in the Dynamic EQ dialog box shows dynamic gain attenuation of 40dB over a duration of 10 seconds.*

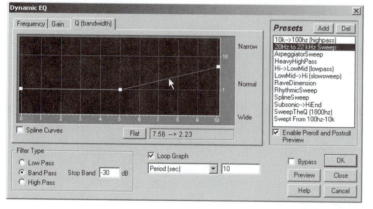

8.43 *The Q tab in the Dynamic EQ dialog box shows Q held at 1 for 5 seconds and gradually changing to a Q of 5 by the end of the period.*

8.44 *The FFT Filter dialog box*

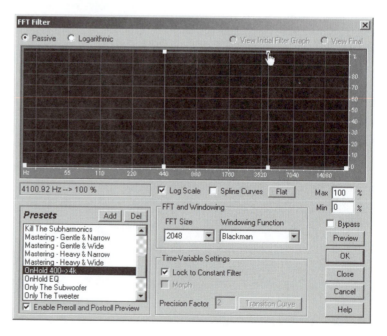

Changes to the equalization curve are made using nodes on the graph control. As with other graph controls in Audition, current cursor data is displayed below the graph, and right-clicking on a node presents a dialog box for precise adjustments. The X-axis displays frequency on a linear or log scale. The **Log Scale** checkbox can be enabled for easier low-frequency adjustments. The Y-axis displays boost or attenuation as a percentage when the **Passive** radio button is selected or in decibels when **Logarithmic** is chosen. The **Max** and **Min** fields set the Y-axis scale limits, with zero always representing no change. The **FFT Size** field controls the quality of filtering. Recommended values range from 1,024 to 8,196. Increasing the **FFT Size** value results in higher quality filtering. The **Blackman and Hamming Windowing Functions** work well for most applications.

One of the surprising features of this filter is the ability to apply dynamic filtering and even morphing. Disabling the **Lock to Constant Filter** checkbox enables the **View Initial Filter Graph** and **View Final** radio buttons above the graph and permit switching between the views. Additional information on use of the **Transition Curve** and **Morph** features are available in the Audition help files.

Graphic Equalizer

The **Graphic Equalizer** window contains three tabs. The first tab divides the frequency range into 10 bands at one-octave intervals. The second tab divides the range into 20 bands at one-half octave intervals. The third tab splits the range into 30 bands at one-third octave intervals. Each band can be boosted or attenuated with the slider, by clicking the arrow buttons on the top or bottom of the sliders, or entering the numeric value directly into the **Gain** field.

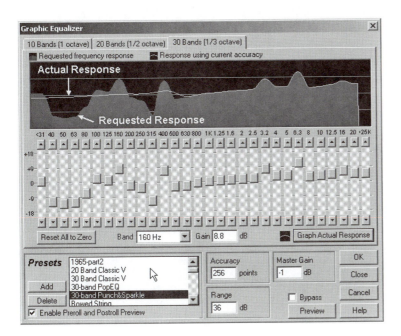

8.45 Graphic Equalizer window

The graphic equalizer has traditionally been used to compensate for the deficiencies of an audio system and room acoustics. The frequency response of the room was measured and plotted on a curve. Then the graphic equalizer was adjusted to offset the peaks or dips of the room. The result was intended to flatten or equalize the frequency response.

Changes are instantly reflected on the graph. The slider range can be set from 4–180dB in the **Range** field. The **Band** value can be selected by clicking on the desired slider or selecting it from the pop-up menu. The equalizer can be returned to a flat response at any time by clicking the **Reset All to Zero** button. The **Master Gain** field provides a means of boosting or attenuating the amplitude as is frequently required when equalization is applied.

The graphic equalizer is a **Finite Impulse Response (FIR)** filter and offers more accuracy than an **Infinite Impulse Response (IIR)** filter. Clicking the **Graph Actual Response** button displays a line on the graph showing the frequency response using the current value in the **Accuracy** field. Increase the value and click the button again. Repeat the process until the requested frequency response shown in solid blue and the actual response shown in light blue line match. Lower frequencies require higher accuracy values, and higher accuracy values require more processing time. In Figure 8.45, the equalizer is set for the lowest accuracy level. The solid shaded area on the graph shows the requested frequency response. Notice the disparity between the line showing the actual frequency response and the requested frequency response. The **Accuracy** setting should be set to about 15,000 to handle the frequency response of the low frequencies.

Graphic Phase Shifter

The **Graphic Phase Shifter** effect allows you to shift the phase of frequencies selected on the graph control. The X-axis can be displayed as a linear frequency scale or a logarithmic frequency scale. The X-axis displays the phase in degrees. The effect quality and processing time are increased as the **FFT Size** value is increased.

In addition to driving a mastering engineer crazy by placing selective frequencies out of phase on one of the tracks, the **Graphic Phase Shifter** effect has the potential to correct phase inconsistencies that may occur during location recording.

8.46 The Graphic Phase Shifter dialog box

Notch Filter

The **Notch** filter was designed to remove narrow bands of frequencies. It can reduce or eliminate 50/60 cycle hum and harmonics and has checkboxes to enable **DTMF (Dual Tone Multi-Frequency)** tones used by telephones. This feature can be handy in preparing material for radio broadcast. A maximum of six frequency bands can be attenuated at one time. Enabling the checkbox allows editing of the **Frequency** and **Attenuation** fields. The **Fix Attenuations** to checkbox forces the same amount of attenuation on every frequency band. Three **Notch Width** values are available: **Narrow, Very Narrow,** and **Super Narrow,** providing filtering with a slope of 12dB (second order) to 36 dB (sixth order) per octave.

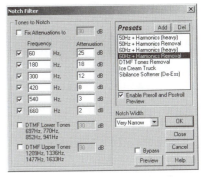

8.47 The Notch filter dialog box

 Maximum attenuation levels of 30dB for **Narrow**, 60dB for **Very Narrow**, and 90dB for **Super Narrow** **Notch Width** are recommended. Exceeding these guidelines can result in attenuation of a wider range of frequencies than expected.

Parametric Equalizer

The **Parametric Equalizer** effect has been the traditional tool of choice for most engineers. The reason for this preference is the versatility of the parameters.

Adjustment of up to five frequency ranges can be enabled simultaneously and are engaged by clicking the checkbox in the **Center Frequency** section. The graph control provides an easy method of adjusting settings. Dragging any of the nodes adjusts the amplitude and/or frequency. Adjustment can also be accomplished with the corresponding sliders or entering the numeric value directly in the associated field. The width of the frequency band can be set using **Constant Width** expressed in Hertz or Constant Q. Either value can be edited directly in the **Width** field. **Low Shelf Cutoff** and **High Shelf Cutoff** are always enabled and are adjusted by the graph nodes, sliders, or numeric input. A **Master Gain** adjustment is provided to compensate for changes in level caused by the filtering (see Figure 8.48).

 Filters, such as the **Parametric Equalizer** effect, can be used to help locate problem frequencies such as a particular resonance or noise. To find the frequency, set a high Q and maximum boost on one of the center frequency controls. Sweep the node across the graph until the problem frequency is very audible. Once the frequency is found, adjust the Q and attenuation to taste.

8.48 *The Parametric Equalizer dialog box showing two different Q values*

Quick Filter

The **Quick Filter** offers an eight-band graphic equalizer that can be used to make static changes in equalization or smooth frequency adjustment across the duration of the selection. The **Lock to these settings only** checkbox determines whether the **Quick Filter** is in static or dynamic mode. Once the checkbox is disabled, the tab labels change to **Initial Settings** and **Final Settings**. In the dynamic mode, the equalization will transform smoothly from the initial settings to the final settings. **Master Gain** sliders control the overall amplitude of each channel. Enabling the **Lock L/R** checkbox forces uniform gain changes to both channels. Gain changes are not dynamic. One drawback to the **Quick Filter** is that the Q or the slope is very wide and affects the entire waveform.

8.49 *The Quick Filter dialog box*

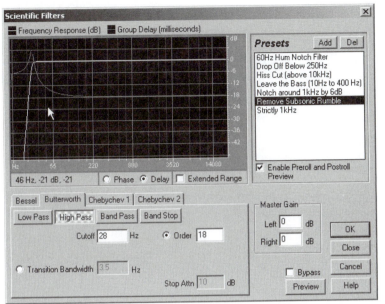

8.50 *The Scientific Filters dialog box*

Dynamic filters such as **Quick Filter** can be used on voice talent that tends to drift off mic during a recording to gradually compensate for the change on tonal quality. It can also be an aid in smoothing transitions when revising voiceover recordings.

Scientific Filters

The **Scientific Filters** effect offers extremely precise filtering not available in any of the other filters. As the name implies, the application and setup of this filter is beyond the needs of the typical user. These filters use IIR (Infinite Impulse Response) filters and are used for designing filters or in situations where extremely accurate filtering is needed such as notching or removing only a specific frequency band.

One of four different types of filters is available: **Bessel, Butterworth, Chebychev 1,** and **Chebychev 2.** These filters are known as high-order filters because of the steep attenuation slope. The settings provide a high degree of filtering control. Note that this is one of the few graph controls that do not use nodes for adjustments (see Figure 8.50).

The Audition help files provide more details regarding the options and use of these filters.

Noise Reduction

A few years ago, if someone told me that it would be possible to remove distortion from a track, I would have thought they were crazy and shoved a copy of the *The New Audio Cyclopedia* into their hands. Today, Audition makes it possible to minimize the effects of clipping

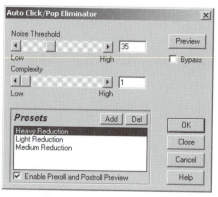

8.51 *The Auto Click/Pop Eliminator dialog box (above)*

8.52 *The Click/Pop Eliminator dialog box (right)*

with the **Clip Restoration** filter. Although it cannot restore the original signal, it can make the distortion less obvious if the clipping is very light. Four other noise-reduction filters provide the ability to remove clicks, ticks, pops, hiss, and other forms of noise. Each of the five filters has a specific forte. Developing skills using these filters requires an investment of time, but they can provide surprising results with little effort. Discussing the function of each parameter along with how they interact with each other and techniques for using the filters could easily fill another chapter, so only a brief overview of each filter is provided here. The Audition help files are an excellent source of additional information on filter functions and usage.

Auto Click/Pop Eliminator

The **Auto Click/Pop Eliminator** is the easiest-to-use filter of the **Noise Reduction** group (see Figure 8.51). It has only two controls. The **Noise Threshold** adjusts the sensitivity to clicks and pops. Lower values detect more noise. A value of 35 is the default. The **Complexity** slider determines the effort used to reduce the noises, however higher values can degrade the audio. The default value is one.

Click/Pop Eliminator

The **Click/Pop Eliminator** can certainly clean up old vinyl recordings. It also does an excellent job of removing digital glitches with little user assistance and the **Fill Single Click Now** button (see Figure 8.52).

The result of filtering depends on the source content. Best results are obtained when the parameters are adjusted for each waveform. Using one of the presets or the **Auto Find All Levels** function provides a good starting point. The dialog box graphs the detection and rejection thresholds and describes the basic functions under the **Presets List**.

The F2 key and **Edit > Repeat Last Command** are quick ways to apply the **Pop/Click Eliminator** when removing multiple anomalies.

 Larger clicks and pops are displayed as vertical lines and are easier to locate using **Spectral View**.

Clip Restoration

Clip Restoration is a tool that can heal digital clipping. Clipping occurs when the audio reaches the maximum level of 0dBFS. A single sample at that level may not be heard, depending upon the audio content, but consecutive samples will be heard as an unpleasant, gritty ripping sound.

Audio files should be converted to 32-bit depth without DC offset before you try to repair clipping. The **Minimum Run Size** sets the number of consecutive clipped samples required before restoration is applied. Overhead determines the largest amplitude variance that will be considered as a consecutive clip.

Let's give the **Clip Restoration** a shot. Make sure that Audition is open in the **Edit View** mode.

1. Press **Ctrl+O** and locate the file named *Clipped Signal.wav* in *Chapter 08-Audio* directory on the CD that accompanies this book and listen to the file.

2. Select the **Effects>Clip Restoration** and press the **Gather Statistics Now** button. An analysis is run, and the **Clipping Statistics** matrix notes the percent of clipped samples in each channel.

3. Because the clipping is significant, set the **Input Attenuation** to –2.5dB.

4. Enable the **FFT Size** checkbox and enter a value of 128. **Overhead and Minimum Run Size** can remain at a value of 1.

5. Click **OK**.

8.53 The Clip Restoration dialog box

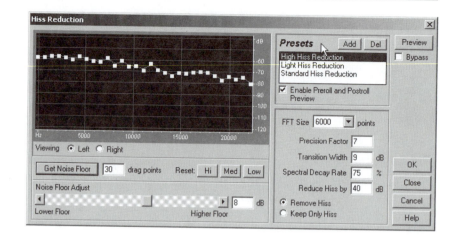

8.54 The Hiss Reduction dialog box

Success in restoring clipped signal will vary with waveform content, extent of clipping, and your experience in using filters. Remember that you are working with destructive effects in **Edit View,** so consider working on a copy of the original.

> Filtering is processor-intensive and can take a long time for larger files. Set parameters on a small selection using the **Undo** command (**Ctrl+Z**) to reverse the effect until satisfactory settings are found.

Hiss Reduction

The **Hiss Reduction** filter is designed to remove hiss such as that heard on a cassette tape. As with the other **Noise Reduction** filters, best results are obtained when the settings are adjusted for each file.

To use the filter, select a short segment (about half a second) of the source file that contains the least amount of audio other than hiss. Open the filter, select a preset, and press the **Get Noise Floor** button. This creates a sort of fingerprint of the hiss used to identify the content that should be removed and displays an adjustable curve of the fingerprint on the graph control. Use the **Preview** button to hear the audio and adjust the settings until you're satisfied. The filter will retain the settings when closed so the filter can be reopened and applied to the desired selection area.

Noise Reduction

The **Noise Reduction** filter removes broadband noise. The function is similar to the **Hiss Reduction** filter. A small segment of the noise is used to create a fingerprint or profile. The segment should be at least 1/2 second and contain as little content other than the objectionable noise as possible. Using the **Alt+N** shortcut or clicking the **Capture Profile** button takes snapshots of the current selection and creates the profile, or a previously saved profile can be used. Nodes can be used on the bottom graph to govern the percentage of reduction applied over

8.55 The Noise Reduction dialog box

the frequency spectrum. The **Noise Reduction Level** slider adjusts reduction level across the entire frequency spectrum. Noise reduction level is displayed in yellow on the upper graph control. The **Preview** button allows auditioning of changes while the profile is fine-tuned.

Capture Noise Reduction Profile

The **Capture Noise Reduction Profile** command creates a noise contour or profile for the current selection for use in the **Noise Reduction** filter. The command can be activated in several ways: pressing the **Alt+N** shortcut, double-clicking the command in the **Effects** tab of the **Organizer** window, right-clicking on the waveform and selecting **Capture Noise Reduction Profile** from the pop-up menu, or choosing **Effects>Noise Reduction>Capture Noise Reduction Profile**.

Use **Capture Noise Reduction Profile** in combination with the marquee tool in **Spectral View** to quickly limit the noise contour to a frequency band.

Special

The **Special** category is compromised of three effects. Although the **Distortion** effect does just as its name implies, **Convolution** and **Music** are not ordinary effects.

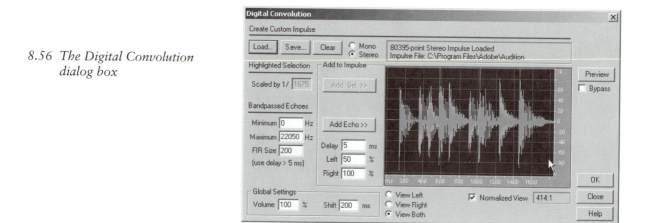

*8.56 The Digital Convolution
dialog box*

Convolution

Convolution uses an impulse to modify another waveform. The samples of the waveform are multiplied by the impulse, resulting in the waveform inheriting or assuming some of the impulse properties. It might be called morphing in a convoluted way.

The concept is that every impulse contains the full spectrum of the sound that includes characteristics such as reverb and that the impulse can be used to model another sound. This effect can create some striking and unusual results, but it takes some effort. Adobe has provided several impulse files in the *IMP* directory located in the *Audition* program directory, or you can create your own from the current selection using the **Add Sel** button. More impulse files and information on the **Convolution** filter is readily available on the Internet.

Distortion

The **Distortion** effect provides a quick and simple method of adding distortion to a waveform (see Figure 8.57). The *X*-axis displays the input signal, and the *Y*-axis shows the output signal. Adjustment is done using nodes as with most other graph controls. The effect defaults to **Symmetric** processing of the signal, meaning that both positive and negative samples will be affected the same way. Disabling the **Symmetric** checkbox allows you to apply separate settings.

Music

Music is a small utility that allows uses drag-and-drop music notation voiced with the current waveform selection as a quarter note (see Figure 8.58). Compositions can be up to 256 notes, titled and stored in the *SONGS.INI* file. The sequence can be previewed on systems configured for MIDI. See "What Is MIDI?" on page 267 in Chapter 12 for a brief overview of MIDI. Additional information regarding using the **Music** utility is available in the Audition help files.

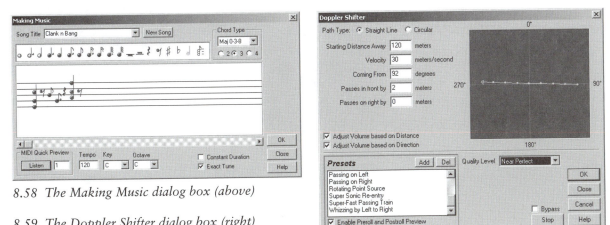

8.57 *The Distortion dialog box*

Time/Pitch

The **Time/Pitch** category provides some effects that were not easily achieved, if even possible, in the analog world. These three effects make it possible to simulate motion, bend the pitch of an instrument or voice, and stretch the audio without altering the pitch.

Doppler Shifter

The **Doppler Shifter** is one of those simple effects that is just cool. Although its application is typically limited to use on sound effects, don't rule it out to enhance station promos or an unusual intro for a track. The effect provides a number of good presets to use as a starting point (see Figure 8.59).

8.58 *The Making Music dialog box (above)*

8.59 *The Doppler Shifter dialog box (right)*

The **Doppler Shifter** simulates the sound of an object in motion by altering the pitch in relation to the location. The **Path Type** can be **Straight Line** or **Circular**. The parameters displayed depend on the path type and allow adjustment of variables such as starting location, velocity, and radius. Checkboxes enable automatic volume adjustments based on distance and direction values. Six quality levels are available. The **Perfect** quality level requires the most processing time.

> **Doppler Effect:** The concept behind this effect is based on the phenomena called the Doppler Effect. The Doppler Effect is the shift in frequency or pitch caused by compression of the sound waves as an object travels toward the listener. As the object passes by the listener, the waves are no longer compressed by the forward motion of the object, and the frequency or pitch is heard as lower.

Pitch Bender

The **Pitch Bender** effect allows you to alter the pitch over a period of time. The best example of the effect is demonstrated by the **Turntable Losing Power** preset with the pitch falling 48 semitones or four octaves within a couple of seconds.

The effect contains few parameters because most adjustment are made with nodes on the graph control. The X-axis displays the selection duration, and the Y-axis displays semitones or beats per minute depending on the range selected. The **Zero Ends** button returns the end of the effect to zero or the starting point, should the effect need to be inserted or looped. Five degrees of quality are available from the **Quality Level** pop-up menu. Perfect quality requires the most processing time.

TIP!! Right-clicking on a node allows accurate entry of semitone values. Vocal pitch can be adjusted with varying degrees of success using the **Pitch Bender** effect.

8.60 The Pitch Bender dialog box

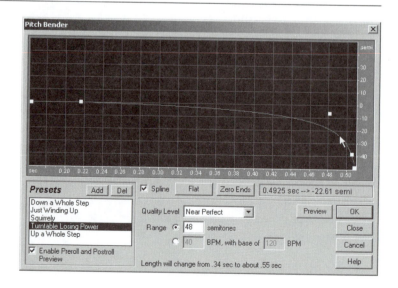

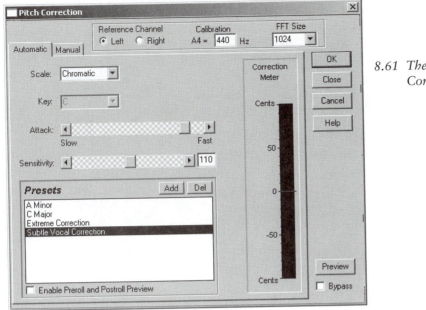

8.61 *The Automatic tab of the Pitch Correction dialog box*

Pitch Correction

The **Pitch Correction** effect functions in either automatic or manual mode and can be used to correct pitch on vocals or other periodic waveforms such as violin, cello, or saxophone. **Pitch Correction** works on mono and stereo; however, one channel must be selected to use as a reference channel. Higher **FFT Size** values generally offer better quality but require longer processing time. The **Calibration** field enables you to define a reference other than A4=440. The **Pitch Correction** effect functions most accurately when used on short phrases.

The **Automatic** tab of the **Pitch Correction** effect offers relatively few controls. The **Scale** pop-up menu permits selection of **Chromatic, Major,** and **Minor** scales and keys. Major and minor scales can result in more defined results. The **Attack** slider determines how quickly the effect corrects the pitch. Slower attacks usually sound more natural. The **Sensitivity** slider sets the threshold that triggers pitch correction and is expressed in cents. There are 100 cents per semitone. Therefore, a setting of 25 means the pitch would have to be more than 25 cents sharp of flat from the target pitch before the effect would make a correction. The **Correction Meter** displays correction during preview. Positive values indicate that the pitch is flat, and negative numbers indicate that the pitch is sharp.

The **Manual** tab of the **Pitch Correction** dialog box allows much greater accuracy in making pitch corrections than the **Automatic** tab. The top graph, called the pitch reference graph, displays the original pitch profile in red and pitch corrections in green. Pitch adjustments are made using nodes on the pitch edit graph (see Figure 8.62).

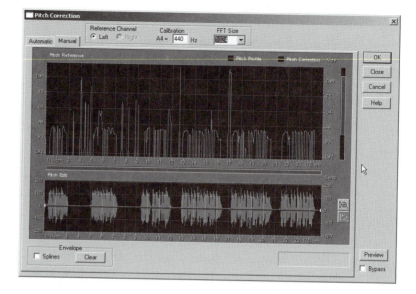

8.62 *The Manual tab of the Pitch Correction dialog box*

Stretch

The **Stretch** effect enables you to alter the pitch or duration of a selection. Compressing or expanding the time can be accomplished without altering the pitch by selecting the **Time Stretch (preserves pitch)** radio button and adjusting the **Stretch** slider. The desired change can also be entered directly into the **Ratio** field or **Length** field. The **Transpose** pop-up menu allows adjustment in semitones. The **Pitch Shift (preserves tempo)** radio button works in the same manner, maintaining the selection duration. The **Resample (preserves neither)** radio button alters both pitch and duration. Three levels of quality are available. **High Precision** requires longer processing time. The **Choose appropriate defaults** checkbox allows Audition to determine the best splicing frequency and overlapping. The value in the **Splicing Frequency**

8.63 *The Constant Stretch tab of the Stretch dialog box*

field determines the number slices of audio that are inserted or removed to alter the time scale. Higher values produce more precise results; however, audible artifacts are more likely to occur. Overlapping sets the percentage of slices that overlap. Overlapping smooths the slicing but tends to sound artificial at higher values. Use the automatic settings as a starting point and alter them if necessary. The **Gliding Stretch** tab enables a dynamic transition between the **Initial** slider and **Final** slider values.

 The length of radio and TV spots can be changed by selecting the **Time Stretch** (preserves pitch) mode and entering the desired length. Variations of 7–10 percent can usually be made without objectionable artifacts from the stretch; however, results depend on the content and the values in the **Pitch** and **Time** settings.

 Stretching tracks in **Edit View** is destructive. The effect can be applied in **Multitrack View** nondestructively.

Unsupported

Fortunately, Audition is not the only application that uses DirectX and VST plug-ins. Unfortunately, not all plug-ins were meant for use with Audition or other applications. Unsupported DirectX, DXi, VST, VSTi plug-ins will show up under this submenu.

VST

Audition supports VST (Virtual Studio Technology) plug-ins. Audition automatically scans and adds any VST plug-ins located in the *Steinberg* directory in the *Program Files* directory. Audition will also automatically find and load Adobe Premiere VST effects if Adobe Premiere Pro is installed on the system. Additional VST plug-ins can be added by selecting **Effects>Add/Remove VST Directory**. It may be necessary to select **Effects>Refresh Effects List** to see any added plug-ins.

Add/Remove VST Directory

The **Add/Remove VST Directory** window is used to manage VST plug-in directories. To add VST plug-ins, click the **Add** button and locate the directory that contains the plug-in. Audition will scan the listed directory and subdirectories for VST plug-in. Click the **Remove** button to delete the highlighted directory.

8.64 VST directories are managed using the Add/Remove VST Directory dialog box.

8.65 The Effects Rack dialog box

USING EFFECTS IN MULTITRACK VIEW

The use of effects in **Multitrack View** is nondestructive. Effects are stored as part of the session information and can be removed at any time without consequences. Many of the effects in **Edit View** can also be used in **Multitrack View**, and there are three additional effects not available in **Edit View** mode: **Envelope Follower, Frequency Band Splitter,** and **Vocoder.** There are some specific conditions that must be met before two of these filters can be applied. These conditions are detailed in the discussion of each effect.

Unlike **Edit View,** only the three effects listed above appear under the **Effects** menu. Audition provides other ways to select effects in **Multitrack View.** Effects can be activated by double-clicking or dragging and dropping an effect from the **Effects** tab of the **Organizer** window on a clip. Another method to select an effect is by clicking the **FX** button in the track controls. Clicking the **FX** button opens the **Effects Rack** and presents a number of options for configuring the effects or multiple effects.

 Note   The focus of this chapter is effects and settings. The **Effects Rack**, along with techniques to add multiple effects to a track or tracks, is discussed in detail in the chapter on mixing, Chapter 10.

Real-Time versus Offline Effects

Audition provides the ability to apply and adjust effect settings in real time while hearing the adjustments. The effects that support this ability are called real-time effects and when used in **Multitrack View** are nondestructive effects that can be removed or modified at any time (see Figure 8.66). Real-time effect names appear highlighted in the **Organizer** window, and the **Effects Rack** will display only real-time effects.

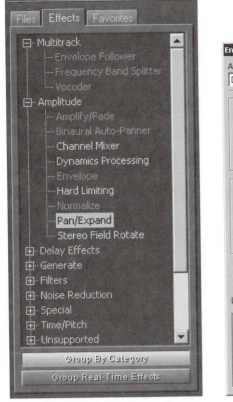

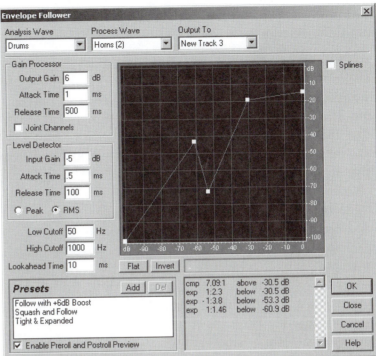

8.66 Highlighted effects are real-time effects that can be applied in Multitrack View.

8.67 The Envelope Follower dialog box

Offline effects can be applied only in the **Edit View** mode. Most of the offline effects permit you to audition the effect before applying it, but the effects are destructive.

Envelope Follower

The **Envelope Follower** is used to control the amplitude of one waveform by the envelope or input level of another waveform (see Figure 8.67). The result when the effect is setup successfully is the sound of one instrument triggering another sound.

One difficulty that users find is enabling the effect. Note that two tracks have to be selected, and segment of the waveform must be highlighted. It's simple, but it can seem tricky. First, drag the cursor to make the selection and hold down the **Control** key while clicking on each track. Each track should become brighter when clicked. Select the **Effects** tab of the **Organizer** window and display the **Envelope Follower** effect. It should be brighter than the effect below it. Double-click the effect name, and the dialog box will open.

Select the desired value in the **Analysis Wave** and **Process Wave** fields and confirm that the **Output To** selection is set to the desired track. Most of the parameters are the same as those used by the **Dynamics Processing** dialog box. Using waveforms that lend themselves to this effect and some patience can produce pleasing results. Additional tips are available in the Audition help files.

Frequency Band Splitter

The **Frequency Band Splitter** adds the ability to divide the current selection by frequency content. The effect can work only on a selection in one clip at a time and cannot be enabled when more than one clip is highlighted. Each division or band of frequencies is added to the next available track and listed in the **Organizer** window; however, they have not been saved to hard drive at this point.

Once a selection is made, open the effect dialog box by double-clicking the effect in the **Organizer** window, choosing **Effects>Frequency Band Splitter**, or dropping the effect on the selection. The number of bands is determined by the **Bands** radio buttons, and the **Crossover** fields are enabled for those bands. The crossover frequency is the highest frequency that will be contained in the band. In other words, the content crosses over to the next band at that frequency. The **Output Waves** are named with the source filename appended with the frequency range contained in the band. It should be noted that frequency content of the bands can overlap, meaning that the same frequencies can be contained in more than one band if desired. The recommended FIR (Finite Infinite Response) Filter Size is 320, but that value may need to be increased if the quality is not satisfactory.

The **Frequency Band Splitter** can be a valuable tool when used creatively. For example, different bands of frequencies can be compressed with unique settings for each band. A reverb can be added to a specific range of frequencies without crowding the effect with low- or high-frequency.

Vocoder

The **Vocoder** modulates one sound, called the process wave, with the control wave, which is frequently a vocal. The result is an instrument that sounds as if it were singing.

The **Vocoder** does not have a lot of parameters; however, getting a good effect takes some time and effort. Like the **Envelope Follower**, two tracks have to have focus with an active selection. First, drag the cursor to make the selection and then hold down the **Control** key while clicking on each track. Both tracks should become brighter as they receive the focus. Select the **Effects** tab of the **Organizer** window and display the **Vocoder** effect. It should be brighter than the effect above it. Double-click the **Vocoder**, and the dialog box will open.

Select the desired values for **Control Wave** and **Process Wave**, and confirm that the **Output To** selection is correct. Start with the presets and experiment until the desired effect is

8.68 *Frequency Band Splitter effect*

8.69 *The Vocoder dialog box*

obtained. Higher **FFT** values render a higher-quality effect at the cost of longer processing time. The **Help** button offers additional information regarding parameter settings.

> Some of the real-time effects such as **Pan/Expand**, **Stereo Field Rotate**, and **Dynamic Delay** have parameters that can be adjusted with envelope controls on the waveform. Controlling envelopes is discussed in detail in the chapter on mixing, Chapter 10.

THIRD-PARTY PLUG-INS

Audition ships with effects that will satisfy most users, however additional third-party effects can be added through Audition's use of the DirectX plug-in architecture. Audition also support VST (Virtual Studio Technology) plug-ins. There are an abundance of plug-ins available on the Internet as well as some demos on the CD that accompanies this book.

> Appendix B contains a listing of web sites for commercial, shareware, and freeware plug-ins, but this listing of plug-ins is a courtesy and not an endorsement or recommendation.

DirectX

DirectX is a suite of Application Programming Interfaces (API) developed by Microsoft to enable program developers with direct access to hardware. DirectX is an updateable component of the Microsoft Windows operating system and provides the software routines required to communicate directly with computer hardware. These routines or programming codes not only lessen the programming required to develop plug-in effects but also provide standardization across the platform.

With that being said, there are other APIs or plug-in architectures that are not supported by Adobe Audition. Among those not supported are DirectX Instruments (DXi), Steinberg's Virtual Studio Technology Instruments (VSTi), DigiDesign's Real-Time Audio Suite (RTAS), and DigiDesign's Time Division Multiplexing (TDM).

Enable DirectX Effects

Installation of DirectX plug-ins is typically very simple. Follow the publisher's installation instructions and make sure that the **Effects>Enable DirectX Effects** option has been activated. Once this option is enabled, it will no longer appear as an option on the menu.

Refresh Effects List

Once a new DirectX of VST plug-in is installed, it may be necessary to tell Audition that the plug-in is now available. **Effects>Refresh Effects List** directs Audition to scan the system for any available effects. Once the DirectX plug-in is registered in Audition, it will be available whenever the application is started.

Chapter 9

A Critical Review

WHAT IS ANALYZATION?

Since the earliest days of audio recording, engineers have used tools to monitor the accuracy of recording equipment and the performance of recording media. One simple device is the volume unit meter. The VU meter gauged the signal voltage, giving the engineer an indication of the amount of signal applied to the tape. This was an invaluable tool, because the recording would be noisy if the voltage was too low, or the magnetic tape would saturate and distort when the voltage was too high.

The VU meter was a great tool; however, engineers were keenly aware that high frequencies require less power and saturate at lower voltages. The need to monitor the voltage of multiple frequencies simultaneously spawned the invention of real-time analyzers. The RTAs provided a picture of the frequency content of the waveform during the recording or playback.

During the past century, a number of methods and devices have been added to the arsenal of analyzation devices. Only a handful have proven their worth, but these few tools can give a comprehensive view of the frequency content and amplitude of the waveform. Combined with a trained ear, they can be important aids in fine-tuning and polishing audio for the desired medium.

Purpose of Analyzation

Applying a spotlight to an actor on stage may draw the attention of the audience to that actor, but it can also affect how the audience sees the other actors, or whether the audience can see the other actors at all. Consider the result of adding a bank of yellow stage lights to an array of blue stage lights. Any changes in color or lighting affect the appearance of the stage and actors.

The same effect occurs in audio. Accenting a particular sound or frequency can affect the sound of the entire recording. Boosting the bass guitar can not only cover or mask other instruments, but it can also color the sound by increasing the amount of low frequencies in the mix.

Unless you were born with a golden ear and perfect pitch, determining these problem frequency ranges can be tricky. Fortunately, we have some tools that provide the ability to analyze and monitor the waveform and any changes that are applied to it. Audition includes not only the basic tools for analyzing the signal, but also some highly advanced tools. These tools include **Frequency Analysis**, **Phase Analysis**, and **Statistics**. Another useful analysis tool is the **Spectral View** available in the **Edit View** mode.

Using Analysis

Using the tools under the **Analyze** menu can help determine and resolve many problems. For example, dominant sibilant frequencies vary with different voice talent. Using **Frequency Analysis** can help pinpoint the problem frequencies. That frequency range can be notched or reduced without having to apply a broad equalization filter across all the high frequencies. **Frequency Analysis** can also help locate the resonating frequency of drum or a hum in an audio track and reduce the time wasted on trial and error.

The **Phase Analysis** tool shows the phase relationship of the waveform. An inverted channel of a stereo waveform could have a disastrous result. A stereo signal with one channel out of phase may not be obvious to the untrained ear, but when played back over a small TV set with one small speaker, the two channels cancel each other, and little if any audio is heard. The **Phase Analysis** tool provides an instant view of the waveform's phase relationships.

The **Statistics** tool reveals a wealth of information about the waveform such as the average level, peak level, and samples that may have clipped. The statistical data can be easily exported through the clipboard to another Microsoft Windows application. Reviewing the statistical data can provide key information to assist in maximizing levels and utilizing compression or other signal processing.

It could easily take a tome to explain Fast Fourier Transform (FFT) and how it is used in analysis. You can drag out your old calculus books if you like, but the key is to understand how to interpret the results rather than understanding the significant math involved. Let's take a closer look at each these analysis tools.

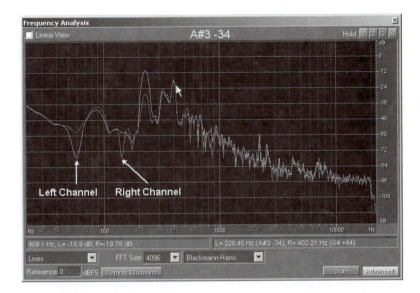

9.1 *Frequency Analysis window showing a snapshot of the amplitude of left channel and right channel frequency content on a logarithmic scale*

FREQUENCY ANALYSIS

The **Frequency Analysis** tool is available only in **Edit View**. It is accessed by pressing **Alt+Z** or **Analyze>Show Frequency Analysis**. The analysis window can be moved, resized, and docked. Once open, the **Frequency Analysis** window shows a snapshot of the frequency content versus amplitude at the current cursor location. If the entire waveform or a segment of the waveform is selected, the graph will show the frequency content of the selection. In recording or play-back mode, the **Frequency Analysis** window will also continuously update the display in real time, providing a constant view of the waveform content.

In the default state, one area for each channel will appear on the graph. Each channels displays in a different color. The horizontal scale shows the content expressed in Hertz, and the vertical scale indicates the amplitude of the frequency expressed in decibels. There are a number of options available to change the manner in which the waveform is displayed.

Placing the cursor on either the horizontal ruler or verti-cal ruler causes the cursor to appear in the shape of a hand. Click and drag the hand to move the content display left or right, up or down. Right-click and drag on either ruler until the cursor changes into the shape of a magnifying glass with two arrows above it to zoom in. Right-click to open a pop-up menu with **Zoom Out** and **Zoom Out Full** options.

The musical note and number of cents of the dominant frequency of the selection appears in the title bar of the anal-ysis window.

> **Musical Math:** In our current musical system, each octave, or doubling of frequency, is divided into 12 notes. Each of these notes is divided into 100 subdivi-sions, called *cents*.

Left-clicking on the graph displays the frequency and amplitude currently under the cursor.

Linear View

The frequency scale can be viewed on a logarithmic scale or a linear scale by enabling or disabling the **Linear View** checkbox. The logarithmic scale displays a more detailed look at the low frequency content, and the linear scale provides an equal view of all frequencies.

9.2   *Linear View checkbox in the Frequency Analysis window*

Hold

Four multicolored **Hold** buttons are found at the top right corner of the analysis window. Clicking these buttons captures a snapshot of the current frequency content and outlines the snapshot on the graph in the matching color. Up to four snapshots can be used simultaneously. Clicking the **Hold** button a second time clears the outline.

The **Hold** buttons can be a valuable aid in locating problem frequencies or comparing the frequency content of different mixes.

9.3   *Four Hold buttons store snapshots of frequency content*

Status Bar

The status bar of the **Frequency Analysis** window is divided into two parts. The left side displays the frequency and amplitude of each channel under the current cursor location. The data is instantly updated as the cursor is moved on the graph until the cursor leaves the graph boundaries. The right side shows dominant frequency and equivalent note with cents of each channel. The dominant musical note is based on frequency and harmonic content.

Graphing Options

Several options are provided to draw the frequency analysis graph. The pop-up menu in the bottom-right corner of the window determines the style. The available options are **Lines,**

226 Hz, L=-4.992 dB, R= -22.5 dB   L= 228.73 Hz (A#3 -32), R= 68.335 Hz (C#2 -24)

9.4   *Status bar of the Frequency Analysis window*

Areas, and **Bars. Areas** and **Bars** provide the option of showing the left channel on top or the right channel on top.

Scan

The **Frequency Analysis** window is not a modal window, meaning that it will remain open and permit switching between other windows. This feature makes it easy to switch to the waveform window, select another segment, and return to the analysis window. Once the new area is selected, click the **Scan** button to the analyze the segment.

Advanced

The **Advanced** button displays more options for the Frequency Analysis window, including **FFT Size, Curve,** and **Reference Level.**

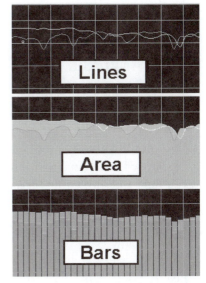

9.5   *The same frequency content graphed in three styles: Lines, Areas, and Bars.*

FFT Size: allows selection of the **FFT size.** This is the resolution of the analysis. Sizes range from 32 to 65,536. Accuracy increases with size; however, the increases in size come at a cost. To demonstrate accuracy versus performance, play back a waveform and right-click to open the **FFT Size** options. Start at **32** and press the **Down Arrow** key to increase the **FFT Size** as playback continues. As the resolution increases, the redraw of the frequency analysis begins to lag and will stop unless the CPU is extremely fast. The default size of 128 is more than adequate for most situations, and a size of 4,096 provides a precise-enough slice to reveal most problems.

Reference: adjusts the zero reference of the graph by the decibel value entered in the field. Entering a value of **10** drops the content on the graph by 10dB. Entering value of **–10** raises the content on the graph by 10dB.

Curve: determines the curve used to display the frequency analysis. The Blackmann-Harris curve is the easiest curve for most users. The other curves are for more advanced functions than those used by the typical user. Use the **Blackmann-Harris** curve unless you have a specific need for one of the other curves.

9.6   *Advanced buttons presents additional options for the Frequency Analysis window.*

Copy to Clipboard: copies the frequency analysis data to the clipboard for easy access from other Microsoft Windows applications (see Figure 9.7). This function is useful for scientific applications and documentation.

PHASE ANALYSIS

The **Phase Analysis** window displays the phase relationships of a stereo waveform and provides a guide to phase issues. The window is available only in **Edit View** mode and is opened by selecting **Analyze>Show Phase Analysis**. The window is moveable, resizable, and dockable. It is a nonmodal window permitting real-time updating and display changes.

Interpreting the phase is simple, but first we have to understand what an in-phase signal looks like. Figure 9.9 shows an in-phase stereo signal. The **Phase Analysis** window shows an oval shape at a 45° angle extending from the lower left to the upper right. Figure 9.10 shows a stereo signal that is 180° out of phase. The angle is the opposite of that of the in-phase signal.

Freq	Left	Right
0	–29.687	–29.9956
10.766	–32.8207	–33.1396
21.533	–41.2783	–42.0064
32.299	–48.4553	–50.269
43.066	–49.0665	–50.4068
53.833	–43.7355	–43.2055
64.599	–31.2208	–32.1907
75.366	–25.6643	–24.0308
86.132	–28.4447	–20.2523
96.899	–37.9152	–16.8438
107.666	–31.4991	–12.0552
118.432	–32.8684	–12.2425
129.199	–32.7954	–18.8251

9.7   *Partial sample of data copied to the clipboard using the Copy to Clipboard button (left)*

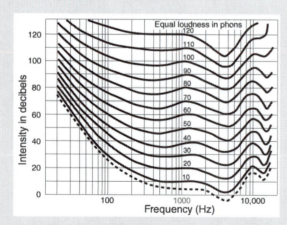

9.8   *Fletcher-Munson Curve*

Sound Perception

There have been thousands of studies on how the human ear perceives sound. One of these 'equal loudness contours' studies is the Fletcher-Munson Curve. This study demonstrates that the ear does not hear frequencies below 1kHz or above 5kHz at lower volumes as well as it does at higher volumes. Many manufacturers of home audio components added a **Loudness** button to compensate for this phenomenon.

Understanding the subtleties of human hearing and acoustics, and a basic knowledge of physics can greatly enhance analysis skills.

Although perfectly in-phase stereo signals would display as a diagonal line from lower left to upper right, this rarely occurs. In fact, the resulting audio would be very boring because it would present no stereo image. There would be no width or depth in the stereo field. The typical stereo mix has some out-of-phase material, and the **Phase Analysis** window will frequently indicate an almost out-of-phase signal, but the display will remain with a mostly in-phase orientation as shown in Figure 9.9.

 It is important to monitor the stereo phase relationship, even if the destination is a DVD or FM radio station. Inevitably, there will be listeners who play the audio through a 2-inch speaker in an inexpensive TV. If the channels are 180° out of phase (by mistake, of course) or the content is not mixed with mono-compatibility in mind, the audio quality will be poor or inaudible. Don't assume that just because you transferred the client CD directly into your system, the phase is correct. One of the channels may have been reversed on the customer's master, or one of the interns may have swapped cables with reversed phase.

Lissajous: The phase image displayed in Audition is called a Lissajous figure (pronounced LEE-sa-zhoo). The Lissajous figure is named for French physicist Jules Antoine Lissajous, who developed a technique for displaying waveforms by attaching a vibrating object to a mirror and reflecting light off the mirror onto a screen.

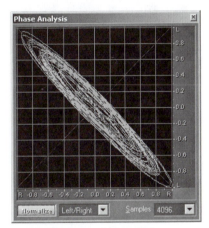

9.9 *Phase Analysis window showing an in-phase stereo signal*

9.10 *Phase Analysis window showing an out-of-phase stereo signal*

The **Phase Analysis** window has only a few settings.

Display Option

The **Phase Analysis** window can be set to display **Left/Right**, **Mid/Side**, and **Spin**.

Left/Right: displays the phase image with the left channel feeding the *Y*-axis and the right channel feeding the *X*-axis. A signal with the left channel displays only a vertical line, and a right-channel signal displays a horizontal line. Left and right channels that contain the same content (mono) are displayed as a diagonal line from the lower left to the upper right, and a stereo signal produces an image similar to that shown in Figure 9.11.

Mid/Side: displays the phase image with the sum of both channels (left plus right) feeding the *Y*-axis and the difference between channels (left minus right) feeding the *X*-axis. The net effect is that the phase image is displayed as a diagonal line from lower right to upper left when only the left channel signal is present and a diagonal line from lower left to upper right when only right channel signal is present. A mono signal produces a vertical line, and a stereo signal produces a signal as shown in Figure 9.12. Some users may find **Mid/Side** easier to use because in-phase material will appear with a vertical orientation, and out-of-phase signal will appear on a horizontal axis. Left and right channel content displays on the relative side of the display.

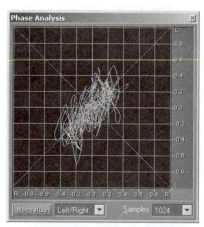

9.11 *Stereo signals will remain with a lower-left to upper-right orientation most of the time.*

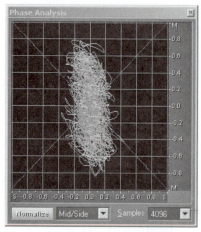

9.12 *Mid/Side — or as frequently called, M-S Phase Analysis — displays a stereo signal.*

Samples

This option might have been better named **FFT Size**. It does not relate to a digital sample as we discussed in Chapter 1. This option increases or decreases the resolution or frequency at which FFT is calculated on the waveform. Increased sample sizes provide a more accurate image, but the required CPU clock cycles can bog the processor down, reducing accuracy. The maximum number depends on your system capabilities and should be adjusted to provide a compromise of performance and accuracy. For most analyses, values of 1,024 or 2,048 are more than adequate.

Normalize

The **Normalize** button expands the image to the window boundaries for easier viewing. This should not be confused with the **Effects>Normalize** function. This button enlarges the display of the signal in the **Phase Analysis** window instead of altering the amplitude of the signal.

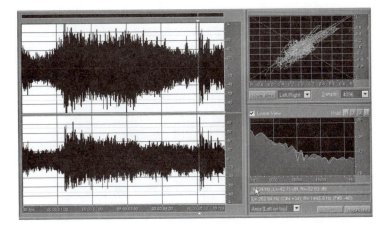

9.13 Edit View mode with real-time Phase Analysis and Frequency Analysis

PEAK VERSUS AVERAGE LEVELS AND SOMETHING CALLED "RMS"

Before we go onto the next section, let's discuss amplitude and methods of determining amplitude. Most normalization algorithms search for the highest-value sample and increase the entire program by the difference between that peak and the highest possible level of 0dBFS. For example, if the amplitude of the highest sample found during the peak search is –10dB, the program level will be normalized by boosting the value of all the samples in the waveform by 10dB.

This type of level adjustment is fine if all segments of the program are consistent and the objective is simply to boost the entire program to the highest possible level without clipping or distortion. But what if this is not the case? Consider two audio segments. Each segment is a recording of the same content but a sudden loud noise occurs during the second recording. When these two segments are normalized to the highest peak, there is a marked discrepancy between the average levels. The first segment sounds considerably louder. The same issue occurs in music recordings as well. A cymbal, percussion, or other transient sounds often peak significantly above the track's average level. In Figure 9.14, the two soundtracks have the same background level, but very different peak levels are shown when normalized. Segment 1 will sound considerably louder than Segment 2 even though they have the same maximum peak level.

One should be aware of both the peaks and average levels when working with audio. Average levels are what the ear perceives as loudness, but digital peaks are how technology perceives loudness. Fortunately, Audition provides not only the tools to measure peaks, but also displays root-means-square (RMS) statistics about the average levels. The RMS method of measuring amplitude divides the total peak to peak value of a sine wave by two and multiples that value by 0.707, effectively calculating a mean or average value. The RMS values are

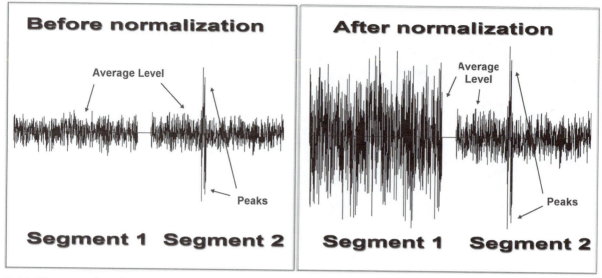

9.14 *Two soundtracks with the same background level*

much more accurate in representing amplitude the way we hear it. For most audio production, RMS power values provide more usable data.

RMS statistics will become more predominant in the industry. For example, the U.S. government recently issued a specification for digital audio production that specifies minimum and maximum RMS power values.

 Normalizing the signal to 0dBFS is great for use on nonlinear editing systems, digital audio workstations, and other systems in which the signal remains in the digital domain. However, it can have disastrous results if recorded to an analog device. It's recommended to reduce the signal to the ATSC (Advanced Television System Committee) standard of −20dBFS nominal level for outputting to an analog video tape recorder such as a BetaCAM deck.

Note The ATSC standard is −20dBFS; however, be aware that the meters on digital decks may not be calibrated to −20dBFS translating to 0VU. The meters may have been calibrated to some manufacturer recommendations of −14dBFS or −18dBFS.

STATISTICS

The **Waveform Statistics** window is available only in the **Edit View** mode and is selected from the **Analyze** menu. There are two tabs: the **General** tab and the **Histogram** tab. The statistics presented are extrapolated from the selection or the entire waveform if no selection is high-lighted.

RMS Settings

The RMS settings are the same for both the **General** tab and the **Histogram** tab. Radio buttons enable you to select whether 0dB is equal to a sine wave or a square wave at full scale.

Account for DC Offset: adjusts the RMS level and compensates for any DC offset found in the signal. Disabling this option and calculating RMS values on a signal with DC offset will cause the RMS values to be skewed because the waveform centerline is not actually at zero.

Window Width: determines the windows width in milliseconds used to calculate the minimum and maximum RMS values. Incase the value for more accuracy on audio with an extended dynamic range.

Recalculate RMS: recalculates RMS values. Any changes to the **Window Width** value require recalculation before the new values are displayed.

General Tab

The **General** tab provides an abundance of detailed information about the waveform, including peak amplitude and location, DC offset, possible clipped samples, and the ability to transfer the statistics to another application.

 Click any of the arrow buttons next to the left or right channel values to close the **Waveform Statistics** window and place the cursor at that location on the waveform. This feature is great for locating waveform peaks.

Minimum Sample Value: shows the minimum sample value for each channel.

Maximum Sample Value: shows the maximum sample value for each channel.

Peak Amplitude: shows the value in decibels of the highest peak amplitude and coincides with the maximum sample value.

Possibly Clipped Samples: the number of samples that hit 0dB full scale.

 Click the arrow and review any locations that show possible clipping. The clipped samples may cause distortion.

DC Offset: Positive values indicate that waveform is above the centerline, and negative values indicate the waveform is below the centerline.

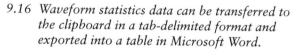

9.15 *General tab of the Waveform Statistics window*

	Left	Right
Min Sample Value:	−32392	−22960
Max Sample Value:	32392	30323
Peak Amplitude:	−.1 dB	−.68 dB
Possibly Clipped:	0	0
DC Offset:	−.005	.035
Minimum RMS Power:	−20.8 dB	−23.77 dB
Maximum RMS Power:	−8.35 dB	−10.46 dB
Average RMS Power:	−13.52 dB	−17.26 dB
Total RMS Power:	−13.12 dB	−16.86 dB
Actual Bit Depth:	16 Bits	16 Bits
Using RMS Window of 50 ms		

9.16 *Waveform statistics data can be transferred to the clipboard in a tab-delimited format and exported into a table in Microsoft Word.*

Minimum RMS Power: shows the minimum RMS amplitude. The minimum RMS value can help establish the lower range of the average levels.

Maximum RMS Power: shows the maximum RMS amplitude. The minimum RMS value can help establish the higher range of the average levels.

Average RMS Power: displays the average RMS power of the waveform or selection.

Total RMS Power: shows total RMS power of the waveform or selection.

Actual Bit Depth: displays the waveform's resolution, such as 8 bit, 16 bit, 24 bit, and float.

Copy Data to Clipboard: makes the **Waveform Statistics** data available to other Microsoft Windows applications via the system clipboard.

Histogram Tab

The **Histogram** tab is a bar chart that shows how the RMS amplitude is distributed in the waveform. The horizontal scale displays decibels, and the vertical scale displays percentage of the time the program is at a particular amplitude. The histogram, when used properly, can aid in evaluating waveform levels and options for additional processing.

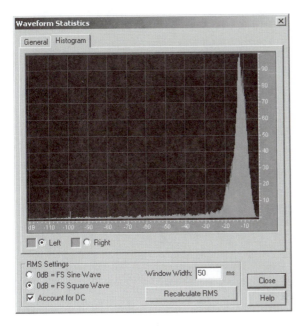

9.17 *Histogram showing a highly compressed signal with the most amplitude occurring in the range of –4–20dB (left)*

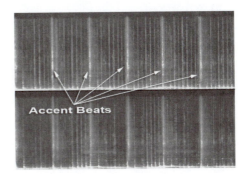

9.18 *Spectral View displaying a rhythmic pattern. Notice the bold lines as each of the accent beats is hit and the fainter lines of the other beats (above)*

Left/Right: The **Left/Right** buttons select the channel that is displayed in front overlaps the other channel on the **Histogram**. The left channel is colored blue, and the right channel is colored red.

SPECTRAL VIEW

Spectral View is an alternate view to **Waveform View** and is available only in **Edit View** mode. **Spectral View** is selected from the **View** menu. It displays the time on the X-axis and frequency on the Y-axis. Waveform content is displayed in real time with brighter colors representing higher amplitudes.

Judicious use of effects such as EQ, compression, de-essing, and other signal processing can fine-tune and polish the audio. Understanding how to use the analysis tools in Audition can certainly aid in making decisions; but remember that the analysis tools are only tools. There is no substitute for using your ear and common sense. The chapter on mixing, Chapter 10, provides some keys to aid you make sensible decisions.

Chapter 10

Mixing It Up

WHAT IS MIXING?

Attending a performance where all the actors remained grouped tightly together at the front of the stage would probably not convey the emotional exchange the author intended. The dialog would probably sound jumbled, and any facial expressions or physical motions of the actors would be hard to distinguish.

In professional theater, the stage is usually set with the actors placed at locations that draw the most from the scene. The placement of the actors on the stage is in itself, a form of mixing. The actor toward the front has more presence and demands more attention than the subtle acts of those toward the rear of the stage. The entrance of an actor from the right calls our interest in that direction, but the width and depth of the stage still allow understated actions to be noticed.

We are accustomed to this form of mixing in our daily lives whether the mixing is natural, such as the sound of ocean waves, or a staged theater performance. If the sound is too soft, we will move toward it. Too loud and we will move away. This act of mixing is the balancing of the variety of available sounds to make them sound as appealing as possible.

There are times when the ability to mix sounds is limited or is just not possible. For example, recording the Moody Blues in concert with a couple of microphones would not require much effort to set up. The recording would entail little, if any, work to complete. However, it provides few alternatives if the guitar amplifiers overpower the orchestra, and it's doubtful that the band would acquiesce to someone coming on and off stage to adjust amplifiers in the middle of a performance.

This method of what-you-hear-is-what-you-get has been in use since the very first recordings. The obvious drawback is the inability to make changes to individual instruments or vocals. The only alternatives are to filter or use some phasing tricks in an attempt to change the tone or balance of the instrumentation.

An alternative to this type of recording is multi-track recording. Each instrument or group of instruments is recorded on discrete channels or tracks. This separation provides the ability to change the volume relationship, or balance between instruments, and other characteristics of the instruments such as the pan, or where the instruments are heard in the stereo field. In addition to balance and pan, frequency content can be equalized and effects added until the desired sound is achieved. This process of balancing, equalizing, processing, and imaging is called mixing.

THE ACT OF MIXING

Mixing is an art form. Yes, you are an artist. There are no concrete rules. It is completely subjective. That

10.1   *Recording studio mixing console*

is, unless you're not the client. In which case, we should discuss some suggestions before beginning the section on mixing. The following are some suggestions to consider when mixing.

Pick a good set of reference monitors. The monitors will affect the sound of your mixes more than any other single piece of gear. Listen to the mix at various volumes, on various systems, from different distances, and don't hesitate to run the mix through a little two-inch speaker in your TV.

Mix for the medium. If you mixing a television commercial, make sure that the words are intelligible. The underscore will generally lose some presence when broadcast, but the client expects the message to be delivered. If mixing a big-band recording, don't compress the dynamic range as though it were a heavy-metal track.

Use EQ judiciously. There are two schools of thought on using equalization. One school prefers to add or boost frequencies to achieve the desired sound, but the other school uses a subtractive method so that the desired high frequencies will become apparent as the low frequencies are attenuated. Try to use the subtractive method, but this method does not work all the time. Use whatever works for you.

Don't overuse effects. Effects are a form of distortion. They modify the original signal, and artifacts occur. Effects have their place and can, if used sparsely, add magic to the mix. But their novelty can wear thin quickly.

Finally, remember that the mixing field is a canvas. It's a three-dimensional canvas. Use the sounds as colors and the effects to add textures and depth. Too many colors in one spot turn to mud, and too many textures mask the other textures. The same applies to audio. Too many overlapping sounds with the same dominant frequencies or too many effects can cloud the mix and obscure the essential elements. Remember, mixing is an art form, and you are an artist. So go create a masterpiece.

Mixing Formats

There are a number of different configurations or formats for mixdowns; however, mono, stereo, and surround-sound are the most frequently used formats.

Mono Mixing

The mono format was the de facto broadcast standard just a few years ago when most televisions had only a single speaker. The mono mix is the simplest format but sometimes the hardest to achieve. When mixing to mono, all tracks are balanced and combined to a single channel or track. It can be challenging to mix to mono and still have depth and clarity.

It is still a good idea to check your stereo mix for mono compatibility. If possible, listen to the stereo mix to a small video monitor or single-speaker boom box. This could also help detect stereo channels that are out of phase.

Stereo Mixing

The stereo format is the most commonly used mixing format. It is a two-channel format consisting of discrete left and right channels. Most networks, television, and radio stations broadcast in stereo, and it is the standard for compact disc.

Left   **Right**   *10.2   Stereo audio playback system*

Surround-Sound Mixing

The advent of DVDs has been a strong factor in the home theater revolution by providing a format for multichannel audio mixes. People had become fond of the movie theater sound system, and the electronics manufacturers were more than happy to oblige. There are and probably always will be new formats being introduced to the market; however, Dolby Digital (AC-3) is the current forerunner.

Dolby Digital provides a format for recording five main channels of audio: left, center, right, left-rear, and right-rear. The term 5.1 comes from these five main channels plus the low-frequency effects or LFE channel. The LFE is referred to as the point 1 because the channel contains only a percentage of the total frequency spectrum.

Audition provides the tools to mix and export surround-sound files with the multichannel encoder. If the destination is a DVD, the surround-sound files require Dolby Digital or DTS encoding with third-party software such as the Surround Dolby Digital AC-3 Encoder and 5.1 Surround DTS Encoders from the SurCode division of Minnetonka Audio Software. The multichannel encoder is discussed toward the end of this chapter on page 245.

10.3   *5.1 Audio playback system*

MIXING WITH BASIC CONTROLS

Basic mixing controls are readily accessible in Audition. Track volume, panning, and equalization can be quickly adjusted for any track using several methods. The easiest way to make adjustments to a track is often through the track controls. Let's take a closer look at these controls.

Volume Tab   **EQ Tab**   **Bus Tab**

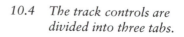

10.4   *The track controls are divided into three tabs.*

Make certain the **Lock in Time** for each track is enabled before starting a mix. This eliminates the possibility of moving a track by accident and causing it to be out of sync other tracks.

Volume

One of the most important functions in mixing is the volume control. The track controls offer easy access. To make volume adjustments, click in the field with the letter **V** and drag or right-click to open a fader. The fader permits volume adjustment with the slider, pressing the top or bottom arrows, or direct numeric entry. Fine-tune the level using the arrow keys.

 Right-click on the fader to move the fader to that location.

Mute: The green **Mute** button is an easy way to shut off a track during playback without affecting other tracks. This is useful when mixing versions with alternate instrumentation. Muting tracks is also possible by selecting **Mute Clip** after right-clicking on the clip.

Solo: Solo is the opposite of the **Mute** function. Clicking the **Solo** button mutes all other tracks. The **Solo** function is useful for reviewing tracks for distortion, noises, or anomalies or the results of an effect without changing or muting the other tracks. Hold the **Control** key while clicking to solo multiple tracks.

10.5   *The Pan slider sets where the track is heard in the stereo image.*

Panning

The panning control determines the placement of the track in the stereo image and displays the percentage of the tracks applied to the channel. Click and dragging left or right will place the track in the image. Right-click in the **Pan** field to open the **Pan** slider.

10.6   *The Pan slider sets where the track is heard in the stereo image.*

EQ

EQ or equalization is the process of adding or subtracting specific bands of frequencies Two equalizers are available from the **Track Controls** tab; however, they cannot be used simultaneously. Click the **EQ\A** or **EQ\B** to switch equalizers. Fields to adjust low, mid-range, and

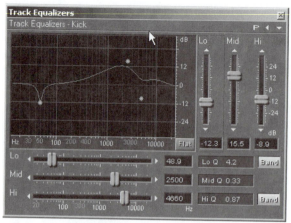

10.7   *The Track Equalizer window.*   10.8   *The Track Properties window*

high frequencies are accessed in the same way as the volume and pan controls. Right-clicking on any of the **EQ** fields opens the **Track Equalizers** window and provides a way to make adjustments that are more accurate. **Alt+5** will also open the **Track Equalizer** window.

> Right-click on the **EQ** button and then press the button labeled **p** to quickly access favorite EQ Presets.

Equalization adjustments in the **Track Equalizers** window can be made using nodes on the graph control or sliders. The sliders on the bottom are used to set the frequency of each band, and the sliders to the right of the graph determine the amount of boost or cut applied at each of these bands. The Q or width of the band of frequencies affected can also be changed in this window.

Track Properties

The **Track Properties** window contains volume, panning, and basic EQ controls as well as input, output, and track configuration settings. The **FX** button can be used to open the **Effects Rack** and once effects have been applied, the **Lock** button can be enabled to force pre-mixing of the effects on the track. Bus fields permit adjustment of the source to original effect balance.

Using Basic Mixing Controls

Now that we're familiar with the basic mixing tools, let's try using them from the **Track Properties** window along with another tool, the mixer. Make certain that Audition is open and in the **Multitrack View** mode. Use the **File>Close All** command if any files or sessions are already open.

1. Select **Ctrl+O** and locate the session file named *Basic Mixing.ses* in the *Chapter 10-Audio* directory on the CD that accompanies this book.

2. Press **Alt+9** to close the **Organizer** window.

3. Open the **Mixers** window with the **Alt+2** shortcut and expand the window by dragging the corner until all 10 tracks are shown and turn off all the buttons next to the **Master** fader except the **Pan** and **M/S** buttons.

1. Reduce the overall level by 10dB using the **Master** fader in the **Mixers** window to allow for the increase in level when the tracks are combined to a stereo mix.

10.9   *The Mixers window*

2. Click on the **Pan** field of each track and drag the cursor left or right to set where the track will be in the stereo image. Moving the dot above the **Pan** field moves the pan instantly to hard left, center, or hard right.

3. Click the **Play** button and begin creating a rough mix by adjusting the faders for each track until the balance between each track sounds acceptable.

> There are many methods of mixing. Many engineers start with all tracks open and massage each track until satisfactory, and others prefer to work with groups of instruments such as drums or keyboards and building upon each group. There is no right or wrong way.

4. Drag the **Mixers** window to the left edge of the screen until it docks and shows only the **Master** fader.

5. Open the **Track Equalizers** window with the **Alt+5** shortcut and drag it to the right side of the screen until it docks. Expand the **Track Equalizers** window so that the graph control is displayed.

6. Click the **Solo** button on one of the tracks and listen to the changes as you make adjustments in the **Track Equalizers** window.

7. Monitor the mix output. Adjust the **Master** fader to prevent overloading or clipping.

8. Continue using a combination of the basic mixing controls until you're satisfied with the rough mix.

> Use the **Looped Play** button to play the tracks continuously as you make adjustments. The selected area can also be looped to assist in making adjustments to a specific area.

That's an overview of using the mixing controls. Audition offers many other tools for mixing. In fact, many of these tools need to be applied before getting the rough mix together. Next we'll discuss how to get the signal processing and effects where you want them in the mix.

MIXING WITH BUSES AND EFFECTS

Audition provides a sophisticated set of mixing tools; however, it doesn't stop by offering its own effects. Many third-party DirectX and VST plug-ins are also accessible. To route the signal flow and apply effects, Audition uses the concepts of buses and effects racks that are already common technology in recording studios. Before we get into buses and FX, let's look at the background mixing setting and the mixing gauge.

Background Mixing

Background mixing attempts to render the mix before playback. Background mixing reduces the load on the CPU and can prevent stuttering or dropouts in complex sessions. There are a variety of settings. The best choice depends system capability and need. Select **Window>Load Meter** to help gauge the burden on the processor and adjust the **Background Mixing** settings.

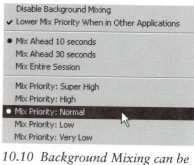

10.10 *Background Mixing can be set for various degrees of CPU usage.*

Mixing Gauge

The mixing gauge displays the progress of background mixing. A full bar indicates that all background mixing has been completed. This tool is helpful in determining when to begin recording or playback.

10.11 *Mixing gauge*

The Bus

In recording terminology, a bus is a common electrical path through which multiple signals can merge on the way to a common destination, much like traffic entering onto a freeway and exiting at the same or different exits. In Audition, each track can be assigned or routed to an output such as a soundcard or a bus, and multiple tracks or buses can also be routed to the same soundcard. For example, the outputs of the background vocal tracks could all be assigned to a bus that sends the combined signal on the bus to a reverb effect.

To add a new bus, click on the **Output** button and then the **New Bus** button of the **Playback Devices** window. Existing buses can be modified by clicking the **Properties** button.

FX/Rack Effects

The **FX/Rack** is modeled after the rack of effects typically found in recording studios. The rack can be fitted with a multitude of effects by dragging them from the **Effects** tab of the **Organizer** window to the clip or track. The **FX/Rack** can also be equipped by right-clicking the **FX** button and selecting **Rack Setup**. Move the desired effects from the left list to the right list, and adjust the device order

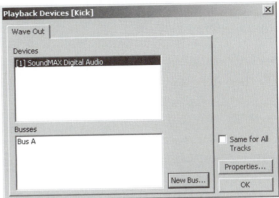

10.12 *New buses are configured by clicking the New Bus button on the Playback Devices window.*

using the **Move Up** and **Move Down** buttons. The **FX/Rack** is similar to the bus with the exception that only one track can be assigned to the **FX/Rack**, and it will be routed to the **Track Output Device**. The **Friendly Name** field allows you to name the **FX/Rack**. Presets of favorite **FX/Rack** configurations can be saved.

Wet/Dry

The **Wet** and **Dry** fields of the **Bus** tab set the amount of effect or wet signal, and the amount of original source signal or dry audio, that is added to the bus. This balance can also be set on the **Mixer** tab of the **FX Bus**.

10.13 *FX/Rack (left)*

10.14 *Bus Tab*

Locking Effects

Applying effects to a multitrack mix in real time can bog down even the fastest processors. Pressing the **Lock** button on tracks using the **FX/Rack** can reduce the load by rendering the effects before playback.

Serial/Parallel

The **Serial** button places the **FX/Racks** effects in a daisy-chained mode, where each effect outputs its signal to the next. The **Parallel** button feeds the original source signal to all effects in the **FX/Racks** equally. The **SRC** (Source) and **PRV** (Previous Effect) fields can be changed from the automatic settings.

 The **Master** fader is positioned in the signal path before the FX bus. There are times you send a track or tracks to an FX bus and you want the **Master** fader to affect the level Post-Bus FX. This setting is made in the **Mixing** tab of the **Advanced Session Properties** window.

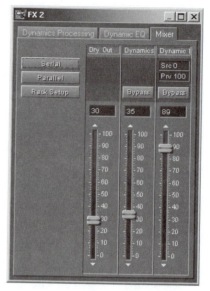

10.15 *Mixer Tab of the FX Bus*

Using FX/Racks

The next tutorial demonstrates how to place a few effects in the tracks. Make sure that Audition is open and in the **Multitrack View** mode. Use the **File>Close All** command if any files or sessions are open.

1. Select **Ctrl+O** and locate the session file named *Adding Effects.ses* in the *Chapter 10-Audio* directory on the CD that accompanies this book.

2. We'll apply some compression to the bass guitar. Drag the **Dynamics Processing Effect** from the **Organizer** window and drop it on the bass track.

3. Select **SharpAttackBass** from the pop-up menu and make any adjustments to taste. Use the **Solo** button to make monitoring easier.

4. Click the **Lock** button to pre-render the effect on the bass track.

5. Click the **Out** button on the **Guitar 1** track and click **New Bus**.

6. Enter the name **Flanged Echo** in the **Friendly Name** field

7. Highlight **Flanger** under the **Delay Effects** on the **Real-Time Effects** list and click the **Add** button.

8. Add **Studio Reverb** and click the **OK** button.

9. Press the **Solo** button on the **Guitar 1** track and select **Flanged Echo** from the **Buses** list and click **OK**.

10. Now we'll add the same effects to **Guitar 2** by clicking the **Output** button and selecting **Flanged Echo** from the **Buses** list.

11. Click the **Looped Play** button, right-click on the **Bus A** button, and adjust the effects to your satisfaction. Click the **Output Device** button on the **Lead Vocal** and add it to the **Flanged Echo** bus (Bus A).

That's a quick tour of the potential available in Audition using buses and effects. Take some time and work with the effects and buses with this or your own material. When you tire of the built-in effects, there are a number of demos on the CD-ROM that accompanies this book.

Let's move on to automating volume and effects changes using fades, crossfades, and envelopes.

MIXING WITH FADES, CROSSFADES, AND ENVELOPES

Audition has the traditional mixer functions of muting, soloing, and fading for those who are comfortable with conventional methods of mixing; however, envelopes offer an alternative to the software mixing console and provide the ability to automate the mixdown. This style of automated mixing may be a little different for anyone who has routinely used moving fader automation. It may take some time to get accustomed to working with envelopes, but the speed and convenience is well worth the time spent developing the skills. Envelopes are easily visible on the clip and allow precise adjustment of individual clips or groups of clips. Best of all, the envelopes are not limited to volume adjustments. When enabled, envelopes can control panning, MIDI tempo, effect settings, and effect levels. Let's see how these tools work.

Fades

The dictionary defines the word *fade* as "to lose brightness, loudness, or brilliance gradually." In audio, the term is used to characterize the continuous attenuation of the signal until the audio is inaudible, but it can also mean to fade in or gradually increase the audio until the desired level is achieved.

Fades can be applied to any track by double-clicking the clip, selecting the area the fade will affect, and applying a fade from the **Amplify/Fade** effect. The drawback to using fades in **Edit View** is that they are destructive. The **Crossfade** function is another method of applying a fade in or fade out and does so in a nondestructive way in **Multitrack View**.

To create a fade, highlight the area of the clip where the fade should be applied and select **Edit>Crossfade** or right-click on the selection area and choose **Crossfade** from the pop-up menu. The **Crossfade** option has four submenu choices: **Linear, Sinusoidal, Logarithmic In,**

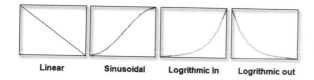

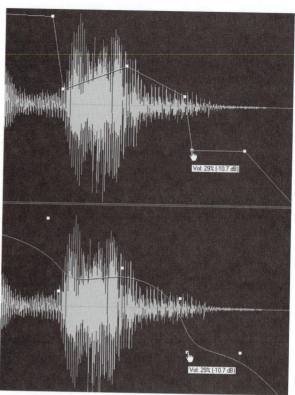

10.16 Four types of crossfades (above)

10.17 Envelopes and nodes (right)

and **Logarithmic Out**. Select the desired type of crossfade. The differences in the four cross-fades have to do with the slope, or how smooth the crossfade occurs.

 To apply a crossfade to multiple tracks, select the area to which the crossfade will be applied and **Ctrl**+click each clip that should be included in the fade.

Crossfades

The terminology for fades and crossfades can be confusing in Audition. We will defer to Adobe's terms; however, fades generally refer to either the gradual increase or the decrease of volume of a single track or mix, and a crossfade is best described as overlapping tracks with one track fading out as the other track fades in.

Applying a segue or crossfade requires at least two tracks that overlap on the timeline. To perform a crossfade, select the area of the clips where the crossfade should occur, **Ctrl**+click to select the tracks to be included, and select the desired crossfade from **Edit>Crossfade** sub-menu.

Envelopes

Envelopes are a powerful feature in Audition. Five different types of envelopes can be displayed by selecting the corresponding **Show Envelope** command from the **View** menu. The **View>Enable Envelope Editing** command toggles the envelope editing nodes on and off, making it possible to change volume, pan, effects settings, and even tempo of MIDI tracks by dragging the nodes on the envelope line. Splines can be enabled to smooth the envelopes, or the envelope nodes can be cleared by right-clicking and selecting one of the **Volume, Pan,** or **FX Mix** submenu options.

Click anywhere on the envelope line to add a node or grab the node and drag it off the track to remove it. Envelopes can be adjusted by dragging single nodes, or groups of nodes can be adjusted using modifier keys. For example, holding the **Alt** key while dragging on a node adjusts all nodes in the clip by the same amount. Pressing the Control key while moving a node causes a rubber band-like adjustment where all nodes reach the maximum or minimum value. The **Shift** key prevents the node from moving left or right while you're making adjustments. Audition also provides a useful feature that adjusts the relative value of all nodes on the volume envelope. This is a valuable function when the clip has complex level changes and the entire clip needs an overall level adjustment. Holding the **Control** key and moving a volume node accomplishes the same task.

> **TIP!!** The default setting for volume envelopes is 100 percent. This initial setting limits any level changes to attenuation. To provide a greater initial range, select the **Mixing** tab of **Advanced Session Properties** window to change the range of the volume envelopes. Choose the 0 – 200 percent range and click the **Set As Default** button. If necessary, reduce the **Master** fader to compensate for this reduction.

Using Crossfade and Envelopes

The next tutorial uses the **Crossfade** and **Envelope** functions. We'll also use the **Auto-Cue** function to separate two takes of a voiceover tag and add them to a video clip. Make sure that Audition is open and in the **Multitrack View** mode. Use the **File>Close All** command if any files or sessions are already open.

1. Select **Ctrl+O** and locate the session file named *Envelopes.ses* in the *Chapter 10-Audio* directory on the CD that accompanies this book.

2. Choose *View>Show Volume Envelopes*.

3. Select **View>Enable Envelope Editing** and make certain **Snap to Clips** is on.

4. Select **Import** and locate the file named *ET Tag.aif* in the *Chapter 10-Audio* directory. (This is a Macintosh AIFF file, so the **Files** of type filter needs to be set for **All files(*.*)**).

5. Double-click on the waveform and choose **Edit>Auto-Cue>Find Phrases and Mark**. Press **F12** to return to **Multitrack View.**

6. Click the plus sign next to *ET Tag.aif*, highlight the cues under the filename, and then press **Ctrl+M** to insert the cues into **Multitrack View.**

7. Listen to the voice tag and then highlight the last second or so of **Tracks 3** and **4**. Press the **Control** key and left-click **Track 3** and **4**. Right-click and choose **Crossfade>Sinsoidal**. Notice the fades have numerous nodes on them.

8. Right-click on the second clip in **Track 3** and choose **Remove Clip**.

9. Highlight the first clip in **Track 4** and drag the two nodes down the bottom of the waveform. This sets the volume to zero. Press **Home** and play the session back.

 Right-click on the video to open the video playback settings. Reduce the quality level and/or size if the video does not play smoothly.

Once the levels are adjusted and any effects in place, the session is ready for mixdown. If you're planning to use the mixdown in other Adobe Video Collection applications, press **F4** to enable the **Embed Project Link** data for **Edit Original** functionality on the **Data** tab. The **Save extra non-audio information** checkbox must be enabled or the **Edit Original** links will not be saved with the files.

PERFORMING THE MIX

After all of the balancing, processing, and endless hours of toil are complete, the final stage of the mix is ready for execution. However, there is one other element to the mixing process that we should discuss before moving on to the mixdown.

 Don't overmix a track. In the real world, some of the best mixes happen relatively quickly. Working a mix too long can flatten the dynamics, fatigue your ears, and frustrate your mind.

The Session

Session files are crucial to the operation **Multitrack View** mode of operation. Although the session file does not contain any audio or video content, it does contain the instructions necessary to create the mix. Audio engineers and video editors may be familiar with the acronym EDL (Edit Decision List). The Session file is essentially the EDL and contains the instructions that tell Audition which files to open in which tracks. The session also keeps track of the buses, effects, pans, levels, envelopes, and EQ used during the mix. Virtually any non-audio, video, or MIDI information set up in the mixing session is stored in the session file. It is the session file that tells Audition how to render the files to create the mixdown.

Enabling the **Lock In Time** option on any tracks with effects will speed up reloading the session at a later time.

The Mixdown

The actual mixdown is an extremely complex task; however, the CPU will be doing all the work. After the session is mixed to your satisfaction, select one of the **Mix Down** or **Export** commands, and Audition will use the session information to render the audio to the chosen format. Depending upon program length and complexity, this can take a while.

Mix Down to File: The **Mix Down to File** command has four options. You can mix down the entire session to a stereo mix or mix down only the selected audio clips. The same two options are available for mono mixes. The mixdown will be placed in the **Edit View** waveform display.

Mix Down to Empty Track (Bounce): The **Mix Down to Empty Track** command offers the same options as **Mix Down to File**; however, the mixdown will be placed on the next available track instead of the **Edit View** display. This is a great way to submix or mix group of instruments to a single track.

Mix Down to CD Project: **Mix Down to CD Project** renders a mix down of the selected clips or all clips if none are selected, along with the cue mark information, to the **CD Project View** window.

Export: The **Export Audio** command renders the audio to the format selected in the **Export Audio** window. Note that the 16-bit or 32-bit mixdown settings chosen on the **Multitrack** tab of the **Settings** window determine the output resolution. Other options such as 24-bit resolution can be selected with the **Options** button in the **Export Audio** window.

The **Export Video** command renders the audio back to the video track with optional codecs available from the **Option** button in the **Export Video** window.

 Audition sessions can be opened from Adobe Premiere Pro or Adobe After Effects using the **Edit Original** command; however, the **Embed Project Link** data for **Edit Original** functionality must be enabled, and the **Save extra non-audio information** option must be checked in the **Export** window. The **Embed Project Link** option is located on the **Data** tab of the **Settings** window.

Dithering

A sample is the binary value representing the amplitude of a waveform. The number of bits or resolution used to store the sample determines the range of values that can be stored. For example, a 1-bit sample can represent two values: zero and one. An 8-bit sample can represent 256 different values, and the standard resolution for compact disc audio can represent 65,536 unique values.

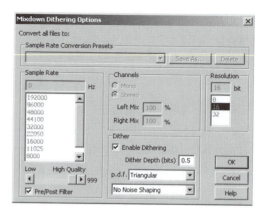

10.18 *The Mixdown Dithering Options window*

It would appear that this would be adequate for even the most critical audio. It's not. In fact, Audition does all internal processing using 32-bit resolution. That's great! So what's the problem?

The problem occurs when higher resolutions need to be reduced. For example, a 32-bit mixdown in Audition would have to be converted to 16-bit resolution to master to a compact disc. As the resolution is lowered, the number of unique amplitude values decreases, and the dynamic range is reduced. At a resolution of 16-bits, the transition between the lowest sample value and off can be audible. Given that the digital signal is either on or off, the transition can be audible. In fact, if the signal is fluctuating between on and off, the effect can become even more noticeable. This may not be extremely noticeable on material recorded at 16-bit resolution; however, the effect can be significant when a 24-bit file is truncated to 16-bits.

To resolve this issue, a small amount of low-level noise is added to the signal. This process is called dithering. Adding the low-level noise turns the last few bits on and off randomly. The result is a smoother transition. Audition provides a number of methods of adding noise to keep the added noise to a minimum.

 Use dithering when converting resolutions from 24 bit or above to 16 bit or below. Converting to lower resolutions without enabling dithering can result in anomalies on low-level audio transitions, such as fades.

Enable Dithering: Dithering can be enabled on the **Mixdown Dithering Options** window accessed by pressing the **Dithering** button on the **Multitrack** tab of the **Options>Settings window**. The **16-bit** radio button must be enabled before the **Dithering** button can be pressed.

Dither Depth (bits): The **Dither Depth** determines the amount of dither applied. Recommended values are 0.2 to 0.7 with higher values adding harmonic distortion.

p.d.f. (probability distribution function): The **p.d.f.** pop-up menu sets the method of noise distribution. Triangular is typically the best compromise between signal-to-noise ratio, distortion, and noise modulation.

Noise Shaping: The **Noise Shaping** pop-up menu presents a number of noise-shaping curves that introduce noise to the signal differently. The best selection is dependent on the content.

 iZotope's Ozone 3 is a DirectX plug-in that provides an alternative to the dithering available in Audition. Ozone 3 also provides a number of other features that make it well worth a test drive. A PDF file on dithering and a demo of Ozone 3 courtesy of iZotope are located on the CD-ROM that accompanies this book.

THE MULTICHANNEL ENCODER

One of the surprise features in Audition is the ability to create surround-sound mixes. The **Multichannel Encoder** provides an interface that is both intuitive and versatile. Signals are tracked visually as they are panned anywhere in the surround-sound image field. Subchannel and center-channel levels are individually attenuated with sliders. **Pan Envelopes** can be enabled for each track or bus. The **Multichannel Encoder** offers the ability to export one interleaved six-channel .wav file or six discrete wave files for DVD production. The MCE can also encode the Windows Media Professional 9 Multichannel format.

MCE System Requirements

Use of the **Multichannel Encoder** requires a sound card or device capable of outputting six-channel audio and a driver compatible with Microsoft DirectSound. DirectX 9.0 or later is recommended; however, DirectX 8.0 will work for exporting .wav files. Windows Media 9 runtime is installed by default during the Audition 1.5 installation and is necessary to output WMA Professional 9 files.

Encoder Window

The **Multichannel Encoder** is available only in **Multitrack View** mode. A stereo mix should be set up before beginning a surround mix. Open the **Multichannel Encoder** window with the **Ctrl+E** shortcut or by select it from the **View** menu. At first glance, the window can seem intimidating; however, the interface is easy to navigate. The settings reflect the currently highlighted track. The **Surround Panner** and **Track Options** will affect only the selected track.

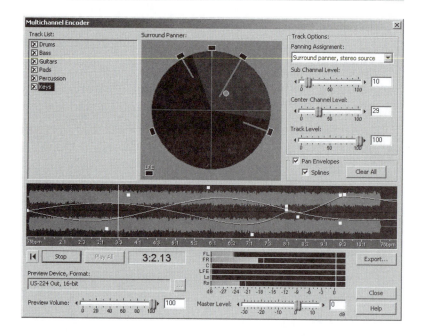

10.19 Multichannel Encoder window

Track List

The **Track List** displays a list of all tracks and buses in the session. The checkbox to the left of the track or bus name determines whether the track or bus is included in the surround mix.

Surround Panner

The **Surround Panner** depicts a surround-sound image field with the left, center, and right speakers represented by black boxes or blocks across the top of the circle and left-rear and right-rear speakers placed appropriately. The LFE or Low Frequency Effects speaker block is located in the lower-left corner. The darker blue area indicates the spread of the track in the image field, and the lighter blue lines projecting from the speaker blocks signify signal strength.

Panning or placement of the track or bus in the image field can be managed in several ways, including dragging the white dot in the **Surround Panner**. The light and dark blue areas update as the dot is moved to display the approximate coverage in the surround-sound image field. Selecting the desired location from the **Panning Assignment** pop-up menu, clicking on the speaker block, or dragging the white dot onto the speaker block are other methods of placing the track in the surround-sound image field.

Pan Envelopes

In addition to the panning methods discussed in the previous section, the **Multichannel Encoder** allows you to use pan envelopes to adjust placement in the surround-sound image field. Pan envelopes can be used to dynamically adjust the pan over the duration of the track.

Click on the **Pan Envelopes** checkbox to enable the envelopes. The yellow envelope line controls left and right balance, and the green line is used to adjust front and rear balance. Additional nodes can be added by clicking on the envelope line. Drag the white squares or nodes to make panning changes, and the **Surround Panner** will update to reflect any envelope changes. Fine adjustments can be made using zoom functions available by right-clicking on the horizontal ruler below the waveform. Enabling the **Splines** checkbox smooths the panning transitions, and the **Clear All** button resets the **Pan Envelopes** to their default position.

Track Options

The **Sub Channel Level** slider controls the signal level that feeds the LFE channel of the currently selected track. The **Center Channel Level** slider sets the balance between the left, right, and center channels. The **Track Level** slider determines the signal level or balance of the selected track in the overall surround mix.

Playback Controls

The highlighted track or the entire mix can be previewed using the **Play Track** and **Play All** buttons, respectively. The **Preview Device** pop-up menu and the **Preview Volume** slider permit changing the sound card setting, playback format, and monitoring volume. Real-time metering provides display of each of the six channels. The **Master Level** slider controls the output level of the final mix.

Most Dolby Digital encoders are set up with the channel configurations listed below.

Channel 1	Left Front
Channel 2	Right Front
Channel 3	Center
Channel 4	LFE
Channel 5	Left Rear
Channel 6	Right Rear

TIP!! Consumer surround-sound systems often use a bass-management circuit that boosts bass content and sends lower frequencies to the LFE channel. It is recommended that a bass-management system is used in the monitoring system to avoid mixes that may overload the typical consumer system. Most hardware cards provide software that will offer a management preview to give you an idea of what this might sound like on a typical system.

10.20 The Multichannel Export Options window (left)

10.21 The Fold down to stereo settings dialog box (below)

Export

Once the surround-sound mix is completed and ready for output, click the **Export** button, enter a new session name if desired, and set the location to which the files will be saved in the **Save In** field. Exported mixes can be saved in three different formats.

Export as six individual mono wave files: the preferred format for outputting surround mixes that will be used on other systems such as Sonic Solutions DVD Creator, Fusion, or Scenarist or stand-alone Dolby Digital and DTS encoders such as those from SurCode.

Export as one interleaved, 6-channel wave file: outputs the mix as one interleaved PCM file; however, this format may not be compatible with many applications.

Export and encode as Windows Media Audio Pro 6-channel file: exports the mix as a single WMA file. The file can be output as a Constant Bit Rate, Variable Bit Rate, or as a Lossless VBR encode. Various quality levels are available via the **Format Options** dropdown.

The **Fold down to stereo** settings are used to determine how the rear, center, and LFE channels fold down when played back on a system that is not equipped for 5.1 playback. The settings determine the attenuation of channels when combined into a stereo mix.

Audition, coupled with Adobe Premiere Pro, After Effects, and Encore DVD, provides a powerful arsenal of tools for creating and editing audio and video content, but Adobe doesn't stop at just supplying a great set of tools. Adobe has built some tools that not only work together with you and your equipment, but also work with each other. Let's look a new way of handling your workflow.

THE ADOBE WORKFLOW

The past decades have brought some amazing changes to the way graphics and prints are created. Manually typesetting, striping, and paste-up are processes of the past. Today, graphic design, typesetting, and printing can be completed in single office, using one suite of software tools, by one individual.

Adobe deserves much of the credit for this revolution, and now Adobe is bringing that integration of creation and production processes to audio and video production.

The Adobe Video Collection

The Adobe Video Collection is a suite of applications specifically designed for media production. The Standard Collection contains Premiere Pro, Encore DVD, Audition, and the standard version of After Effects. The Professional Collection contains Premiere Pro, Encore DVD, Audition, the professional version of After Effects, and Photoshop CS. Either package includes the necessary software to create stunning video and audio content.

After Effects creates 2D and 3D video titling, animation, and effects. Premiere Pro provides real-time video editing. Encore DVD combines video, audio, and images and transforms them into the DVD-Video format. The addition of Photoshop CS makes the Adobe Video Collection the most powerful way to manage the design, creation, and production workflow.

What Is the Adobe Workflow?

Most video production entails certain or steps to complete the project. Often these steps require multiple workstations such as a nonlinear editing system for video editing and a digital audio workstation for working with audio. It may also require a workstation for creating animation and special effects and even another for designing graphics. Encoding the video and authoring a DVD or multimedia files for use on a web site or CD generally adds even another workstation or two to the process. Operating these various systems usually requires different operators, editors, engineers, and designers and a host of different formats.

Adobe has changed this awkward and confusing way of working by integrating all of these processes into the Adobe Workflow. A single person with a single computer can now handle the entire project from beginning to end without the hassles of incompatible formats and the costs of multiple workstations. The Adobe Workflow allows the Adobe Video Collection applications to work in concert. Premiere Pro and After Effects can open Audition sessions with a simple **Edit Original** command. Photoshop files are easily changed and updated in Encore DVD, and video effects can be applied in Premiere Pro using the After Effects engine.

The best part is that all the files are compatible. Let's take a look how the Adobe Workflow is used.

Using Audition with Premiere Pro and After Effects

It's not uncommon to produce an audio soundtrack with a voiceover, music bed, and sound effects before any video editing begins. This is the perfect situation for using the Adobe Workflow. Using Audition, the voice elements are recorded and edited, music is added, created from loops, sweetened with sound effects, and mixed down to an audio file with the **Embed Project Data** link for **Edit Original** functionality. Once the audio mixdown is imported into Premiere Pro, the video is edited using the audio as a guide, and any special effects and titling are added with After Effects.

It looks good and everything is working well, but the sound effects need to be moved a little, and the client needs to revise a line in the copy. Here's where the Adobe Workflow shines. Right-click on the audio track in Premiere Pro and select **Edit Original**. Audition opens the mixdown session and audio source files with all pans, volumes, and effects exactly as they were in the mixdown session. Revise the voice element, move the sound effects, and mix down again. Premiere Pro will recognize the mix as if all the audio work were done in Premiere Pro.

That's just part of the Adobe Workflow. There's more. Remix the session in Audition's **Multichannel Encoder** and export the files. Premiere Pro will automatically conform the audio when it's launched and the audio can be encoded with the Surcode Dolby Digital plug-in and authored in Adobe Encore DVD. It's Amazing. All the production completed... in a single office, with a single suite of applications, by one person.

 Note Premiere Pro will process 32-bit mixdowns. After Effects 6.0 will work only on 16-bit mixdowns.

Using Audition with Other Applications

Audition supports industry-standard formats, and exchanging audio files with most other audio or video applications is routine; however, swapping multitrack sessions between digital audio workstations or nonlinear editing systems can present incompatibility problems.

There are third-party translators such as EDL Convert Pro by Cui Bono Soft that provide a solution to transferring projects between various systems. A demo of EDL Pro Convert is included on the CD-ROM that accompanies this book.

Chapter 11

The Finale: Producing a Master Piece

WHAT IS MASTERING?

Mastering is probably the least understood but most important aspects of music production. To some, mastering is viewed as a mystical process practiced by only a few wizards. To others, the process is simply part of the mixing process. In truth, mastering occurs after the music has been recorded, edited, and mixed. Mastering is the process of homogenizing the tracks and making them flow from one track to the next. It is an art form, so it is generally done with varying degrees of success by the novice or seasoned mastering engineer. Perhaps the best analogy is that of finishing a collection of rough diamonds. Each is precious, but it is not until the jeweler facets them and creates the necklace that they become a work of art.

The techniques required for mastering include editing the sequence of tracks and setting the space between tracks. Equalization may be used to brighten the tracks, add an airy feel, or give them more warmth, as well as making the tracks sound more consistent with each other. Compression and limiting can be used in combination with level adjustments to keep the volume comparable from track to track and making the tracks consistent with other recordings of the same genre. There are also a number of signal-processing techniques that can be used in the mastering stage from enhancing the stereo image to using an old tube device to remove the harshness of some recordings. There is no formula that works for every project. Much like acting, experience combined with common sense, feel, and a good ear are the keys to creating a great-sounding master.

MASTERING FOR COMPACT DISC

The mastering process can be divided into five steps:

Sequencing: the act of assembling the tracks with the desired order and timing between cuts.

Signal Processing: the process of compressing, limiting, equalizing, or adding other signal processing enhancements.

Level Adjustment: the adjustment or normalization of the volume of the tracks.

Track Mark Placement: the placement of start-of-track, end-of-track, or index cues.

Burning the CD: the output of the finished sequence to a Pre-Master Compact Disc (PMCD).

Step 1 Sequencing Tracks

The first step in preparing a compact disc master is determining the track order. This is called sequencing. The sequence and timing between songs can have a significant impact on the mood and emotions created when listening to the final CD. Sequencing, like music itself, is subjective and should be given adequate consideration.

Before beginning, make sure you have chosen **View>Display Time Format>Compact Disc 75 fps** as shown in Figure 11.1 and that the **Edit>Snapping>Snap to Frames (Always)** is chosen as shown in Figure 11.2. This will force the cue marks or track marks to always begin on a frame, preventing any clicks caused by tracks beginning in the middle of a frame.

As with most functions in Audition, there are several ways to place the tracks into the final sequence. If your tracks are already in one audio file, select the **File>Open** command and locate the desired file. The **File>Open Append** command will open multiple files at one time, appending each file to the next; however, they will be sequenced in alphabetic or numeric order by track name.

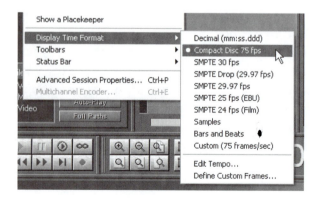

11.1 *The Compact Disc 75 fps setting (left)*

11.2 *The Snapping to Frames (Always) setting (below)*

> Unless you are running Windows XP, the result of a sort of filenames containing numbers may not be as expected. Computers sort numbers using the value of each character in sequence as it appears in the filename. If you're naming multiple files with numerals, it is a good practice to use the zero placeholder. Figure 11.3 illustrates filesnames sorted in ascending order.

The following method will provide the most flexibility during the mastering process and allow overlapping tracks called a *segue*. You will be able to compress, equalize, or add other signal processing to each track without affecting the other tracks.

11.3 *Sorting filenames with numbers shows the effects of adding a leading zero.*

Using Multitrack View to Sequence Tracks

1. Select **Multitrack View** mode.

2. Chose **File>Import** and open the six .wav files in the directory titled *Sequencing* in the *Chapter 11* directory of the companion CD. The selected tracks will appear in the **Organizer** window.

3. Drag and drop the file that will be the first cut on the CD from the **Organizer** window onto **Track 1** of the timeline in **Multitrack View.**

4. Right-click and drag the clip to the left edge of **Track 1** in the timeline.

5. Drag and drop the file that will be the second cut on the CD from the **Organizer** window onto **Track 2** of the timeline.

6. Right-click and drag the second clip to the desired position on the timeline.

7. Audition the transition between the cuts and continue moving the clip until the spacing or segue is acceptable. A crossfade can also be added to create a unique segue.

8. Continue alternating placing cuts between **Track 1** and **Track 2** of the timeline until all cuts have been placed in the tracks as demonstrated in Figure 11.4.

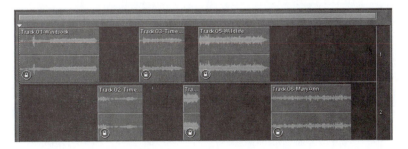

11.4 *Sequencing*

Once you are satisfied with the placement of the clip, right-click on the clip and select the **Lock in Time** option. A padlock icon will appear in the lower-left corner indicating that the clip cannot be moved left or right.

 Sequence your tracks with an energy curve in mind. Placing all ballads or all driving rock tracks together will not make for the most exciting listening experience. Use the sequence of tracks to create a journey for the listener with peaks and valleys.

Step 2 Signal Processing

The most common processing done during mastering is equalizing. Equalizing is the act of increasing or decreasing the volume of specific bands of frequencies. Unfortunately, no room is acoustically perfect, but sometimes the personality of a room shows through too much. The result may be a mix with accented low-end frequencies, making a track sound dark or muddy. Or perhaps a track was mixed in a room with very bright monitor speakers and the tracks sound dull when played back in an accurately tuned room on professional audio monitors. Although having consistently good-sounding tracks to begin with would be preferred, equalization is key in correcting these issues and making the tracks sound more consistent throughout the disc.

Audition offers a wide selection of signal processing tools. Several equalization filter presets are included. The **FFT Filter** has four mastering presets specifically for mastering. The **Graphic Equalizer** and **Parametric Equalizer** are preferred in many situations and **Dynamic EQ** has its specialized applications. There are many other equalization-type filters that could be used during the mastering process.

Some effects are offline effects and require application from **Edit View**. The **Effects** tab of the **Organizer** window dims **Off-Line Effects**. **Real-Time Effects** can also be grouped with the button at the bottom of the **Organizer** window.

Compression and limiting are also frequently used during mastering. Using compression properly will maintain a minimum and maximum level, narrowing the dynamic range. Limiting will prevent the levels from exceeding a threshold. **Effects>Amplitude>Dynamics Processing** and **Effects>Amplitude>Hard Limiting** are two of the processes you may consider using.

Noise Reduction is probably the least-used process in mastering. Audition has some incredible noise-reduction filters that not many years ago cost tens of thousands of dollars. Noise-reduction filters can be used to remove hiss, ticks, and clicks, and in some cases Audition can diminish the impact of clipped audio.

There are multitudes of ways to use these effects. Most of the time, there is no right or wrong way. It all depends on the mixes you are going to master. The best advice is to use your ear and experiment. See Chapter 8 for a detailed look at each of these processes.

Take the time to experiment with some signal-processing on these files. You can replace them from the companion CD should the files become unusable.

 A solid understanding and use of the analyze tools built into Audition will make a noticeable difference in the final result of the mastering process.

Step 3 Level Adjustment

One of the most distracting things about a poorly mastered CD is inconsistent levels from track to track. Listeners want to sit down and enjoy the music without adjusting the volume from track to track. Therefore, needless to say, level adjustment is a crucial part of the mastering process. Level adjustment should be done after any type of signal processing such as equalization, compression, or limiting, because these processes will generally alter the track level.

The easiest way to make manual adjustments is to right-click on the volume field in the **Track Properties** window and adjust the pop-up fader. Consider docking the **Track Properties** window for easy access while making level adjustments. Dual-monitor users can place control windows or the **Mixers** window on the second monitor for greater convenience.

Nothing beats using your ears and making manual levels adjustments. Audition also provides some advanced level-adjustment tools. These tools are **Effects>Amplitude>Normalize** and **Edit>Group Waveform Normalize**. The **Normalize** function will locate and raise the highest sample, called a peak, to absolute zero. **Group Waveform Normalize** uses a technique more akin to how the human ear perceives loudness to maximize levels. Regardless of whether you've used these automated level functions or not, the best advice is to carefully review the final master before burning to disc.

The following method uses **Edit>Group Waveform Normalize** to perform level adjustments on the sequenced tracks.

Using Group Normalize

1. Open the session titled *Levels.ses* in the *Level Adjustment* directory in the *Chapter 11-Audio* directory of the companion CD.
2. Select **Edit>Group Waveform Normalize**.
3. Hold the **Shift** key while clicking on each track to highlight all tracks in the **Choose Files** tab as shown in Figure 11.5.
4. Select the **Analyze Loudness** tab and press the **Scan for Statistical Information** button as shown in Figure 11.6.

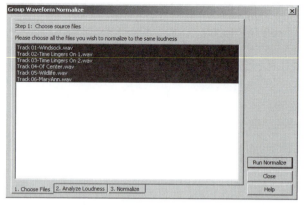

11.5 *The Choose Files tab of the Group Waveform Normalize window*

11.6 *The Analyze Loudness tab of the Group Waveform Normalize window*

5. Click on the **Normalize** tab and select the **Normalize to a Level of** radio button.

6. Enter a value of **–15** in the **dB** field and notice the message directly below showing the percentage of clipped signal if normalized at the current settings.

7. Experiment with these settings, and then click the **Run Normalize** button as shown in Figure 11.6.

Analyze Loudness Tab

Click the **Scan for Statistical Information** button to present statistics. Double-click any file to view an **Advanced Statistical Report**. The RMS histogram shows relative amounts of audio at each loudness level, and the clipping profile shows clipping versus level of amplification.

EQ Loud: the loudness value based on an RMS value with the Equal-Loudness Compensation. The value is modified to approximate how the human ear hears sound. The human ear is less sensitive to low and high frequencies, and this curve takes that factor into account.

Loud: the loudness value based on an RMS value without the **Equal–Loudness Compensation** value.

Max: the maximum RMS value found in the file.

Avg: the average RMS value of the file.

% Clip: the percentage of samples that would be clipped when normalized. This value should be zero if limiting is not selected in the **Normalize** tab. It is not recommended to exceed 5 percent when using limiting.

Reset: clears all normalization statistics.

Normalize Tab

Click **Run Normalize** to **Group Normalize** the selected files.

Normalization: allows normalization based on the maximum average level value determined in the **Analyze Loudness** tab or a user-entered decibel value.

Use Equal Loudness Contour: enables or disables a human-ear compensation curve. Enabling the checkbox is recommended.

Out of Band Peaks: enables or disables limiting.

Lookahead Time: determines the time in milliseconds that it will take to attenuate the audio. The default value is 12; however, it is recommended that the value stay above 5.

Release Time: determines how long in milliseconds it will take after attenuation to return to the normal level. The default is 200 milliseconds.

Advanced: determines window width or duration in milliseconds use to gather RMS Stastistics. The default value is 50.

11.7   *The Normalize tab of the Group Waveform Normalize dialog box*

Step 4 Track Mark Placement

Once the tracks have been sequenced, all signal processing has been done, and the levels have been adjusted, the project is ready to be divided into tracks. Making those divisions is referred to placing track marks or cue marks.

There are four types of cue marks. Each type can be a point within the file or a range with a start time and an end time. The types are as follows:

Basic: marks a point or range for reference. This is a great way to mark a pop or an edit that needs to be made at a later time. They are also used as stop and start points in the playlist.

Beat: marks a musical beat.

Track: marks the point that will begin a track on a compact disc.

Index: marks points within a CD track. Very few CD players in production today allow access to an index, and even fewer listeners know how to use them. I do not recommend using index marks.

Placing track marks or cues is simple. Once placed, the marks can be easily moved, deleted, renamed, and the type of cue can be changed. The only caveat is that cues will not be saved if **Save extra non-audio information** is disabled when saving the file. Let's take a look at the process of adding cues.

Using Cues as Track Marks

1. Open the session titled *Cues.ses* located in the *Track Mark Placement* directory in the *Chapter 11-Audio* directory of the *Using Audition* CD.

2. Select **Window>Cue List** or press **Alt+8**. This will open the **Cue List** window. You may want to close the **Organizer** window for now by pressing **Alt+9** and docking the **Cue List** window in its place.

3. Press the **Home** key or drag the cursor all the way to the left in **Track 1** of the **Multitrack View** window and press **Shift+F8**. The F8 function key is the shortcut for adding cue marks, and **Shift+F8** places track marks. You should see **Cue 01** in the **Cue List** window.

4. Using the cursor, find the start of the next track and press **Shift+F8**.

5. Continue placing track marks until all tracks have been marked.

6. Move the cursor to the end of the last track and press **Shift+F8**. This will mark the end of the CD. The **Cue List** window should show **Cue 01** through **Cue 07**.

7. Select all cues in the **Cue List** window by **Control**-clicking or clicking and dragging. Click the **Merge** button. This will create the cue range as shown in Figure 11.8.

8. Select **Edit>Mix Down to File>All Audio Clips**. This will mix the mastered files down to a single stereo file and open it into the **Edit View** window while retaining the cues. Select **No** if prompted to activate the **Embed Project Link** data for **Edit Original** functionality.

 The cues can also be mixed directly to the **CD Project View** workspace by selecting **Edit > Mix Down to CD Project > All Audio Clips**. Skip the rest of this tutorial if selecting this option.

9. Press **Alt+8** to open the **Cue List** window in **Edit View**. Highlight all the cues in the **Cue List** window and click the **Batch** button.

10. Select the **Save to files** radio button and type a name for the files in the **Filename Prefix** checkbox. A sequential number will be appended to the **Filename Prefix** starting with the value in the **Seq. Start** filed.

11. Click the **Browse** button and select a destination for saving the files.

12. Click **OK**.

Now all the files have been saved as separate tracks with all the modifications. These files can be used with any commercially available CD authoring applications such as Roxio's CD EZ CD Creator or Ahead's Nero, you can use the built-in CD-burning capability of Audition.

11.8   *The Cue List window (above)*

11.9   *The Batch Process Cue Ranges dialog box (right)*

> **TIP!!** If you need to create any other type of CD such as an Enhanced CD or Philips Blue Book, you will need to use another application. Audition cannot burn discs other than standard audio discs as defined by the Philips Red Book specification.

The **Cue List** window has several features and functions.

Column Bar: runs along the top of the **Cue List** window. Cues can be sorted by clicking on any of the headings. The sequence of the headings can also be rearranged by simply dragging the heading horizontally.

Edit Cue Info: brings up the cue information and allows it to be edited. **Begin, End, Length, Label, Description,** and **Type** can be changed. This is a good time to name your cues. Note that the last cue will lose its name when the cue range is created.

Auto-Play: automatically plays the highlighted cue when clicked.

Add: adds cues to the cue list.

Del: deletes a cue from the cue list.

Merge: creates a cue range from the highlighted cues in the cue list. Note that any cues marks between the first highlighted cue and the last highlighted cue will be lost when the cues are merged.

Batch: opens the **Batch Process Cue Ranges** dialog box when in **Edit View** mode in preparation to save the cue ranges to discrete files (see Figure 11.9). The **Batch Process Cue Ranges** dialog box has several options.

Set amount of silence: adds silence to the beginning and/or end of each cue range in the current waveform.

Save to files: saves each cue range to a separate file.

Filename Prefix: saves the files with the text entered into the field followed by a sequential number and the correct extension.

Seq. Start: determines the beginning number of the sequential numbering scheme used with **Filename Prefix.**

Destination Folder: determines the location to which the files will be saved.

Output Format: determines the desired format of the file that is being saved. The **Options** button provides options for selected file formats.

Step 5 Burning the CD

Burning a compact disc is often the final output format of the master used for replication. The replication master is called a Pre-Master CD (PMCD). It is important to make sure that this master is free from anomalies and has been reviewed in entirety.

If you are using a CD authoring application, it is best to burn the disc in Disc-At-Once (DAO) mode rather than Track-At-Once (TAO) mode. DAO mode will burn the entire disc without shutting the laser off, but TAO mode shuts the laser off between tracks. Although this is not generally a problem, it can cause audible clicks and affect the timing between tracks. Now we'll burn a CD with Audition.

Using Audition to Burn a CD

1. Using the **Multitrack View** mode, press **Ctrl+0** to open the *Burn.ses* file in the *Burning the CD* directory of the *Chapter 11-Audio* directory, and then select **Edit>Mixdown to File>All Audio Clips**. Select **No** if prompted to activate the **Embed Project Link** data for **Edit Original** functionality.

 You can skip steps 1 through 4 by opening the *Burn.ses* file and choosing **Edit** > **Mix Down to CD Project** > **All Audio Clips**.

2. Select the **CD Project View** tab or press the **0** key.
3. Click the plus sign to the right of **Mixdown** in the **Organizer** window to show the cues.
4. Drag and drop the cues from the **Organizer** window to the **CD Project View** window.

11.10 *The CD Project View window*

5. Use the **Move Up, Move Down,** and **Remove** buttons to arrange the tracks in the order they will be recorded on the CD.

6. Insert a blank CD into the recording drive and click the **Write CD** button.

7. Select the CD or DVD recorder from the **Device** pop-up menu.

Note The CD length and disc size are noted in the **Project Size** box on the lower right-hand corner of the **CD Project View**. This information is based on the **Free space based on 74 min CD** or **Free space based on 80 min CD** option on the **View** menu.

8. Choose **Write** from the **Write Mode** pop-up menu.

9. Click the **Write CD** button.

It's that easy to burn a CD. There are more options available, and some of those options are described next.

Device: determines which recorder will be used to write the disc. The recorder will be configured automatically when only one recording device is present on the system.

Note Local administrator rights are necessary to burn compact discs in Windows 2000 and Windows XP.

Write Mode: allows selection of the recording modes. **Test** mode permits simulating writing the disc to confirm that the write will be successful. **Test** and **Write** will begin recording provided the test did not fail, and **Write** mode will burn the disc without any testing.

Eject CD when complete: ejects the media upon completion.

Write CD: starts the selected **Write** mode. The **Track** and **Disc** progress bars will display the percentage completed once the write is initiated.

Write CD-Text: enables writing CD-Text information provided the recording device supports CD-Text. The **Project Title** and **Artist** fields as well as the **Track Title** and **Artist** entered in the **Track Properties** window will be displayed on CD players that support CD-Text.

Note   CD-Text should not be confused with music recognition services such as Gracenote CDDB. CD-Text is written on the CD-R. Music recognition services use an algorithm based on the CD Table of Contents to locate a match to an on-line database.

UPC/EAN: permits entering a Universal Product Code Identification Number or European Article Numbering code. The UPC/EAN identifies a product using a unique 13-digit code.

Device: selects the recording device for configuration.

Buffer Size: determines the amount of RAM allocated for disc burning. The recorder uses the data from the buffer before requesting more data from the hard drive. This buffering process allows the recorder to continue uninterrupted burning even when the CPU may be momentarily busy handling routine system tasks. Disc failures that occur when the buffers are too small and empty before the write is complete are called Buffer Underruns. Set the buffer for as large as possible to avoid this type of failure.

Write Speed: determines the disc writing speed. Faster speeds typically provide better recording by exposing the media to the laser for a shorter duration, however the opposite result can occur if the media is not certified for the selected recording speed.

11.11 The Write CD window

11.12 The CD Device Properties window (above)

11.13 The Track Properties window (right)

Buffer Underrun prevention: enables buffer underrun protection provided it is supported by the recording device.

Track Properties Window

The **Track Properties** window displays specifics of each track and allows using default or custom settings. The **Use default track properties** should be selected unless there is a specific need to change the **Track Property** settings. The **Track Title** and **Artist** fields will be written to the CD-R when **Write CD-Text** is enabled in the **Write CD** dialog box provided the CD or DVD recorder supports CD-Text.

Pause: allows you to adjust the pause between tracks. The default is 2 seconds. This option should be enabled and set to zero if the tracks segue.

Copy Protection: enables a flag bit indicating that the track is copyrighted.

Pre-emphasis: sets a flag that enables the pre-emphasis circuitry in CD players. Pre-emphasis is an equalization curve that boosts the high frequencies to improve frequency response. Most audio professionals do not consider this curve necessary for digital audio, and it is not typically used anymore.

Set as default: saves the current track properties settings as the default values for future CD projects.

Same for all tracks: sets the tracks properties of all tracks to the values of the current track.

ISRC: displays the ISRC (International Standard Recording Code) that is used to identify audio recordings.

ISRC

The ISRC (International Standard Recording Code) was developed to aid in collecting royalties and as a tool in anti-piracy effects. The code format consists of four parts: a two-character country code, a three-character registrant code, a two-digit code for the year, and a five-character code designated by the copyright holder.

ISRC Code Example: US-D77-03-UAB01

The Recording Industry Association of America administers the program, and registration is free. Contact the RIAA at www.riaa.com for registration information.

When creating your CD, make sure to use a premium brand. Even though the other brands may sound okay and are cheap, your player masks errors that may not be acceptable when used as a master for replication. Your burner may also have particular brands that it prefers, so you may need to experiment to find the brand that works best.

MASTERING FOR ANALOG TAPE FORMATS

Although analog tape and audiocassette sales are an extremely small percentage of the market today, a chapter on mastering would not be complete without mentioning a few words about analog formats. There are still a number of audiophiles who swear that analog audio sounds much better than digital. I had the opportunity to work with both formats in extremely critical environments, and I agree that there are advantages and disadvantages to both digital and analog recording, but for flexibility and creativity, I prefer working in the digital realm. With that being said, I will briefly touch on mastering for analog tape formats.

Most of the mastering techniques are the same for analog and digital formats. The main difference in these formats, aside from the obvious, is the ability to retain and regenerate signal without distortion. Digital formats can be hundreds of generations from the original master and still have very little, if any, signal degeneration. Analog on the other hand, deteriorates to an unacceptable quality within a few generations.

The main consideration when mastering to analog should be level. Analog formats cannot handle the amount of signal that most digital formats can without severe distortion. For example, the output level for cassette production should be at least 8–12dB lower than for a compact disc. Even with that level reduction, you should be very careful with high-frequency and extremely low-frequency content. These frequencies can saturate the tape and result in erasing the higher frequencies or distortion. The lower frequencies can also cause an undesired modulation of the audio content. When working with analog formats, it is also critical that the tape equipment be calibrated properly.

Whatever the final product, there is no substitute for using your ears. Experiment and listen. Learn the medium for which you are mastering. You'll be surprised at the results.

Chapter 12

Bonus Features

CONDUCTING MUSIC

Audition offers the ability to use MIDI (Musical Instrument Digital Interface) files while simultaneously playing and/or recording other audio tracks and video and including ReWire compliant music and audio applications.

WHAT IS MIDI?

In the early 1980s, a group of musical instrument manufacturers agreed upon a protocol or system of communicating between electronic instruments such as synthesizers. The protocol, named MIDI, provided the means for a device called a MIDI controller to transmit a musical performance or sequence to devices made by different manufacturers. The MIDI specification has advanced with technology, and today a wide range of MIDI products is in use from multi-timbral sound modules and samplers to software-based sequencers used to compose and run MIDI files.

12.1 *The Ozone from M-Audio is a portable USB MIDI controller. Copyright: (Copyright symbol) 2004 by M-Audio, used with permission.*

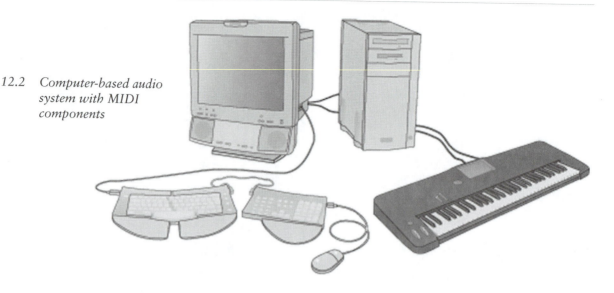

12.2 Computer-based audio system with MIDI components

Although MIDI can record virtually all the nuances of a musical performance, it is not digital audio. It is a stream of computer data that instructs a keyboard or sound module what to do and when. Think of it as a text file that sends musical notes instead of letters.

Using MIDI in Audition

Using a MIDI file in Audition is easy; however, before the MIDI file can be played, the MIDI devices must be properly connected and configured. Chapter 2, on page 36, provides information on configuring MIDI devices in the **Device Properties** and **Device Order** windows.

 Audition supports MIDI file *Note* formats with the .mid and .rmi extensions.

MIDI files can be opened into the **Organizer** window while in **Edit View** mode; however MIDI files will only playback when placed into a track of the **Multitrack View**. MIDI files are inserted into tracks in **Multitrack View** by selecting **Insert>MIDI** or right-clicking on a track and selecting the same option. Although Audition is not a sequencer and therefore cannot create a MIDI sequence, MIDI tracks can be treated like most other tracks. The clips can be split, moved, copied, and deleted. Unlike inserting video into the **Multitrack View**, MIDI files are not limited to a single instance; however, MIDI files can only be placed into tracks one at a time.

 It's a good practice to patch the MIDI outputs into the Audition inputs and record them to hard disc. Doing so will make the tracks available even if the keyboard or synth is not.

There are five commands that affect only MIDI tracks and appear on the **Edit** menu or the pop-up menu when a MIDI track has the focus.

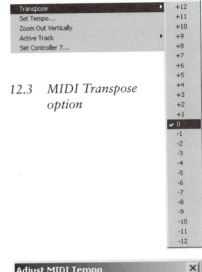

Transpose: The **Transpose** function allows you to transpose the key of the selected MIDI track up to an octave up or down.

12.3   *MIDI Transpose option*

Set Tempo: The **Set Tempo** function determines the MIDI track tempo. Three options are available from the pop-up menu. Authored means the MIDI track will remain at the tempo set when the MIDI file was created. **Match Session** uses the current session tempo, and **Custom** enables the **Tempo** field that is used to set the tempo for the MIDI track only. The tempo is displayed by a red horizontal line on the clip with the numeric value at the beginning of the clip.

Zoom In Vertically/Zoom Out Vertically: This function provides another method to magnify the MIDI track view.

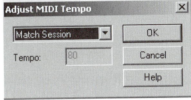

12.3   *The Adjust MIDI Tempo dialog box*

Active Track: **Active Track** determines whether only a single track or all tracks in a MIDI clip play. If a single track is chosen, the **Active Track** name displays in the lower left corner of the track.

Set Controller 7: Audition can issue a MIDI command to set the volume of a MIDI device. The default **MIDI Controller for Volume** is 7. Values range from 0–127; higher values are louder.

> On occasion, and usually at the worst possible time, the MIDI controllers jam, and it seems that only an act of God or pulling the power plug can stop it. Fortunately, there is another way. The MIDI panic button is the **P** key. Hit it when all else fails.

12.4   *Volume delivered by MIDI keyboards or other sound generators can be set from within Audition with the Set Controller 7 command.*

Map: The tracks in each MIDI file can be assigned to any available MIDI device or channel using the pop-up menus. The **MIDI Device Assignment** window is opened with the **MAP** button.

There is a lot more to MIDI, and other sources of more detailed information are readily available. An excellent overview of the MIDI technology can be found at www.MIDI.org.

WHAT IS REWIRE?

ReWire is a technology that connects two audio applications together with up to 256 channels of audio in real time while maintaining Sample-Accurate Sync or synchronization accuracy to within one sample. ReWire 2.0 also provides cross-application transport control so you don't have to switch applications to stop or rewind the track. ReWire offers more MIDI channels than you could possibly need, and applications can even exchange channel names. These are all great features, but the best part is that there are *no* wires.

12.5   *The MIDI Device Assignment window*

 Note   Audition does not currently support recording or editing of MIDI data. There are a number of MIDI sequencer applications on the market to handle these tasks.

Using ReWire in Audition

Audition supports ReWire 2.0 and later. There are no installation requirements other than having another ReWire compliant application such as Reason from Propellerhead Software, Unity DS-1 from Bitheadz, Sonar and Project 5 from Cakewalk, or ACID from Sony/Sonic Foundry. The list of applications supporting ReWire is growing quickly.

Configuring ReWire in Audition is simple, but it should be noted that ReWire is operable only in **Multitrack View** mode. Select **Options>Device Properties** and click the **Enable** button on the **ReWire** tab. Any ReWire-compliant applications will appear in the window. Enable the checkbox of the desired application, select the track assignment, and fire up the application with the **Launch** button. See "ReWire Tab" on page 41 in Chapter 2 for more information on the **ReWire** tab.

When ReWire channels are patched to a track, the **Input Device** button is labeled **RW**. ReWire track assignments can be changed by clicking the **RW** button on the track controls as shown in Figure 12.6. The **RW** button opens the **Input Devices** window, allowing you to select the desired channel. The **Properties** button on the **Input Devices** window opens the **ReWire** tab in the **Settings** window.

12.6   *Track Control displays RW Button when a ReWire device is assigned to the track.*

ReWire tracks respond to mixing controls such as volume adjustment, pan, EQ, and effects in the same way that controls affect recorded tracks. They can be mixed down or

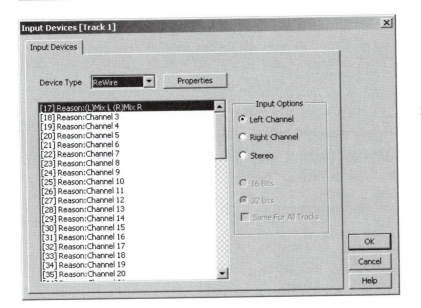

12.7 *The Input Devices window shows a listing of audio tracks open in the ReWire application.*

exported to a file, bounced to other tracks, or mixed down and placed in the **CD Project View**. Bear in mind when using ReWire that there are two applications at work on the CPU. Mixing will take more time, and file housekeeping is required for two applications. Make sure to save the files in both applications before quitting.

> Try reducing the **Playback buffer** on the **Multitrack** tab of the **Settings** window if you notice a timing difference between the ReWire application and Audition.

SHORTCUTS AND MIDI TRIGGERS

One of the reasons computer have gained their popularity in the workplace is their ability to perform repetitive tasks. Audition provides another way for the computer to help with repetitive tasks called *shortcuts*. These shortcuts are a way of activating a function or a series of functions.

Most computer users are familiar with using **Ctrl+C** to copy text. Audition provides the same ability to cut and copy audio using keystrokes; however, Audition puts this ability on steroids and allows shortcuts for virtually every function in the application. The shortcuts feature is enhanced by providing access to these shortcuts and the ability to change them to suit the user. To add even more versatility to this feature, functions can be mapped to MIDI controllers allowing a keyboard or other MIDI device to trigger play, stop, record, and almost any other function in Audition.

If a shortcut fails, click in the waveform or session display areas. The appropriate window must have the focus of the application. Clicking in a docked window or pressing **Alt**+/ shows the active window with a short burst of color around the handle on the window.

Table 12.1   Frequently Used Shortcuts

Shortcut	File Commands
Ctrl + N	New file or session.
Ctrl + O	Opens file or session.
Ctrl + I	Imports file.
Ctrl + M	Insert into Multitrack View.
Ctrl + S	Saves the file or session.
Ctrl + Shift + S	Save As file or session.
Ctrl + W	Close waveform or session.
Ctrl + Q	Quits Audition application.
Alt + Insert	Inserts selection into CD Project View.
	View Commands
=	Zoom In - Horizontally.
-	Zoom Out - Horizontally.
Alt + =	Zoom In - Vertically.
Alt + -	Zoom Out-Vertically.
Alt + Home	Zoom In - Left edge of selection.
Alt + End	Zoom In - Right edge of selection.

Table 12.1   Frequently Used Shortcuts (Continued)

	Cursor/Selection Commands
Left Arrow	Move cursor left.
Right Arrow	Move cursor right.
Home	Move cursor to the start of the waveform or session.
End	Move cursor to the end of the waveform or session.
Ctrl + Left Arrow	Move cursor to previous cue or start of waveform or session.
Ctrl + Right Arrow	Move cursor to next cue or end of waveform or session.
Ctrl + A	Select All or All Clips.
[	Marks left side of selection while in playback mode.
]	Marks right side of selection while in playback mode.
Shift + Left Arrow	Extend selection to the left of the cursor position.
Shift + Right Arrow	Extend selection to the right of the cursor position.
Shift + Home	Extend selection to the beginning from the cursor position.
Shift + Left	Extend selection to the end from the cursor position.
Alt + N	Creates Noise Reduction Profile from selection.
	Editing Commands
Ctrl + C	Copy selection or waveform.
Ctrl + X	Cut selection or waveform.
Ctrl + T	Trim waveform outside of selection.
Ctrl + V	Paste selection or waveform.
Ctrl + L	Edit left channel
Ctrl + R	Edit right channel
Ctrl + B	Edit both channels
Ctrl + Z	Undo last command.
Ctrl + Shift +Z	Redo command.
Delete	Delete the selection.

Table 12.1   Frequently Used Shortcuts (Continued)

	Transport Commands
Alt + P	Play.
Alt + S	Stop.
Alt + W	Plays Preroll, Selections, and Postroll.
Space Bar	Toggles between Play and Stop mode.
Ctrl + Space Bar	Toggles between Record and Pause mode.
J	Rewind while pressed.
K	Fast Forward while pressed.
	Tool Commands
R	Hybrid Tool
V	Move/Copy Tool
S	Time Selection Tool
M	Marquee Selection Tool
	Window Commands
8	Selects Edit View mode.
9	Selects Multitrack View mode.
0	Selects CD Project View mode.
F9	Toggle display between Waveform and Spectral views.
F12	Toggle between Multitrack View and Edit View modes.
Alt + 2	Toggle display of Mixer window.
Alt + 3	Toggle display of Session Properties window.
Alt + 4	Toggle display of Track Properties window.
Alt + 5	Toggle display of Track EQ window.
Alt + 6	Toggle display of Selection/View Controls window.
Alt + 7	Toggle display of Level Meters window.
Alt + 8	Toggle display of Cue List window.
Alt + 9	Toggle display of Organizer window.
Alt + K	Toggle display of Shortcuts and MIDI Triggers window.

Table 12.1   Frequently Used Shortcuts (Continued)

Alt + Z	Toggle display of Frequency Analysis window.
Alt + 1	Sets focus to main display window.
Ctrl + H	Displays Audio Clip Properties window.
Ctrl + P	Displays Wave Properties or Advanced Session Properties window
Misc. Commands	
F1	Opens Audition Help engine.
F2	Repeat last command with dialog box.
F3	Repeat last command without dialog box.
F4	Displays the Settings dialog box.
F5	Refresh Now.
F6	MIDI Triggers Enable.
F7	SMPTE Slave Enable.
F8	Place Cue Mark.
Shift+F8	Place Track Mark.
F10	Toggles Monitor Record Level on and off.
F11	Opens Convert Sample Type window.
P	MIDI Panic command.

Using the Shortcuts Window

Managing shortcuts and MIDI triggers is done through the **Shortcuts** window. The window is accessed with the shortcut **Alt+K** or selecting **Options>Keyboard Shortcuts and MIDI Triggers**.

The **Category** dropdown and **Multitrack**, **Edit View**, and **CD View** buttons determine the functions displayed in the list. In fact, there are even some functions not available via menu options. Adding, changing, or removing a keyboard shortcut or MIDI trigger is as simple as entering or clearing the desired fields. To add or modify an existing shortcut key, locate the desired command and click inside the **Press new shortcut key** field. Type the key or combination keystroke and click the **OK** button. It couldn't be much simpler.

It is worth noting that the **Options>MIDI Trigger Enable** function must be checked for the MIDI triggers to operate. The **F6** function key toggles **MIDI Triggering** on and off.

12.9   Shortcuts Window

When MIDI is properly connected and configured, the MIDI event data will display on the lower left side of the status bar. Check MIDI connections and MIDI configurations in the device settings if MIDI event information is not present on the status bar.

MIDI Channel: 1, Note Off: F# 4 (66)

12.8   Status Bar displays last MIDI event information received.

Set: selects the current shortcut keyset. Audition allows saving keysets so that different keysets could be used for different applications. For example, one set of shortcuts could be set up for editing and sweetening audio for video, and another set could be used for multitrack recording and mixing. I have a hard enough time keeping track on one set of keys, but Audition will allow as many as you so desire.

To save a keyset, make a change to any shortcut or function. Once a change has been made, the **Set** pop-up menu will display [**Custom**]. Click the **Save As** button, enter a name for the keyset, and click the **Save** button.

One of the best applications for multiple keysets is when you have multiple engineers using the same computer. Each engineer can save their own keysets customized for their own style of engineering. Keysets can also be moved to other machines. Moving the keysets involves opening the Windows Registry, so make sure that you possess the necessary technical expertise before opening or making changes in the registry.

Here's the method for saving and restoring keysets for those people who are confident with their registry abilities:

1. Go to **Start >Run** and type in *REGEDIT.*

2. Find *HKEY_CURRENT_USER\Software\Adobe\Audition\1.5\Prefs\en_US\name of your keyset.*

3. Right-click on that key, choose **Export,** and save the file to another location.

4. Transfer the key to the desired PC.

5. Double-click on that saved Registry Key to restore your keyset.

Category: selects which functions are displayed. All functions can be displayed using the **Show All** choice.

Multitrack/Edit View /CD View Buttons: toggle on and off display of functions available in the three views: **Multitrack View, Edit View,** and **CD Project View.**

Press new shortcut key: pressing a key or combination of keystrokes when this field has the focus will set that key or keystroke as the shortcut for the highlighted function. This field can be edited manually.

Clear: resets the shortcut key.

MIDI Trigger: receives the MIDI controller information when the field has focus and sets the MIDI trigger to the event value received for the highlighted function. In other words, pressing a key on a MIDI keyboard will send the necessary MIDI information and fill the **MIDI trigger** field. This field can be manually edited.

Note Options > MIDI Trigger must be enabled, and the MIDI device must be connected and properly configured for this function to work. See "Device Properties" on page 36 in Chapter 2 for information on configuring device properties.

Channel: sets the MIDI trigger channel. Any channel between 1 and 16 inclusive are available. All channels can also be enabled by selecting *(any).

Clear: sets the MIDI shortcut and channel fields.

Conflicting Keys: displays any functions that have the same shortcuts keys. It's not a good idea to have conflicting keys. In fact, Audition will not permit saving a keyset with conflicts.

Restore Defaults: resets all shortcuts to the default settings as if Audition had just been installed.

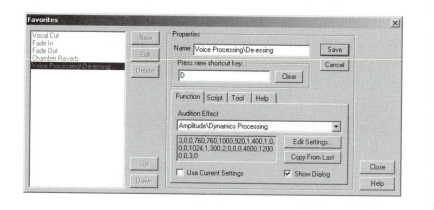

12.10 The Favorites dialog box

 Speed is the name of the game in commercial production and shortcuts can help you lead the race. Consider adding shortcuts for commonly used tasks in your workflow. A few examples of functions you may want shortcuts for are **Arm for Record**, **Lock in Time**, **Loop Mode toggle**, **File Save All**, **Close All**, **Zoom Out Full Both Axis**, **Solo Track**, **Snap to Zero Crossing**, not to mention any of the numerous built-in effects and third-party plug-in effects

 Set up shortcuts for the way you work. Create as many shortcuts as you want, but remember, it's not going to help if you don't use them. Try learning shortcuts one at a time. Work with them until they become habit, and then go for another one. You'll be amazed at how soon you know shortcuts for almost every command.

FAVORITES MENU

The **Favorites** menu is a simple but valuable feature. **Favorites** allow adding frequently used effects as a menu items on the **Favorites** menu as well as the **Favorites** tab of the **Organizer** window, but **Favorites** items are not limited to the built-in effects supplied with Audition. Macros known as scripts, other applications, and third-party effects can be configured as **Favorite** items.

The Favorites Dialog Box

Adding or removing menu items is done through the **Favorites** dialog box. The dialog box is opened by selecting **Favorites>Edit Favorites**.

New: adds a new menu item, group, or separator bar.

Edit: allows you to modify the all settings of highlighted menu item.

Delete: permanently removes the currently highlighted menu item.

Up: moves the currently selected item up in the list and determines the order of display on the **Favorites** menu.

Down: moves the currently selected item down in the list and determines the order of display on the **Favorites** menu.

Name: sets the name of the menu item. The name function can also be used to create separator bars by typing dashes or any other desired character without setting any action for the menu item. Use a backslash between items in the name to add submenu items or separator bars. For example, **Voice\Broad De-ess** would create a menu item named **Broad De-ess** as a submenu of **Voice**.

Save: stores the current settings to a new or existing item.

Cancel: cancels creation of a new menu item or editing of an existing item; however, it does not close the **Favorites** window.

Press new shortcut key: sets a shortcut for the menu item by pressing a key or keystroke combination. Shortcuts already in use for other functions can be overwritten; however, a dialog box will provide a warning before overwriting.

Clear: clears any text currently in the shortcut key field.

Function Tab: allows you to add a custom item using any item on the **Effects** and **Generate** menus or supported DirectX or VST plug-ins. **Generate>Silence** is not included.

- *Audition Effect:* displays a pop up list of effects and plug-ins to use as a **Favorite** menu item.

- *Edit Settings:* opens a dialog box for the selected effect, allowing modification of the effect settings. Any modifications will be used when the item is selected as a **Favorite** item.

- *Copy from Last:* copies the effect and setting from the last effect or function that was opened.

- *Use Current Settings:* disables editing of the effect settings and uses the current parameters.

- *Show Dialog:* forces the **Effects** or **Generate** dialog box to open, enabling adjustment of the settings before the effects is applied.

Script Tab: allows selection of a script as a menu item.

- *Script Collection File:* sets the path for the current script collection file. Script collection files carry the .scp extension and are usually located in the *Scripts* directory in the *Audition* application directory. Click the box to the right to navigate to the desired file.

- *Script:* allows selection of any script in the current script collection file.

- *Pause at Dialogs:* causes the script to pause and wait for user input before continuing at each dialog box the script calls. Enabling this checkbox allows you to customize the specific setting used in the task as the script executes.

Tool Tab: allows running executables, including command-line switches.

Command Line: enter the file path and any required switches or click the box to the right and locate the desired file.

 Utilities such as SMPTE time-code calculators, notepad, and even sequencers can be opened from the **Favorites** menu or by using a shortcut. Although the application is not running within the Audition application, it is still a quick and convenient way to have the commonly used apps at your fingertips.

 Consider adding the Windows Recording Mixer or the third-party mixer supplied with your sound device to the **Favorites** menu. A shortcut could also be added for one key access. To add the Windows Recording Mixer, add the *sndvol32.exe* to the **Command Line** of the **Tool** tab. The file path on most systems is *C:\Windows\System32\sndvol32.exe.*

Help Tab: describes how to create separator bars and submenus.

Close: closes the **Favorites** window.

Using the Favorites Menu

The **Favorites** menu is a standard hierarchical menu and can include items in groups with separator bars. Adding and deleting items is not complicated.

Adding a Favorites Menu Item

Let's create a **Favorites** menu item. We are going to make a menu option named **Voice** with a submenu named **De-esser** that will call the **Dynamics Processing** effect with the **De-Esser Light** preset.

1. Select **Favorites>Edit Favorites** to open the **Favorites** dialog box.
2. Click the **New** button and type *Voice\De-esser*. The backslash between names sets the second name as a submenu item of the first name.
3. Enter the letter **D** in the **Press new shortcut key** field.
4. Choose **Amplitude\Dynamics Processing** from the **Audition Effect** pop-up menu.
5. Click the **Edit Settings** button and select **De-Esser Light** from the effect presets list and click the **OK** button to close the **Dynamics Processing** dialog box.

6. Enable the **Show Dialog** checkbox. This will open the **Dynamics Processor** effect with the **Light De-essing** settings when the menu item is selected. By showing the dialog box, the settings can be adjusted to taste before applying the effect.

7. Click the **Save** button.

8. Click the **New** button again and type 10 dashes into the **Name** field.

9. Click the **Save** button and click the **Up** button to move the new separator bar (the dashes) up above the **Voice Processing\De-essing** in the list.

10. Close the **Favorites** dialog box.

The **Favorites** menu should now look like the Figure 12.11. Additional customized effects can be added to the **Voice** group by setting the name for each additional menu item as **Voice\(new item name)**.

12.11 *Favorites Menu with custom item added. Pressing the D key activates the menu item.*

SCRIPTING AND BATCH PROCESSING

Scripting and batch processing are powerful features, and like shortcuts and favorites, they can save you a lot of time by handling repetitive tasks. The time savings can be multiplied when scripts are combined with batch processing.

Scripts

Scripting is not a revolutionary feature of Audition. It has been in use since the beginning of computing; however, few other audio applications take advantage of this ability. Programming in its simplest form uses segments of code to perform certain tasks. These segments or modules, perhaps not as easily discernible as in Audition, are essentially scripts.

For those familiar with actions in Adobe Photoshop, scripting will seem somewhat familiar, albeit a little more cryptic. Scripts can be created in a word processor, but most people find it preferable to let Audition record the scripts automatically.

Let's see how scripting works. First, we'll create a script that applies two effects to a waveform. After the tutorial, we'll take a close look at the scripts and batch-processing functions.

Using Scripting

1. Open Audition in **Edit View** mode and press **Ctrl+O**, and locate the file *GuitSlow10.CEL* in the *Chapter 12-Audio* directory on the CD that accompanies the book.

2. Press **Ctrl+O** and locate the file *GuitSlow10.CEL* in the *Chapter 12-Audio* directory on the CD that accompanies the book.

3. Click the **Open/New Collection** button and type *Tutorial Scripts*. Then click the **Open** button to complete creating a new script collection named Tutorial Scripts. Scripts carry the

.scp extension and are normally located in the *Scripts* directory within the *Audition* application directory.

4. Enter a name for the script in the **Title** field. We'll call it **Distorted Chorus**.

5. Disable the **Pause at Dialogs** checkbox. This will cause the script to run without pausing to allow changing effect settings.

6. Click the **Record** button to begin recording your actions.

7. Select **Effects>Special>Distortion**, and pick **Bow Curve 1** from the **Presets** list.

8. Click **OK** and the effect will be applied to the current waveform.

9. Select **Effects>Delay Effects>Chorus** and choose **TrippyVox** from the **Presets** list.

10. Click **OK** to apply the effect.

11. Select **Options>Scripts** to open the **Scripts** window.

12. Click the **Stop Current Script** button to stop recording any further actions.

13. If no mistakes were made, press the **Add to Collection** button to complete the script creation. Otherwise, press the **Clear** button and repeat steps 4 –12.

> **Note** Keep the file open. We will continue with the tutorial shortly.

The Distorted Chorus script was recorded and stored as text in the script collection named *Tutorial Scripts.SCP*. The script collection is a text file and can be edited with any text editor such as Notepad. The title can be changed, and any comments added next to the **Description:** will be shown in the **Scripts** window. Scripts can be copied, modified, and exchanged with other users.

12.12 The Scripts window

Start a new script collection by opening a new text file and adding the word "Collection" and the desired collection name with a colon between them. For example, *Collection: My New Script Collection*. Save the file with the collection name and the .scp extension. The script collection is ready to begin adding scripts.

 Notice that the effect is listed beside **cmd:** and the effect settings follow. You can create new versions of the scripts or modify existing scripts using a text editor.

Let's continue with the scripting tutorial.

14. Close the **Scripts** window and press **Ctrl+Z** twice to Undo the effects.

15. Select **Options>Scripts** to open the window again.

16. Highlight the **Distorted Chorus**, and click the **Run Script** button.

The script executes and presents a dialog upon successful completion. Undo the effects and try the script again. This time enable the **Pause at Dialogs** checkbox to allow you to change the effects settings before applying them. The completion dialog box can also be shut off by disabling the **Alert when complete** checkbox.

Scripts can work in three different modes as listed on the bottom of the **Scripts** window: **Script Starts from Scratch, Script Works on Current Wave,** and **Script Works on Highlighted Selection**.

Script Starts from Scratch starts the script with a **New** command and is used to create a new file. **Script Works on Current Wave** uses the current waveform but it should be noted that the script begins at the current cursor position. **Script Works on Highlighted Selection** causes the script to function on the selection.

The **Execute Relative to Cursor** checkbox executes the script based on the current cursor position. Otherwise, the script will function based on the cursor position when the script was created. To avoid timing issues when the script will most likely be run at the current cursor location, it is a good practice to record the script with the cursor at the beginning of the waveform and enable the **Execute Relative to Cursor** checkbox.

```
Collection: Tutorial Scripts
Title: Distorted Chorus
Description:
Mode: 2

Selected: none at 0 scaled 255034 SR 44100
Freq: Off
cmd: Channel Both

Selected: 0 to 255033 scaled 255034 SR 44100
Freq: Off
Comment: Special\Distortion
cmd: {3D8A56EF-01B8-481D-911F-EC93C78E88E6
1: 3
2: 0
3: 0
4: 1638
5: 2560
6: 4096
7: 3925
8: 1
9: 2
10: 0
11: 0
12: 4096
13: 4096
14: 1
15: 0
16: 1
17: 0

Freq: Off
Comment: Delay Effects\Chorus
cmd: {14171CBA-E4AB-4A4E-B384-B950D52E37D:
1: 5
2: 31.4
3: 0.1
4: 0
5: 2
6: 0
7: 0.6
8: 30
9: 0.8
10: 0.1
11: 0
12: 0
13: 0
14: 0

Freq: Off
End:
```

12.13 Each script is stored inside a script collection file and can be edited with any text editor.

12.14 The Files tab of the Batch Processing window

Batch Processing

Audio files can be converted from one format to another using **Edit>Convert Sample Type**; however, that can be a time-consuming and tedious task when multiple files are involved. Batch processing simplifies the conversion of multiple files by running a batch process on the selected files. It's a set-it-and-forget-it mode, and meanwhile you can complete session paperwork and billing.

Selecting **File>Batch Processing** presents the main dialog box with the **Files** tab active. Click the **Add Files** button to locate and add the files requiring conversion. Use the **Open Raw PCM As** button to set specific file attributes if the source files are headerless audio files known as Raw PCM. The files path of the selected files can be long, and the file name can be obscured by the edge of the window. Enabling the **Hide Path** checkbox displays only the file name.

A script can be run on the selected files during batch processing. This is a very powerful feature providing the ability to adjust levels, add effects, and filter the files using custom settings written into the script. Check the **Run a script** checkbox on the **Run Script** tab and locate the script collection with the **Browse** button. Once a script collection is open, select the script from the pop-up menu.

Checking **Conversion Settings** on the **Resample** tab enables the **Change Destination Format** button. Clicking this button opens the **Convert Sample Type** dialog box and permits you to change parameters for sampling rate, format, resolution, and quality. See "Convert Sample Type" on page 81 in Chapter 4 for more details.

The **New Format** tab sets the output format of the file conversion. The output format is selected from a pop-up menu, and specific settings for the selected format are available through the **Format Properties** button (see Figure 12.17).

12.15 *The Run Script tab of the Batch Processing window*

12.16 *The Resample tab of the Batch Processing window*

12.17 *The New Format tab of the Batch Processing window*

12.18 Destination tab of the
Batch Processing window

The **Destination** tab sets filename, output location, and whether the original files should be overwritten by the new files, automatically deleted, or removed from the conversion list after successful conversion.

The file-naming schema can seem rather confusing at first look, but it's simple for those familiar with DOS (Disc Operating System) originally used on PCs. It's not that difficult, even if you're not familiar with DOS. Using an asterisk before the period causes the new file-name to use the source file-name. Placing an asterisk after the period retains the source file extension. A question mark will keep the character at the same location in the source file name. The **Destination** tab provides examples for use of the **Output Filename Template** (see Figure 12.18).

Once the parameters of the **Batch Processing** tabs are complete, click the **Run Batch** button and sit back.

SYNCHRONIZATION

It has been a common practice in the video postproduction world to work on audio and video as separate components and lay back the audio to the video master after the audio had been sweetened. The problem with this process was maintaining synchronization between the audio and video.

To retain synchronization, an electronic signal called SMPTE Timecode was employed. The timecode format is based on a 24-hour clock and divided into hours, minutes, seconds, frames, and though not commonly displayed, subframes. SMPTE Timecode can be thought of as an electronic "sprocket" much like those on a film.

Audition uses a timecode called MIDI Timecode. MTC encapsulates SMPTE Timecode within the MIDI signal. Although Audition can generate MTC and act as a master device, slaving Audition via SMPTE Timecode requires running the SMPTE Timecode through another MIDI device to convert the SMPTE Timecode to MTC.

The **MIDI/Synchronization** status will display in the lower left corner of the status bar. As a general rule, allow five seconds for the system to establish synchronization; however, times of 15 seconds or longer can be required when using analog tape machines as slaves. The SMPTE tab of the Settings window permits fine-tuning synchronization parameters. See "SMPTE Tab" on page 35 in Chapter 2 for more details on the SMPTE tab settings. If necessary, a *SMPTE Start Time Offset* can be entered in the **General** tab of the **Advanced Session Properties** window to delay or offset the start of playback.

> **SMPTE** is an acronym for Society of Motion Picture and Television Engineers. The SMPTE organization sets standards for the film and video industries and is responsible for the development of the SMPTE Timecode specification. A wealth of information on SMPTE may be found at www.smpte.org.

Using Audition as the Master Device

Setting Audition up as a master device, or in other words, setting up Audition so that other devices or machines will follow or chase it, is simple if the MIDI connections and configuration are correct. Make sure that the **MIDI Out** tab of the **Device Properties** shows the correct MIDI device or interface in the **SMPTE Output** field.

1. Once the session is open, right-click the **Time Format Display** window and select the desired timecode display format.
2. Choose **Options>SMPTE Master Enable**.
3. Click **Play**.

Using Audition as the Slave Device

Audition can chase another machine or device using MTC. Again, the steps are simple if the MIDI connections and configuration are correct. Make sure that the MIDI In tab of the **Device Properties** window shows the correct MIDI device or interface in the **SMPTE Slave Device** field.

1. Enable **Record** for any tracks to be recorded.
2. Press **F7** or **Options>SMPTE Slave Enable**.
3. Start playback of the master device.

SMPTE Timecode formats can be confusing. Postproduction facilities prefer Non-Drop Frame timecode to Drop Frame.

Devices reading SMPTE Timecode tend to be finicky when it comes to the code. The **Slave Stability** field on the status bar provides an indication of the signal integrity. If the code is not clean, sync can be intermittently lost, and lock-up can sometimes be impossible. If the timecode is from an analog tape and cannot be regenerated, try EQing the SMPTE signal by filtering lows and boosting 1kHz.

OPTIONS

The **Options** menu presents access to a number of features. Although these options do not require their own menu, these are important features. Even though most of these options have been discussed in previous chapters, each selection is presented with a discussion of the purpose and application for quick reference.

The discussion is divided into several sections: options shown in all views, options shown both **Edit View** and **Multitrack View**, and options that appear in only one mode.

Options Menu (All Views)

Settings: opens the **Settings** dialog box, which is used to configure preferences for Audition. Pressing the **F4** key also opens the **Settings** window.

Device Properties: Opens the **Device Properties** dialog box, which is used to control sound cards and devices and MIDI controller settings.

Keyboard Shortcuts & MIDI Triggers: This command opens the **Shortcuts** window, which is used for managing shortcuts and MIDI triggers.

Options Menu (Edit View and Multitrack View Only)

Loop Mode: Enabling the **Loop Mode** option will cause the **Play** shortcut to toggle between **Play** and **Play Looped** mode. (The default **Play** shortcut is the spacebar.)

Monitor Record Level(s): The option enables the level meters and monitoring. It is used when setting input levels prior to recordings. The **F10** key or double-clicking on the level meters also enable and disable the monitoring function. Clicking **Stop** will also turn the monitoring mode off.

Show Levels on Play and Record: Enabling **Show Levels on Play and Record** activates the level meters.

MIDI Trigger Enable: Enables controlling Audition functions with MIDI events. The **F6** key also toggles the on and off state of this function.

Windows Recording Mixer: This submenu choice opens the **Windows Recording Mixer**, which is used to adjust sound device input levels. Note that many soundcards or devices provide their own mixers for adjusting levels.

Start Default Windows CD Player: This option opens the default audio CD player. The default player is Windows Media Player unless another player has been installed and set as the default.

Device Order: Calls the **Device Order Preference** dialog box, which is used to enable input and output devices and preferred use order.

Options Menu (Edit View only)

The following options are displayed only in **Edit View**.

Scripts: Opens the **Scripts** window used for creating, editing, and running automated functions.

Language Options: Audition can be configured to operate in one of four languages: English, French, German, and Japanese. This menu option sets the desired language; however, Audition must be restarted before the change will be effective.

Timed Record Mode: Checking this option will enable timed recordings and cause the **Recording Time** configuration window to open when engaging record.

Synchronize Cursor Across Windows: Enabling this option causes the cursor location or selected segment to remain consistent when switching between open waveforms.

Preroll and Postroll Options: It is often helpful to hear a second or more of the audio at a transition or edit point. The **Preroll** and **Postroll Options** dialog box is used to set the amount of time before the transition, called preroll, and the amount of time playback continues after the edit, called postroll. Preroll and postroll settings for effects can contain different values than the **Edit View-Play** durations.

12.19 The Preroll and Postroll Options dialog box

Options Menu (Multitrack View only)

The following options are displayed only in **Multitrack View**.

MIDI Panic Button: Selecting this menu option or pressing the **P** key issues an **ALL Notes Off** MIDI command. This command is used when MIDI devices connected to Audition become jammed and are not responsive to normal commands.

Synchronize Clips with Edit View: Checking this option forces the cursor location or selection to remain the same when switching between **Edit View** and **Multitrack View**.

SMPTE Slave Enable: Checking this option enables Audition to follow another machine or device in a synchronized mode using SMPTE (MTC) timecode. The **F7** key also toggles the current state of this function.

SMPTE Master Enable: This option enables Audition to act as the master device by outputting SMPTE timecode.

SMPTE Start Offset: Selection of this option opens the **General** tab of the **Advanced Session Properties** window, permitting you to enter the SMPTE Start Time Offset. The offset is used to adjust the synchronization timing between devices.

Sample Accurate Sync: Enables sample accurate sync timing if your hardware offers the capability.

Pause Background Mixing: The premixing process renders some of audio before playback and frees the CPU for other chores. Clicking the checkbox next to **Pausing Background Mixing** suspends the premixing process. This can be desirable when editing, and it is not necessary to continually render the audio only to render it again after the edit.

Metronome: This command opens the **Advanced** tab of the **Advanced Session Properties** window, which is used to configure metronome settings.

Options Menu (CD Project View only)

The following options are displayed only in **CD Project View**.

CD Device Properties: Selecting this menu option presents a dialog box allowing selection and configuration of the CD or DVD recorder. Buffer size, write speed, and buffer underrun prevention are selected through this window. Larger buffer sizes and enabling buffer underrun prevention will help avoid writing failures. Writing discs at higher speeds can yield better results as well as accomplish the burn sooner, however it is important that the CD-R media is certified for the selected speed.

HELP

Learning Audition involves more than simply opening a program and typing. Even though Audition is a very intuitive application, it's also a professional-quality application, and mastering the use of the program is a task in itself. In addition, knowledge of other subjects such as physics, acoustics, electronics and music are required to make the most of a project. There are a number of resources that can help in the quest for knowledge, from the Internet to the documentation provided with the application.

The Help Menu

Adobe has provided very well-written documentation that is available from the **Help** menu. The documentation is well-organized and displayed in a browser window. The **Help** menu also provides quick access to Adobe's web site, technical support information, a glossary, and some system-specific information.

Contents: Selecting the **Contents** menu or pressing **F1** opens the **Contents** tab of the Audition Help engine. The right frame displays a number of categories and helps you to quickly locating the desired topic.

Search for Help On: This option allows searching the Help documentation for a specific topic. An **Index** tab enables you to locate specific words.

Glossary: Displays an alphabetized list of hyperlinked letters for quick access to brief definitions of computer and audio production related terms.

Multitrack Editing (Multitrack View Only): The **Multitrack Editing** submenu presents a hyperlinked page of the Audition documentation on topics involved in working with tracks in **Multitrack View.**

Technical Support: Technical support displays procedures for obtaining technical support from Adobe Systems along with the top support issues, latest support announcements, and links to forums and other Audition-related support topics.

Online Resources: The **Online Resources** option links directly to the Audition product page on Adobe's web site with links to Loopology content, downloads, tutorials, and other Adobe product information.

About Audition: The **About Audition** option opens the Audition splash screen and presents a button to display the required legal notices; however, there are some other features of the page that might be overlooked by the casual user. One such feature is the display of the application version and build number. Another feature is the **System Info** button that provides the user name, company, and serial number. This information may be requested by Adobe technical support. In fact, the **System Info** button provides a laundry list of information about Audition and the system configuration. The information opens in Notepad and can be sent to tech support, if necessary.

Audition Forums

FAQs, tips and tricks, and a loyal community of Audition users can be found on the Adobe Audition User Forum. Registration is required; however, it is free of charge. It can be found at www.adobeforums.com.

Another excellent forum is www.audiomastersforum.org. In addition to the forum, several Audition video tutorials are hosted on the homepage at www.audiomasters.org. As with most forums, registration is required, and there is no cover charge, and of course you are welcome to visit my site at www.technicalworkshops.com.

Adobe Product Announcements

Adobe offers a free support announcement that will help keep you informed of updates, product news, and special offers. Subscribe to the e-mail service at www.adobe.com/support/emaillist.html.

Appendix A

The Controllers

SURFACE CONTROLLERS

Audition can be controlled using a more traditional but highly evolved outboard mixing console called a *surface controller*. As of this writing, there are several controllers available for Audition. The following is a brief description of these products.

Event Electronics

EZ Bus

The Event Electronics controller offers 24-bit processing and accepts analog, S/PDIF, AES/EBU and ADAT Lightpipe input sources with sampling rates up to 96kHz. The EZ Bus hosts two mic preamps with phantom power, two line inputs, and 16 TRS balanced inputs with two independent MIDI In and MIDI Out ports. The EZ Bus has optical input and output for Lightpipe and S/PDIF. Eight analog outputs provide main outputs, four sends, and cue mix with a built-in amp. A word clock out is also provided. The EZ Bus controller offers more than the usual routing abilities, with pre- and post-patching on most controls and plenty of flexibility in configuring software control. More information is available at www.event1.com.

Mackie

Mackie has developed a reputation for building smaller, high-quality mixers. Mackie equipment is definitely a product line to check out when adding to your studio equipment list. The Mackie Controller is one of the most universal controllers in the industry and works with many video, MIDI, and audio-editing systems.

Universal Control Surface

The Universal Control Surface offers eight channels and a master fader with 100mm Penny & Giles moving faders. Each channel strip has separate controls for mute, solo, record enable, recall, and a rotary pot called a V-pot. Faders and buttons are programmable, offering a great deal of flexibility. The Mackie Controller is a very versatile controller, and unlike the other surface controllers, it uses MIDI to communicate instead of USB or FireWire.

Tascam

Tascam offers the largest array of surface controllers at a surprisingly reasonable cost.

US-224

The smallest of the Tascam surface controller family, the US-224 uses a self-powered USB interface. 16-bit or 24-bit audio is supported by Mic, Line, Guitar, and S/PDIF inputs. Other features include stereo analog and digital outputs, a separate amplified stereo headphone output, and MIDI Input and Output. Audio levels are managed by four individual faders with overall level on a separate master fader. Transport functions, mute, record enable, EQ, and panning can all be controlled directly from the US-224.

US-428

Frontier Design Group and Tascam partnered in the design of the US-428. Building on the features of the US-224, the US-428 essentially doubles the features of its little brother and adds four sends and a dedicated pan control.

FW-1884

The FW-1884 is the flagship of the Tascam surface controller line. Unlike its siblings, the FW-1184 uses a FireWire interface. It ships with a host of features including eight 100mm motorized faders, pan, solo, mute, and four bands of EQ on every channel. Balanced XLR mic/line inputs offer a high-quality preamp and phantom power on every channel. The FW-1884 provides 24-bit/96kHz digital operation on all channels, Lightpipe, S/PDIF, and eight analog channels, word clock in and out as well as four separate MIDI In and Outs. The features of this product are hard to beat.

*A.1   Tascam FW-1884 Surface
Controller Copyright:
©2004 by Tascam, used with
permission.*

Note Audition does not make use of moving faders at this time. There are also other controllers that may require programming or may not function with Audition. Research the products thoroughly and check the Audition forums to determine if the product meets your needs before making a purchase.

MIDI CONTROLLERS

Most electronic keyboards manufactured in the past decade support MIDI. The demand for control of multiple MIDI devices spawned a new device called the MIDI Controller. The controllers generally lacked the capacity to reproduce or synthesize sounds and were designed to generate MIDI commands to control synthesizers, sound modules, or other electronic devices.

M-Audio

Although Audition can accept commands from any MIDI keyboard or controller, many newer controllers are not just built for MIDI commands anymore. The race for portability is on, and controller manufactures are keeping pace. An example is Ozone from m-audio.

Ozone

The Ozone controller offers a lot of bang for the buck, including a 24-bit/96kHz audio interface with eight software-assignable knobs. Even though it is extremely small and portable, it sports a 25-key keyboard, XLR mic input with preamp and phantom power, instrument in with preamp, balanced stereo TRS input, stereo outputs, and headphone outputs.

M-audio offers a great line of MIDI, recording, and music products as do many other companies such as Roland, Yamaha, and Mark of the Unicorn. Appendix B, although not comprehensive, provides a starting point to begin exploring the incredible technology being offered today.

Appendix B

The Players

Note These listings are not meant to be a comprehensive list, recommendation, or endorsement of the products or services suitable for use with Audition.

AUDIO WEB SITES

General

www.audiodirectory.nl
www.audiotoolsdirect.com
www.dolby.com
www.dtsonline.com
www.futureproducers.com
www.harmony-central.com
www.prorec.com
www.sonicspot.com

Educational

www.acoustics101.com
www.audiocourses.com
www.bbctraining.co.uk
www.historicalvoices.org
www.sonicspot.com
www.videouniversity.com

FAQs

www.sourceforge.net/audioformats-1.html
www.transom.org/tools/faq/index.php3

Forms

General Audio

www.audioforums.com
www.dvinfo.net
www.hydrogenaudio.com
www.synthvox.com

Audition-Specific Forums

www.adobeforums.com
www.audiomastersforum.org
www.dmnforums.com

Miscellaneous

www.taxi.com

Onlines Sales

www.audiomidi.com
www.bhphoto.com
www.bigdmc.com
www.cdrecordingsoftware.com
www.gprime.com
www.pcaudiolabs.com
www.sweetwater.com
www.zzounds.com

BOOKS AND MAGAZINES

www.beradio.com
www.cmpbooks.com
www.computermusic.co.uk
www.dv.com
www.e-media.com
www.emusician.com

www.keyboardmag.com
www.mixmag.com
www.prosoundweb.com
www.prosoundweb.com
www.remixmag.com
www.soundonsound.com

CD/DVD REPLICATORS

www.cinram.com
www.evatone.com

www.sonopress.com
www.zomax.com

ORGANIZATIONS

www.aes.org
www.ascap.com
www.bmi.com
www.copyright.gov
www.nab.org

www.namm.com
www.riaa.com
www.sesac.com
www.smpte.org
www.spars.com

RECORDING-EQUIPMENT MANUFACTURERS

Microphones

www.akg.com
www.appliedmic.com
www.audio-technica.com
www.audixusa.com
www.behringer.com
www.beyerdynamic.com
www.bluemic.com
www.cadmics.com
www.crownaudio.com
www.dpamicrophones.com
www.electrovoice.com
www.m-audio.com
www.mictotechgefell.com
www.neumannusa.com
www.rode.com.au
www.schoeps.de
www.sennheiserusa.com
www.shure.com

MIDI Controllers and Surfaces

www.eventelectronics.com
www.mackie.com
www.m-audio.com
www.rolandus.com
www.tascam.com
www.yamaha.com

Mixing Consoles

www.alesis.com
www.behringer.com
www.mackie.com
www.m-audio.com
www.yamaha.com

Monitors

www.abluesky.com
www.alesis.com
www.behringer.com
www.dynaudiousa.com
www.egosys.net
www.electrovoice.com
www.eventelectronics.com
www.fostex.com
www.genelec.com
www.mackie.com
www.m-audio.com
www.rolandus.com
www.yamaha.com

Sound Cards and Audio Interfaces

www.aardvarkaudio.com
www.digigram.com
www.digitalaudio.com
www.echoaudio.com
www.edirol.com
www.egosys.net
www.eventelectronics.com
www.frontierdesign.com
www.lucidaudio.com
www.lynxstudio.com
www.m-audio
www.motu.com
www.pcsound.philips.com
www.sekd.com
www.soundblaster.com
www.steinberg.net
www.tascam.com
www.tbeach.com
www.terratec.net
www.uaudio.com
www.yamaha.com

MUSIC SAMPLES, LOOPS, AND SOUND EFFECTS

General Loops, Samples, and Sound Effects

www.beatbasics.com
www.bigfishaudio.com
www.drumsynth.com
www.entropymusic.com/freeloops.htm
www.findsounds.com
www.loops.net
www.loopwise.com
www.musicbakery.com
www.powerfx.com
www.proloops.com
www.quparts.com
www.samplenet.co.uk
www.sonomic.com
www.sound-effects-library.com
www.soundsonline.com
www.timespace.com

Sample Libraries

www.apomultimedia.com
www.fxpansion.com
www.wizoo.com

Loop Libraries (Including Samples)

www.beatboy.com
www.betamonkeymusic.com
www.discretedrums.com
www.keyfax.com
www.loopmasters.com
www.musicloops.com
www.powerfx.com
www.samplecraze.com
www.smartloops.com
www.smartsound.com
www.sounddogs.com
www.soundscan2.com

www.soundsonline.com
www.spectrasonics.com

Music Construction Kits (Including Loops and Samples)

www.bestservice.de
www.bigfishaudio.com
www.eastwestsamples.com
www.e-lab.se
www.loopkits.com
www.mediasoftware.sonypictures.com/
    loop_libraries
www.multiloops.com
www.newtronic.com
www.primesounds.com
www.zero-g.co.uk

Music Libraries

www.firstcom.com
www.killertracks.com
www.musicbakery.com
www.networkmusic.com
www.omnimusic.com
www.sound-ideas.com
www.twistedtracks.com

Sound Effects Libraries

www.hollywoodedge.com
www.mediasoftware.sonypictures.com/
    loop_libraries
www.networkmusic.com
www.powerfx.com
www.primesounds.com
www.rarefaction.com
www.sonomic.com
www.sounddogs.com
www.sound-ideas.com

OPTIMIZATION

www.musicxp.net

www.toejumper.net/speed5/winex5.htm

www.tomshardware.com

SOFTWARE

Audio Encoding

www.dtsonline.com

www.dolby.com

www.surcode.com

CD/DVD Authoring

www.ahead.com

www.discwelder.com

www.goldenhawk.com

www.roxio.com

www.sonic.com

Plug-ins

www.directxfiles.com

Plug-ins (DirectX)

www.a0audio.com

www.aipl.com

www.alienconnections.com

www.analogx.com

www.antarestech.com

www.anwida.com

www.arboretum.com

www.bias-inc.com

www.cakewalk.com

www.db-audioware.ceom

www.digilogue.de

www.drumagog.com

www.dsound1.com

www.dspfx.com

www.imaginetechnology.net

www.izotope.com

www.jdklein.com

www.mediasoftware.sonypictures.com/
shopping

www.ntrack.com (www.fasoft.com)

www.ohmforce.com

www.pspaudioware.com

www.rbcaudio.com

www.sonicengineering.com

www.sonicfoundry.com

www.sonictimeworks.com

www.soundslogical.com

www.spinaudio.com

www.steinberg.net

www.thelotron.com

www.tonewise.com

www.vb-audio.com

www.virsonix.com

www.virtos-audio.com

www.vocoder-plugins.com

www.vuplayer.com

www.wavearts.com

www.waves.com

Plug-ins (VST Only)

www.digitalfishphones.com

www.fxteleport.com

www.knzaudio.com

www.tcelectronic.com

www.voxengo.com

Utilities

www.analogx.com
www.cdsppped2000.com
www.cuibono-soft.com
www.exactaudiocopy.de
www.fmjsoft.com
www.intelliscore.net
www.minnetonkaaudio.com
www.rcsworks.com
www.stefanbion.de/cueltool/index_e.htm
www.synchroarts.com

www.wavpack.com
www.widisoft.com

ReWire-Compliant Applications

www.adobe.com
www.ableton.com
www.arturia.com
www.bitheadz.com
www.cycling74.com
www.steinberg.net

Glossary

Analog-to-digital converter (ADC): an electronic device used to convert infinitely varying analog signals into finite digital values.

AES/EBU: a digital audio communication standard designed by the Audio Engineering Society/European Broadcast Union.

Algorithm: a routine set of instructions or formula designed to accomplish a task.

Amplitude: the maximum displacement of a cyclical wave, often referred to as signal level.

Analog audio: audio signal represented by an continuously varying signal.

Attenuation: a reduction of the signal level or amplitude.

Bandwidth: the range of frequencies that a device can handle.

Bit: the smallest piece of digital data, represented by a one or a zero. A byte is usually comprised of eight bits.

Bit depth: the level of detail at which the analog signal is sampled. For audio, 16-bit or 24-bit resolution is typical. Larger resolutions can reproduce greater dynamic range.

Bounce: the act of submixing a larger number of tracks to a smaller set of tracks to free up some tracks for other use or to help in managing the final mix. Bouncing is frequently called ping-ponging.

Buffer: a section of RAM used to store data temporarily until the destination device is ready to receive it.

Burn: the process of writing data to a compact disc. The disc is not actually burned; instead the laser causes a chemical reaction in the dye on the disc.

Bus: a routable electrical signal path used to carry audio such as auxiliary sends for cue mixes, effects, and other groups or submixes.

Byte: a group of binary data usually consisting of eight bits.

Center frequency: the frequency that receives the greatest gain or attenuation of amplitude from a filter.

Channel: a signal or data path. Typically referred to in audio as separate information for left and right stereo signals.

Clipping: the amplitude at which a signal begins to distort as the waveform is squared when attempting to exceed physical limitations of the storage media.

CODEC: an abbreviation for encoder/decoder. Codecs are programming routines used to compress and decompress video and audio.

Compression: reduction of the dynamic range of a signal or size of computer data.

Constant-Q: a filter parameter that maintains a constant bandwidth during level adjustment.

Crossfade: the transition between two segments of audio when the amplitude of the first segment is attenuated and the amplitude of the second segment is increased. Commonly called a segue.

Cue: the beginning of a segment of audio. It is also used in audio to refer to the headphone mix for performers.

Cycle: the frequency rate of a sound wave. It is interchangeable with the term Hertz (Hz).

Digital-to-analog converter (DAC): an electronic device that interprets a digital bitstream and converts it into an analog signal.

Disc-at-once (DAO): the preferred method of writing the entire contents of a CD-R without turning the laser on or off.

Decibel (dB): the standard unit of measurement used to describe a signal level or relative loudness.

DC offset: a direct-current component in the audio signal causing a variance of the waveform zero point.

Delay: the postponing of a sound or effect. Delay is most often used to describe the amount of time between the original sound and the repeat of the sound or affected sound.

Dolby Digital (AC-3): an encoded audio format that can play back six channels: left, right, center, left rear, right rear, and a low-frequency effects (LFE) channel predominately used for DVDs.

Digital audio: audio signal represented by finite numeric values.

Digital audio extraction (DAE): the method of capturing the bit stream from an audio CD (Red Book) into computer files. Ripping is another term for DAE.

DirectX: a plug-in architecture that uses Microsoft's DirectX technology to apply effects from within the host application.

Dithering: the process of adding low-level random noise to audio signals to reduce quantization noise in A/D converters.

Dry: an audio signal with no effects added.

DTS: a digital audio-encoding format created by Digital Theater Systems that competes with Dolby Digital. DTS has a five-channel capability and is used primarily on DVDs.

DVD (Digital Versatile Disc): an optical storage medium used to store video, audio, and computer data.

Dynamic range: the distance between the lowest and highest amplitude of a music selection or soundtrack.

Echo: the single repetition of a sound with a delay long enough to perceive it as a separate event.

Effect: signal processing that applies reverb, delay, expansion, and other effects.

Envelope: the way the amplitude of a sound varies over time.

Equalization (EQ): the process of boosting or attenuating selected frequencies of an audio signal using filtering.

Expander: a hardware device or software application used to increase dynamic range by decreasing the level of a signal when it falls below a threshold.

Fader: a control such as a slider attenuator used to make changes to the amplitude of a signal.

Filter: a device, circuit, or algorithm used to reduce selected frequencies within a signal.

Frequency: the number of times per second a sound wave completes a cycle, expressed as Hertz (Hz). Frequency perceived by the ear is often referred to as pitch.

Full-duplex: the ability to send and receive data simultaneously or record and playback audio simultaneously.

Gain: another term for level or amplitude.

Glitch: a digital anomaly producing click, ticks, pops, and other such sounds typically caused because of errors reading the data from DAT or CD.

Harmonics: frequencies that are whole-number multiples of the fundamental frequency.

Hertz (Hz): the unit of measurement used to describe the frequency or number of times per second a sound wave completes a cycle.

Level: a general term for volume or amplitude.

Limiting: controlling the gain of a signal by reducing the amplitude when a preset threshold is exceeded.

Mastering: the final step in the process of preparing a mix for publication or mass duplication.

Mic Level: a low-level signal typically produced by microphones and electric instruments.

MIDI (Musical Instrument Digital Interface): a hardware, software, and protocol specification used to transmit and receive and control electronic devices such as synthesizers.

Mix, mixdown: the final stage of the multitrack recording process, where the tracks are balanced or EQed, or effects are applied.

Mixer: a hardware or software device used to combine, mix, and distribute signal to other devices.

Mono: a single-channel audio signal.

MIDI timecode (MTC): a specification design that uses the MIDI protocol to carry a variation of SMPTE timecode, providing the ability to synchronize MIDI devices, applications, and machines.

Noise shaping: the use of algorithms in the dithering process to shift added noise in the audio spectrum where the human ear is least sensitive.

Normalization: a process that scans the waveform and boosts the entire waveform to the maximum amplitude.

Nyquist Frequency Theorem: a theorem stating that the sampling frequency of a digital audio system must be at least twice that of the highest audio frequency to enable successful reproduction.

Overdub: the technique of recording additional tracks while playing previously recorded tracks.

Out of phase: a point where cycles in one signal reach their peak as the cycles of another signal reach their crest, causing the two signals to cancel each other out.

Octave: a doubling or halving of frequency.

Panning: moving the signal in the stereo or surround-sound image.

Peak: the point in a waveform that contains the highest amplitude.

Phantom power: power required for the operation of a condenser microphone, usually supplied by a mixing console.

Phase: the time relationship between two different waveforms expressed in degrees, with 360° representing a full cycle.

Pink noise: equal amounts of sound energy in each octave of the sound spectrum.

Plug-in: a program that hooks into a host application and is able to communicate with and work within the host application. DirectX and VST are examples of plug-ins.

Q: the parameter used to set a filter's width or slope.

Real time: a process that occurs during recording or playback without affecting the normal speed.

Resampling: the process of converting the sampling rate of the signal to a different sampling rate, often referred to as sample rate conversion.

Resolution: commonly called bit depth, the accuracy with which an analog signal is represented by a digitized system.

Reverberation: an effect consisting of echos that are not distinguishable from each other.

Root means square (RMS): the square root of the mean of the sum of the squares commonly used to determine average amplitude.

ReWire: a cross-application technology used to communicate audio, MIDI, transport commands, and other data between ReWire-compliant applications.

Ripping: a method of capturing the bit stream from an audio CD (Red Book) into computer files.

Roll off: the reduction of level of a particular band of frequencies.

Sample: the smallest piece of data used to represent an audio signal at a given time.

Sampling rate: the number of times per second that analog audio signal values are recorded.

Sampler: a hardware device or software application that uses a group of samples to create reproductions of musical instrument sounds.

SCSI: Acronym for Small Computer System Interface. A system protocol consisting of hardware and drivers used for transferring data between storage devices.

Sequencer: a hardware device or software application used to arrange, store, and repeat a series of MIDI or audio events.

Sibilance: high-frequency distortion that may occur on the sounds, such as the letters s and f.

S/N ratio: signal-to-noise ratio, the range or distance between the noise floor or residual noise and the operating signal level.

Sine wave: a pure tone with no harmonics that forms the basis of all complex periodic sounds.

SMPTE timecode: an electronic identification system based on a 24-hour clock used to control the synchronization of audio and video equipment. SMPTE is an acronym for the Society of Motion Picture and Television Engineers

S/PDIF: the Sony/Philips Digital Interface Format used to transfer consumer-level digital audio.

Synthesizer: a hardware device or software application that uses algorithms or electronics to create or alter sounds.

Stereo: a two-dimensional sound image created by two discrete channels.

Track-at-once (TAO): a method of writing audio or data to a disc with the laser turning off and back on between each track of the session. TAO is not preferred for replication masters.

Tempo: the speed or rate of a musical composition that is usually based on a quarter note as the timing reference.

Threshold: the signal level that triggers an action in a compressor, gate, or expander.

Timbre: the characteristic or qualities of a sound that distinguishes it from other sounds.

Transient: a high-level signal of extremely short duration.

Unbalanced: a type of connection that utilizes only high and ground and therefore lacks shielding from interference and other forms of noise.

Volume: the amplitude or loudness of a signal.

VST plug-in: an application that uses Steinberg's Virtual Studio Technology to apply effects from within the host program.

Waveform: A graphic representation of a wave's amplitude over time.

Wet: signal with effect applied.

White Noise: random noise that contains an equal amount of energy per frequency band.

XLR: a connector commonly used to carry balanced audio signals.

Zero crossing: the point at which a signal waveform crosses from a positive value to a negative value, or the opposite.

Index

DV
MAGAZINE

DV
EXPO AND
CONFERENCES

DV
QUARTERLY

DV
QUARTERLY

DV
.COM

DV
FILM FESTIVAL

DV
EXPERT SERIES
(A DIVISION
OF CMP BOOKS)

INSPIRING AND EMPOWERING CREATIVITY

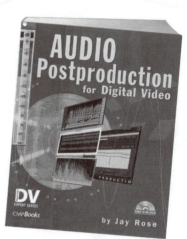

Designing Menus with Encore DVD

John Skidgel

Create engaging, well-structured menus with the latest version of Encore DVD. This full-color book guides you through all of the essential DVD authoring concepts and shows how to plan and manage projects and inter-application workflows. The companion DVD contains tutorial media and plug-ins.

$49.95, 4-Color, Softcover with DVD, 240 pp, ISBN 1-57820-235-3

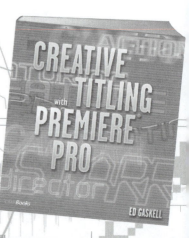

Premiere Pro Editing Workshop

Marcus Geduld

Master the craft of editing with Premiere Pro. This editing workshop gives you firsthand experience with the art and technique of editing with tutorial lessons that cover the gamut—from proper installation to sound editing, special effects, titling, and output. The companion CD contains tutorial media and plug-ins.

$49.95, Softcover with CD-ROM, 400 pp, ISBN 1-57820-228-0

Creative Titling Premiere Pro

Ed Gaskell

Create compelling title sequences using Premiere Pro. Packed with four-color illustrations, explanations, instructions, and step-by-step tutorials, this book teaches and inspires editors to produce work that is a cut above the rest. Covers conceptualization, design, methodology, and the mechanics of successful title sequences.

$44.95, 4-Color Softcover, 198 pp, ISBN 1-57820-233-7

Creating Motion Graphics with After Effects

Volume 1: The Essentials, 3rd Edtion

Trish Meyer & Chris Meyer

Master the core concepts and tools you need to tackle virtually every job, including keyframe animation, masking, mattes, and plug-in effects. New chapters demystify Parenting, 3D Space, and features of the latest software version. **Available September, 2004**

$59.95, 4-Color, Softcover with CD-ROM, 448 pp, ISBN 1-57820-249-3

Photoshop CS for Nonlinear Editors

2nd Edtion

Richard Harrington

Use Photoshop CS to generate characters, correct colors, and animate graphics for digital video. You'll grasp the fundamental concepts and master the complete range of Photoshop tools through lively discourse, full-color presentations, and hands-on tutorials. The companion DVD contains tutorial media and plug-ins.

$54.95, 4-Color, Softcover with DVD, 336 pp, ISBN 1-57820-237-X

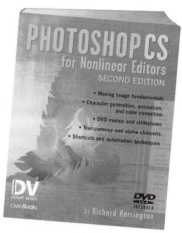

After Effects On the Spot

Richard Harrington, Rachel Max, & Marcus Geduld

Packed with more than 400 expert techniques, this book clearly illustrates all the essential methods that pros use to get the job done with After Effects. Experienced editors and novices alike discover an invaluable reference filled with ways to improve efficiency and creativity.

$27.95, Softcover, 256 pp, ISBN 1-57820-239-6

What's on the CD?

The Using Audition accompaniment CD contains files for use with chapter tutorials, audio samples for experimenting with Audition's features, and demos that provide an 'audition' of the loop content bundled with Adobe Audition and other commercially available music loop libraries. The disc also contains third-party DirectX and VST plug-in demos, filtering and encoding demos, and software utilities for file conversion and format exchange. Supplemental reading material is also included on miking techniques, mastering, and dithering.

Updates

Want to receive e-mail news updates for *Using Audition*? Send a blank e-mail to audition@news.cmp-books.com. We will do our best to keep you informed of software updates and enhancements, new tips, and other Audition-related resources.